Salvaging Corporate Sustainability

NEW HORIZONS IN SUSTAINABILITY AND BUSINESS

Books in the New Horizons in Sustainability and Business series make a significant contribution to the study of business, sustainability and the natural environment. As this field has expanded dramatically in recent years, the series will provide an invaluable forum for the publication of high-quality works of scholarship and show the diversity of research on organization and the environment around the world. Global and pluralistic in its approach, this series includes some of the best theoretical and analytical work with contributions to fundamental principles, rigorous evaluations of existing concepts and competing theories, stimulating debate and future visions.

Titles in the series include:

Pioneering Family Firms' Sustainable Development Strategies
Edited by Pramodita Sharma and Sanjay Sharma

Personal Sustainability Practices
Faculty Approaches to Walking the Sustainability Talk and Living the UN SDGs
Edited by Mark Starik and Patricia Kanashiro

Salvaging Corporate Sustainability
Going Beyond the Business Case
Michael L. Barnett, Irene Henriques and Bryan W. Husted

Salvaging Corporate Sustainability

Going Beyond the Business Case

Michael L. Barnett

Professor of Management, Rutgers Business School, Rutgers University, USA

Irene Henriques

Professor of Sustainability and Economics, Schulich School of Business, York University, Canada

Bryan W. Husted

Professor of Management, EGADE Business School, Tecnológico de Monterrey, Mexico

NEW HORIZONS IN SUSTAINABILITY AND BUSINESS

Edward Elgar
PUBLISHING

Cheltenham, UK • Northampton, MA, USA

Cover image by Victoria Sadorsky.

Published by
Edward Elgar Publishing Limited
The Lypiatts
15 Lansdown Road
Cheltenham
Glos GL50 2JA
UK

Edward Elgar Publishing, Inc.
William Pratt House
9 Dewey Court
Northampton
Massachusetts 01060
USA

A catalogue record for this book
is available from the British Library

Library of Congress Control Number: 2022931165

This book is available electronically in the **Elgar**online
Business subject collection
http://dx.doi.org/10.4337/9781800378940

Printed on elemental chlorine free (ECF)
recycled paper containing 30% Post-Consumer Waste

ISBN 978 1 80037 893 3 (cased)
ISBN 978 1 80037 894 0 (eBook)

Printed and bound in the USA

Mike dedicates this book to his wife, Lisa, and his children, Lauren and Jack, who still don't really know what he's doing in front of the computer in the makeshift office in the laundry room as the days of the pandemic wear on, but encourage him to keep at it, nonetheless.

Irene dedicates this book to her husband, Perry, and her children, Michelle and Victoria, who provided inspirational conversations throughout.

Bryan dedicates this book to the memory of Jane and Bill, his parents, who enthusiastically supported him in all of his projects, adventures, and about-faces.

And jointly, we dedicate this book to future generations, who we hope are able to read it from the comfort of a sustainable planet and society, and not as they face increasingly harsh threats to their survival and prosperity.

Contents

List of figures viii
Preface ix
Authors' acknowledgments xi
Acknowledgments xii

PART I CORPORATE SUSTAINABILITY: PREMISES AND PROMISES

1 Surveying sustainability 2

2 Profiting from sustainability 9

3 Sustaining society 30

PART II THE REALITIES OF CORPORATE SUSTAINABILITY

4 Satisfying stakeholders shan't sustain society 43

5 Baked-in biases of the business case 64

6 Digital detours are dubious 78

PART III GETTING GOOD WITH GOVERNMENT

7 Sussing out the scope of social control 107

8 Gripes against government 129

9 Learning to lean on Leviathan 145

Index 165

Figures

2.1	Corporate benefits of sustainability	12
3.1	Societal benefits of corporate sustainability	31
4.1	Mapping the business case	49
4.2	A CSR logic model	56
5.1	The business case for sustainability	68
6.1	Stakeholder influence in the digital age	87
6.2	Aggregate change in stakeholder influence in the digital age	97
8.1	Process change to achieve sustainability goals	140
9.1	A research framework for corporate sustainability	154

Preface

In 2015, the Tecnológico de Monterrey created a program to bring distinguished visiting professors to campus to guide the work of the various faculty research groups. Irene and Mike were invited into the program, to work with the Research Group in Social Innovation and Sustainability headed by Bryan. Over the course of six years, this program enabled Irene and Mike to make three week-long pilgrimages a year to Monterrey, with many overlapping visits. Though we knew each other prior to the start of this program, these frequent visits allowed for a depth of interaction that is rare in academia. As a result, we were able to quickly find common ground and publish numerous papers, alongside the myriad of events and writing camps that we held.

Alas, all good things come to an end and, as we saw that the program was drawing to a close in 2020, we asked: What's next? Each of us had come to the conclusion that much of what we were teaching and writing about corporate sustainability was just not turning out as expected. After a combined 80 or so years of teaching and researching various aspects of corporate sustainability and related topics like business and society, business ethics, and strategic management, we were frustrated with how little progress was actually being made toward sustaining people and the planet. Whether the topic was climate change, income inequality, or cultural diversity, the tools stemming from our research and taught in our classrooms, such as the business case and stakeholder theory, were not meeting the grand challenges of our day.

It was not easy to come to the realization that much of what we had taught and written was ineffective. Although our colleagues in critical management studies might have said, "We told you so," we did not come to this realization because of any ideological orientation. At heart, the three of us are positivists and optimists and had hope that business and business scholars could contribute to solving global challenges. This hope was dashed after we engaged in a major review of the literature to determine the social impact of corporate social responsibility (CSR) and sustainability initiatives. To our dismay, the answer was: almost nothing. That is, after thousands of studies extending over decades, the field offers no evidence of significant social impact. Corporate sustainability talks a mean game, but it is not sustaining society.

As corporate sustainability programs have become omnipresent over the last several decades, business school coursework at the interface of business and government has faded away. The role of government has been replaced, by design, with reliance on social control and market forces. Stakeholder theory has demoted government to only one of many stakeholders with whom firms need to be concerned. The erosion and even erasure of the role of government in business curriculum and reliance on the business case in its stead caused us grave concern about what we were studying and teaching. We concluded that a correction was overdue, and so this book was born.

Although the last year of our official collaboration occurred during the first year of the pandemic, we were blessed with five years of face-to-face collaborations in wonderful settings like Chipinque in the Sierra Madre, over many coffees and beers and great Mexican cuisine. So, this book is the fortuitous result of a worthwhile university academic endeavor, but it is built on the good times and friendship that we developed over those years. Putting this book together was not as easy as we had planned but working together was always enjoyable. Yes, we had fun. But our message is serious. We hope that this book challenges readers to take a broader view of the resources we use, the biodiversity this planet possesses, and the knowledge (both technological and traditional) we possess in assessing and addressing our global challenges. As Einstein stated, "We can't solve problems by using the same kind of thinking we used when we created them." Yet all too often, we leave the fox to guard the henhouse, even after seeing the destruction it has caused. So, what's next? We hope that this book provides new directions to uncover new and better answers.

Authors' acknowledgments

This book would not have been possible without inspirational and intellectual discussions with many colleagues, friends, and family. First, we wish to thank the EGADE Business School for developing the Distinguished Star Visiting Professor program and selecting Mike Barnett and Irene Henriques to participate in Bryan Husted's research group from 2015–2020. This program provided us with an amazing venue to develop and discuss our ideas amongst ourselves and with an exciting group of faculty, post-docs, and PhD students. We thank two vice deans for research, Teo Ozuna and Osmar Zavaleta, who supported the visiting professor program and some of our zany ideas. We are also thankful for the administrative support of Mary Garcia, Martha Sanchez, and Maria Livas. Special thanks to Gaby Maldonado who always went the extra mile to ensure that the visits of Irene and Mike as visiting distinguished professors were well organized.

We thank Victoria Sadorsky for the original book art. We appreciate your patience as we bounced around a range of ideas – your obvious talents are very much respected. We also thank Michelle Sadorsky for her laborious copy-editing services. Having a layperson edit our scholarly work with a fresh set of eyes challenged us to reduce jargon and to improve the clarity and flow. Every author should be so lucky as to have access to such services. Finally, to complete the family involvement, we would like to thank Perry Sadorsky for providing feedback on artwork and engaging in inspirational discussions.

We thank our myriad co-authors for their important roles in developing the papers over the decades that we integrated into this book, including Perry Sadorsky, Ivan Montiel, Charles Fombrun, Naomi Gardberg, Mike Russo, Carlos Basurto-Meza, Suzanne Tilleman, Ben Cashore, Rajat Panwar, Jonatan Pinkse, Sanjay Sharma, Hari Bapuji, Jane Lu, Raza Mir, José Salazar, Itzel Palomares, and Francisco Layrisse (in the order in which their co-authored works appear in the book).

Finally, many thanks go to Alan Sturmer, Executive Editor at Edward Elgar Publishing, for encouraging and guiding the production of this book, and providing nearly instantaneous answers to our many questions.

Acknowledgments

CHAPTER 1

Draws from:

Barnett, M. L., Henriques, I., & Husted, B. W. 2021. Sustainability strategies. In I. Duhaime, M. Hitt & M. Lyles (Eds) *Strategic management: State of the field and its future*. Oxford University Press: Oxford: 647–662.

CHAPTER 2

Draws from:

Barnett, M. L. 2007. Stakeholder influence capacity and the variability of financial returns to corporate social responsibility. Academy of Management Review, 32(3): 794–816.

Barnett, M. L., Henriques, I., & Husted, B. W. 2020. Beyond good intentions: Designing CSR initiatives for greater social impact. Journal of Management, 46(6): 937–964.

Henriques, I., & Sadorsky, P. 1999. The relationship between environmental commitment and managerial perceptions of stakeholder importance. Academy of Management Journal, 42(1): 87–99.

Husted, B. W. 2005. Risk management, real options, and corporate social responsibility. Journal of Business Ethics, 60(2): 175–183.

CHAPTER 3

Draws from:

Henriques, I., Husted, B. W., & Montiel, I. 2013. Spillover effects of voluntary environmental programs on greenhouse gas emissions: Lessons from Mexico. Journal of Policy Analysis and Management, 32(2): 296–322.

Fombrun, C. J., Gardberg, N. A., & Barnett, M. L. 2000. Opportunity platforms and safety nets: Corporate citizenship and reputational risk. Business and Society Review, 105: 85–106.

Husted, B. W. 2015. Corporate social responsibility practice from 1800–1914: Past initiatives and current debates. Business Ethics Quarterly, 25(1): 125–141.

CHAPTER 4

Draws from:

Barnett, M. L. 2019. The business case for corporate social responsibility. Business & Society, 58(1): 167–190.

Barnett, M. L., Henriques, I., & Husted, B. W. 2020. Beyond good intentions: Designing CSR initiatives for greater social impact. Journal of Management, 46(6): 937–964.

CHAPTER 5

Draws from:

Husted, B. W., Russo, M. V., Basurto-Meza, C. E. B., & Tilleman, S. G. 2014. An exploratory study of environmental attitudes and the willingness to pay for environmental certification in Mexico. Journal of Business Research, 67(5): 891–899.

Barnett, M. L., Cashore, B., Henriques, I., Husted, B. W., Panwar, R., & Pinske, J. 2021. Reorient the business case for corporate sustainability. Stanford Social Innovation Review, Summer 2021: 35–39.

CHAPTER 6

Draws from:

Barnett, M. L., Henriques, I., & Husted, B. 2020. The rise and stall of stakeholder influence: How the digital age limits social control. Academy of Management Perspectives, 34(1): 48–64.

Barnett, M. L., Henriques, I., & Husted, B. 2021. Family matters? The effects of size and proximity in the digital age. Academy of Management Perspectives, 35(3): in press.

CHAPTER 7

Draws from:

Barnett, M. L. 2014. Why stakeholders ignore firm misconduct: A cognitive view. Journal of Management, 40(3): 676–702.

CHAPTER 8

Draws from:

Barnett, M. L., Henriques, I., & Husted, B. W. 2020. The rise and stall of stakeholder influence: How the digital age limits social control. Academy of Management Perspectives, 34(1): 48–64.

Barnett, M., Henriques, I., & Husted, B. W. 2018. Governing the void between stakeholder management and sustainability. Advances in Strategic Management, 38: 121–143.
Henriques, I., & Sadorsky, P. 2008. Voluntary environmental programs: A Canadian perspective. The Policy Studies Journal, 36(1): 143–166.
Husted, B. W. 2002. Culture and international anti-corruption agreements in Latin America. Journal of Business Ethics, 37(4): 413–422.
Sharma, S., & Henriques, I. 2005. Stakeholder influences on sustainability practices in the Canadian forest products industry. Strategic Management Journal, 26(2): 159–180.

CHAPTER 9

Draws from:

Bapuji, H., Husted, B. W., Lu, J., & Mir, R. 2018. Value creation, appropriation, and distribution: How firms contribute to societal economic inequality. Business & Society, 57(6): 983–1009.
Barnett, M. L., Henriques, I., & Husted, B. W. 2021. Sustainability strategies. In I. Duhaime, M. Hitt & M. Lyles (Eds) *Strategic management: State of the field and its future*. Oxford University Press: Oxford: 647–662.
Barnett, M., Henriques, I., & Husted, B. W. 2018. Governing the void between stakeholder management and sustainability. Advances in Strategic Management, 38: 121–143.
Henriques I., Husted B. W., & Montiel, I. 2013. Spillover effects of voluntary environmental programs on greenhouse gas emissions: Lessons from Mexico. Journal of Policy Analysis and Management, 32(2): 296–322.
Husted, B. W., & Salazar, J. 2020. Reducing inequalities: Toward the development of a market for income inequality. Journal of Cleaner Production, 245, 118931.
Palomares, I., Layrisse, F., Barnett, M. L., & Husted, B. W. 2018. Built to scale? How sustainable business models can better serve the base of the pyramid. Journal of Cleaner Production, 172: 4506–4513.

PART I

Corporate sustainability: premises and promises

1. Surveying sustainability

Born in 1893, Sears, Roebuck & Company grew to become one of the largest and most recognizable retailers in the world. More than a century later, the company suffered a period of declining corporate health, and either despite or due to extreme life-saving measures, went belly up in 2018. In contrast, Pets.com, an online pet supply company, was founded in February 1999, quickly developed a national profile, went public in February 2000, and collapsed in November 2000.

Some corporations live long, prosperous lives. Many more do not survive their infancies. Interesting, right? Well, no. Not to us, dear reader. This book is not about sustaining corporations. Corporations are but a dispensable means to a much more important end: that of sustaining society.

Listen up: society is in peril (IPBES, 2019). Our oceans are acidifying and filling with plastic and other toxic debris (Avio, Gorbi & Regoli, 2017). Our forests are disappearing at an alarming rate (Lambin et al., 2018). Our soil is turning toxic (Loska, Wiechuła & Korus, 2004). CO_2 emissions rise unabated (Lindsey, 2020) as our planet's temperature pushes to dangerous levels (IPCC, 2018). If we are to sustain society—if humans are to prosper on this planet in perpetuity—then we must sustain our planet and the ecological and social systems thereupon.

Corporations can help—or hinder—in sustaining humanity. In this book, we seek a way to turn corporations into more of a help and less of a hindrance. There is potential for healthy, positive interdependence by which, in helping to sustain people and the planet, corporations can more profitably sustain themselves. Belief in the viability of a "business case" has driven an explosion in corporate sustainability programs over recent decades (Bonini & Gorner, 2011). Unfortunately, the business case can also spiral out of control, with the quest for profits hindering and harming humanity (Barnett et al., 2021). Many in academia and practice primarily view corporate sustainability programs as a means of sustaining corporate profitability, providing only fleeting concern and flimsy evidence for any contributions to sustaining society (Barnett, Henriques & Husted, 2020).

It is time to reverse what has become a perverse means–ends inversion between business and society. But this is a complex undertaking, as the convolutedness of the prior sentence evokes. Yet it is a necessary undertaking. We must do it to ensure that society's end won't be so mean.

To achieve our complex aim, we have organized the book into three sections—each containing three chapters—that collectively chart the path from where corporate sustainability now stands, through where it has gone wrong, and on to where it needs to go. Part I, *Corporate sustainability: Premises and promises*, defines and overviews corporate sustainability (Chapter 1), explains how corporate sustainability programs can benefit corporations (Chapter 2), and how society can benefit from corporate sustainability programs (Chapter 3). Part II, *The realities of corporate sustainability*, clarifies how corporate sustainability programs have contributed to sustaining society (Chapter 4), explains why the business case proves inadequate to bring about socio-ecological sustainability (Chapter 5), and discusses why the digital age, with all of its promise of democratizing corporate governance, has failed to strengthen sustainability outcomes (Chapter 6). In Part III, *Getting good with government*, we move beyond the present two-dimensional world of business and society by reintroducing a critical third dimension: government. Chapter 7 explains why stakeholder influence is inadequate to bring about sustainability, while Chapter 8 clarifies how government fell out of favor in the corporate sustainability literature. Chapter 9 closes with a discussion of how to bring government back in, and outlines a research agenda to find a working balance between free market and formal governance that can better sustain substantive corporate sustainability.

1 WHAT IS CORPORATE SUSTAINABILITY?

This book integrates the insights of three senior scholars spread across three countries, drawing on more than three decades of published work. We weave together and augment key aspects of our extensive joint libraries of publications to address the current state of, and the prospects for, business helping to sustain society.

All the scholarship integrated into this book is relevant to corporate sustainability, but often we use terms other than corporate sustainability. As has the broader field in which our studies are embedded, our terminology has evolved over time. Dating back to the prior millennium, we have published work using related concepts such as corporate citizenship (Fombrun, Gardberg & Barnett, 2000), corporate social responsibility (Barnett, 2007), corporate social performance (Barnett, 2007), corporate social innovation (Barnett, 2020), sustainability strategy (Barnett, Henriques & Husted, 2021), corporate environmentalism (Henriques & Sadorsky, 1996), and environmental management (Henriques & Sadorsky, 1999). We view corporate sustainability as an umbrella term that encompasses these other concepts and sometimes completely overlaps with them. Where there are distinctions to be made between terms, we clarify them as they arise throughout the book.

By corporate sustainability, we specifically mean *a firm's set of programs for achieving environmental integrity, social equity, and economic prosperity.* This is the same definition we have used for sustainability strategy (Barnett et al., 2021). It is based on the three dimensions of sustainable development put forth by the World Commission on Economic Development (WCED, 1987) and reiterated by leading sustainability practitioners (e.g., Elkington, 1998) and strategy scholars (e.g., Bansal, 2005). It is not just about sustaining the natural environment, but also about continuously prospering as a society. Said more simply, it is a plan to preserve people, the planet, *and* profits.

Corporate sustainability is a common term in the scholarly and applied literatures, but it is often used in generic ways and sometimes muddled with contradictory concepts, especially in the corporate strategy literature. Much of this confusion is due to a difference in perspective on what is to be sustained. Sustainable competitive advantage, for instance, is common business jargon that refers to resources and strategies that sustain a firm's competitive advantage over its rivals. Sustaining a firm's profitability is quite different from sustaining society. Though both corporate sustainability and sustainable competitive advantage share a concern with sustaining performance over time, corporate sustainability looks beyond the firm. Corporate sustainability can be a source of sustainable competitive advantage, which is why we adopt the same definition as we have previously used for sustainability strategy. However, a firm's strategic efforts to sustain its competitive advantage through corporate sustainability may also be to the detriment of the sustainability of society. It is far too easy to recall instances of firms seeking financial gains in ways that ultimately had harmful impacts on ecology and society (e.g., BP Deepwater Horizon, Union Carbide at Bhopal, and Purdue Pharma and the opioid crisis). Thus, we distinguish corporate sustainability from the sustainability of corporations.

Though we define corporate sustainability at the firm level, sustainability is characteristic of a system (Ostrom, 2009), not of any individual organization within it. A system consists of four broad subsystems: resource systems, resource units, governance systems, and users (Ostrom, 2009). Sustainability is achieved at the level of the system, while firms are only part of the subsystem of users. Firms can implement programs that aim to have a positive impact on the sustainability of a system, but they cannot independently ensure the system's sustainability. Nevertheless, we retain the burden of achieving the three elements of sustainable development in our definition of corporate sustainability. Doing so indicates that firms have the responsibility to manage their interdependence with and influence on the system in a way that helps the system to achieve sustainability.

Tragic consequences can arise when firms do not understand or manage their interdependence within the system. The coronavirus pandemic provides a too-salient example. Although the full coronavirus causal chain has not yet been proven, the role of globalization in emerging infectious diseases has been well traced (Frenk, Gómez-Dantés & Knaul, 2011). The globalization of supply chains made firms more efficient and brought work to millions of impoverished people, but it also drove deforestation. Deforestation destroys ecosystems, which stresses animal species. As with humans, when animals are stressed, their immune responses are hindered, and they become susceptible to viruses. Once infected, animals can transmit viruses to humans. The results, as we are experiencing, can be devastating, millions returned to poverty, the deaths of millions globally, and unprecedented social upheaval. Profitable firms and a roaring economy are not sustainable if they lead to global pandemics, irreversible climate change (Lenton, et al., 2019), or worse.

Decades ago, Shrivastava (1995), Starik and Rands (1995), Stead and Stead (1994), and others called on management scholars to develop strategies that would keep firms from breaching the social-ecological limits of our planet. However, the literature did not fully heed their calls. Instead of critically assessing assumptions and developing new theories of sustainability, it concentrated on ways to improve a firm's financial or operational performance (cf. Barnett, Henriques & Husted, 2020). This led to many studies applying existing management theories, such as the resource-based view (Barney, 1991), stakeholder theory (Freeman, 1984), institutional theory (Oliver, 1991), and competitive advantage (Porter & Van der Linde, 1995) to the sustainability context (Hart, 1995; Henriques & Sadorsky, 1999; Hoffman, 1999; Porter & Kramer, 2006, respectively).

Despite the prevailing focus on firm profitability, some corporate sustainability scholars have heeded calls to address the planetary and social limitations of business behavior. For example, Whiteman, Walker, and Perego (2013: 324) argued that effective strategic options require managers to consider "symbiotic solutions for resource issues" to effectively govern within our planetary boundaries (Rockström et al., 2009) and highlight the need to understand "how firms are connected to cumulative, systemic environmental problems" (Whiteman et al., 2013: 326). To understand the interaction between human and natural systems, Winn and Pogutz (2013: 219) looked to ecology and ecological economics to "sketch the myriad interconnections between ecosystems and human, and thus organizational, life." Both papers underscore the need for multidisciplinary perspectives, cross-sector partnerships, and data collection and measurement across levels.

2 TOWARD A BETTER UNDERSTANDING OF HOW TO BE MORE SUSTAINABLE

The self-interested actions of independent firms operating in deregulated global markets will not add up to a sustainable world. This book explains why this ongoing, widespread experiment in the business case for corporate sustainability is failing society. The poorly regulated hand of the free market has incentivized firms to behave in ways that leave humanity hanging by its fingertips amidst constant and worsening environmental calamities. Instead of focusing on sustaining the social-ecological systems in which they are embedded, the corporate sustainability programs developed in recent decades have concentrated on sustaining firms (Barnett et al., 2021).

Government must intervene to gird, guide, and goad firms to treat environments as systems that they are responsible for and must take an active role in sustaining. Even coordinated forms of corporate self-governance such as voluntary environmental programs and certifications require greater government involvement to be effective (Henriques, Husted & Montiel, 2013). Firms cannot continue to perfect constrained optimization by packaging it in more publicly palatable ways. Rather, firms must be regulated in ways that require them to manage rather than ignore their interdependencies with the social-ecological system in which they are embedded (Williams et al., 2017). To move from sustaining firms to salvaging the social-ecological system, governments will need to actually govern, beginning with mandating collaborative actions across firms and between business, government, and global stakeholders across society.

Of course, government travels with a great deal of baggage. Much more management research is needed regarding how to design and implement efficient and effective forms of government regulation that can help tear down firm-level thinking and embed firms in social-ecological systems to co-create collaborative solutions for sustainability problems—and to do so without destroying corporations' incentives to intervene and innovate in ways that make the most of their substantial skills and resources. This book builds up to such a research agenda. We hope you, dear reader, will join us in moving forward with it.

BIBLIOGRAPHY

Avio, C. G., Gorbi, S., & Regoli, F. 2017. Plastics and microplastics in the oceans: From emerging pollutants to emerged threat. Marine Environmental Research, 128: 2–11.

Bansal, P. 2005. Evolving sustainably: A longitudinal study of corporate sustainable development. Strategic Management Journal, 26(3): 197–218.

Barnett, M. L. 2007. Stakeholder influence capacity and the variability of financial returns to corporate social responsibility. Academy of Management Review, 32(3): 794–816.

Barnett, M. L. 2020. Helping business help society: Overcoming barriers to corporate social innovation. Rutgers Business Review, 5(2): 137–144.

Barnett, M. L., Cashore, B., Henriques, I., Husted, B. W., Panwar, R., & Pinske, J. 2021. Reorient the business case for corporate sustainability. Stanford Social Innovation Review, Summer 2021: 35–39.

Barnett, M. L., Henriques, I., & Husted, B. W. 2020. Beyond good intentions: Designing CSR initiatives for greater social impact. Journal of Management, 46(6): 937–964.

Barnett, M. L., Henriques, I., & Husted, B. W. 2021. Sustainability strategies. In I. Duhaime, M. Hitt & M. Lyles (Eds) *Strategic management: State of the field and its future*. Oxford University Press: Oxford: 647–662.

Barney, J. B. 1991. Firm resources and sustained competitive advantage. Journal of Management, 17(1): 99–120.

Bonini, S., & Gorner, S. 2011. The business of sustainability: Putting it into practice. Survey Results. McKinsey & Co. Available at: www.mckinsey.com/~/media/mckinsey/dotcom/client_service/sustainability/pdfs/putting_it_into_practice.ashx. Accessed August 1, 2021.

Elkington, J. 1998. *Cannibals with forks: The triple bottom line of 21st century business*. New Society: Stony Creek, CT.

Fombrun, C., Gardberg, N., & Barnett, M. 2000. Opportunity platforms and safety nets: Corporate citizenship and reputational risk. Business and Society Review, 105: 85–106.

Freeman, R. E. 1984. *Strategic management: A stakeholder approach*. Pitman: Boston, MA.

Frenk, J., Gómez-Dantés, O., & Knaul, F. M. 2011. Globalization and infectious diseases. Infectious Disease Clinics of North America, 25(3): 593–599.

Hart, S. L. 1995. A natural-resource-based view of the firm. Academy of Management Review, 20(4): 986–1014.

Henriques, I., Husted, B. W., & Montiel, I. 2013. Spillover effects of voluntary environmental programs on greenhouse gas emissions: Lessons from Mexico. Journal of Policy Analysis and Management, 32(2): 296–322.

Henriques, I., & Sadorsky, P. 1996. The determinants of an environmentally responsive firm: An empirical approach. Journal of Environmental Economics and Management, 30(3): 381–395.

Henriques, I., & Sadorsky, P. 1999. The relationship between environmental commitment and managerial perceptions of stakeholder importance. Academy of Management Journal, 42(1): 87–99.

Hoffman, A. J. 1999. Institutional evolution and change: Environmentalism and the US chemical industry. Academy of Management Journal, 42(4): 351–371.

IPBES 2019. Intergovernmental Science-Policy Platform on Biodiversity and Ecosystem Services (IPBES). United Nations General Assembly: New York, NY.

IPCC 2018. Special Report: Global warming of 1.5°C. World Meteorological Organization, United Nations: Geneva, Switzerland.

Lambin, E., Gibbs, H., … (thirteen others) ... & Walker, N. 2018. The role of supply-chain initiatives in reducing deforestation. Nature Climate Change, 8: 109–116.

Lenton, T. M., Rockström, J., Gaffney, O., Rahmstorf, S., Richardson, K., Steffen, W., & Schellnhuber, H. J. 2019. Climate tipping points—too risky to bet against. Nature 575(7784): 592–595.

Lindsey, R. 2020. Climate change: Atmospheric carbon dioxide, ClimateWatch Magazine. Available at: www.climate.gov/news-features/understanding-climate/climate-change-atmospheric-carbon-dioxide. Accessed April 4, 2020.

Loska, K., Wiechuła, D., & Korus, I. 2004. Metal contamination of farming soils affected by industry. Environment International, 30(2): 159–165.

Oliver, C. 1991. Strategic responses to institutional processes. Academy of Management Review, 16(1): 145–179.

Ostrom, E. 2009. A general framework for analyzing sustainability of social-ecological systems. Science, 325(5939): 419–422.

Porter, M. E. & Kramer, M. R. 2006. Strategy and society. Harvard Business Review, 84(12): 78–90.

Porter, M. E. & Van der Linde, C. 1995. Toward a new conception of the environment–competitiveness relationship. Journal of Economic Perspectives, 9(4): 97–118.

Rockström, J., Steffen, W., Noone, K., Persson, Å., Chapin, F. S. III, Lambin, E. F., et al. 2009. A safe operating space for humanity. Nature, 461: 472–475.

Shrivastava, P. 1995. The role of corporations in achieving ecological sustainability. Academy of Management Review, 20(4): 936–960.

Starik, M., & Rands, G. P. 1995. Weaving and integrated web: Multilevel and multisystem perspective of ecologically sustainable organizations. Academy of Management Review, 20: 908–935.

Stead, W. E., & Stead, J. G. 1994. Can humankind change the economic myth? Paradigm shifts necessary for ecologically sustainable business. Journal of Organizational Change Management, 7(4): 15–31.

WCED. 1987. *Our common future*. Oxford University Press: Oxford.

Whiteman, G., Walker, B., & Perego, P. 2013. Planetary boundaries: Ecological foundations for corporate sustainability. Journal of Management Studies, 50(2): 307–336.

Williams, A., Kennedy, S., Philipp, F., & Whiteman, G. 2017. Systems thinking: A review of sustainability management research. Journal of Cleaner Production, 148: 866–881.

Winn, M. I., & Pogutz, S. 2013. Business, ecosystems, and biodiversity. Organization & Environment, 26(2): 203–229.

2. Profiting from sustainability

Corporations are designed to make money, not to give it away. A firm starved of money will eventually die. Thus, explaining the activity of a firm means explaining how that activity, in one way or another, sooner or later, contributes to the bottom line. That is, it entails making a "business case" for it.

Some business cases are easier to make than others. Voluntarily allocating the firm's private resources to projects that promote the public good is, on the surface, not an easy business case to make. When that public good is something as amorphous as sustaining society, the complexity of making a business is amplified. How can a firm possibly make money by using its limited resources to regrow forests, protect endangered species, or ameliorate climate change, for example? In this chapter, we provide background on the business case and outline how firms can profit from investing in corporate sustainability.

1 BUILDING UP THE BUSINESS CASE FOR SUSTAINABILITY

Why would a firm willingly take any responsibility for sustaining society? Corporations are popularly described as "externalizing machines" who, in the pursuit of profit, avoid voluntarily accepting responsibility to such a degree that it could be considered pathological (Bakan, 2006). Obviously sustaining society is a huge responsibility for any firm to voluntarily accept. Yet, in the 1990s, as government regulations (Henriques & Sadorsky, 1996; Stead & Stead, 1995, 1996) drew attention to how firms managed information about their environmental performance (Sharbrough & Moody, 1995; Turner & Stephenson, 1994) and how they responded to environmental crises (e.g., Fink, 1986; Mitroff, Pauchant & Shrivastava, 1989; Shrivastava & Siomkos, 1989), firms began to recognize sustainability as one of the most important issues they were facing and to take responsibility for their actions (Hart, 1995; Russo & Fouts, 1997).

Firms, of course, vary in the degree to which they accept responsibility for sustaining society. Henriques and Sadorsky (1999) traced this variation to how differently firms perceived the importance of stakeholders. They examined whether more environmentally committed firms differ in their perceptions of the relative importance of different stakeholders in influencing their natural environmental practices. Blending financial and survey data of Canada's largest firms, they found that managerial perceptions of stakeholder importance do matter.

Table 2.1 Conceptual classification of firms' approaches to the natural environment

Roome (1992)	Hunt and Auster (1990)	Carroll (1979); Wartick and Cochran (1985)	Characteristics
Noncompliance	Beginner	Reactive	• No support or involvement of top management • Environmental management is not necessary • No environmental reporting • No employee environmental training and involvement
Compliance	Firefighter	Defensive	• Piecemeal involvement by top management • Environmental issues only dealt with when necessary • Satisfy environmental regulations • Little employee environmental training and involvement
Compliance plus	Concerned citizen	Accommodative	• Some involvement by top management • Environmental management is a worthwhile function • Internal reporting but little external reporting • Some employee environmental training and involvement
Commercial and environmental excellence	Pragmatist	Proactive	• Top management supports and is involved in environmental issues • Environmental management is an important business function • Internal and external reporting • Employee environmental training and involvement encouraged
Leading edge	Proactivist		

Source: Adapted from Henriques & Sadorsky (1999: 88).

As shown in Table 2.1, firms were categorized according to their approach to the natural environment: reactive, defensive, accommodative, and proactive. Henriques and Sadorsky (1999) found that proactive leaders viewed environmental management as an important business function. However, the only stakeholder reactive firms viewed as important was the media. In other words, reactive firms appear to be more concerned about being caught doing something wrong (e.g., releasing toxic emissions) by a reporter than by a regulator. Moreover, both proactive and accommodative firms placed great importance on community stakeholders. Their perceived importance supports the position that successful environmental policy planning requires industry members to work with community leaders and to look at environmental issues through the eyes of their stakeholders.

Over the last several decades, management scholars have helped firms to become more environmentally proactive by framing sustainability not as an obligation or cost, but as an investment (Dyllick & Hockerts, 2002; Porter & Kramer, 2006). This investment can pay off for firms in a myriad of ways. As shown in Figure 2.1, we sort the corporate benefits of sustainability according to how quickly a firm can realize them (short term versus long term) and how easily they can be codified (tangible versus intangible), creating four broad categories.

Short-term, tangible benefits are the low-hanging fruit that firms tend to quickly harvest when launching sustainability programs. Firms can immediately cut costs through technological and process improvements that increase eco-efficiency. Near-term tangible gains arise by reducing the costs associated with energy usage, waste production, and manufacturing (Dutt & King, 2014). Hart and Milstein (2003) showcase examples of companies who grew their profits and reduced risk through pollution prevention and eco-efficiency, including 3M's "Pollution Prevention Pays" and Dow Chemical's "Waste Reduction Always Pays." A recent review of the industrial sector worldwide suggests that there are vast energy-saving opportunities that firms have yet to adopt (Abdelaziz, Saidur & Mekhilef, 2011). Why are firms not adopting these savings? A recent paper by Dowell and Muthulingam (2017) examines firms' choices regarding the implementation of energy-saving initiatives and finds that the degree of disruption, the number of prior local adopters, and the strength of environmental norms affect a firm's decision to adopt such initiatives. Hence, it is no surprise to see governments try to hasten greater firm adoption of energy efficiency initiatives by introducing taxes on energy use, encouraging the exchange of technical information, and providing energy management training and tax incentives (Abdelaziz, Saidur & Mekhilef, 2011). Thus, the business case is relatively easy to make here, given that waste reduction and improved sourcing, production, and distribution processes can provide quick, tangible "win–win" outcomes.

The second kind of short-term benefit is more intangible. Rather than realize direct savings from lower input and production costs, here firms gain pricing power. As we will discuss in Chapter 5, some consumers have a greater willingness to pay (WTP) for products and services that are more sustainable (Schäufele & Hamm, 2017). Researchers have found that green consumption is part of a broader human engagement with the environment. For example, Delmas (2018) speaks to the importance of framing product benefits to motivate green behavior. Firms producing products and services such as organic wine (Delmas & Gergaud, 2021), sustainable tourism (Kim, Barber & Kim, 2019), and green products (Nuttavuthisit & Thogersen, 2017) have all succeeded in growing their markets over time. Thus, corporate sustainability initiatives may enable firms to immediately raise prices, thereby increasing revenue.

Though increases in pricing power can be more difficult to predict than gains from cost cutting, business-case calculations are relatively easy to make for sustainability initiatives that promise immediate returns. But as the expected benefits become more distant, it becomes more difficult to make the business case. Therefore, we focus this chapter on how firms achieve long-term benefits from their sustainability initiatives. Specifically, we outline how corporate sustainability programs help firms build capacity to influence stakeholders over time, which provides these firms with improved access to new market opportunities while buffering them from a myriad of risks.

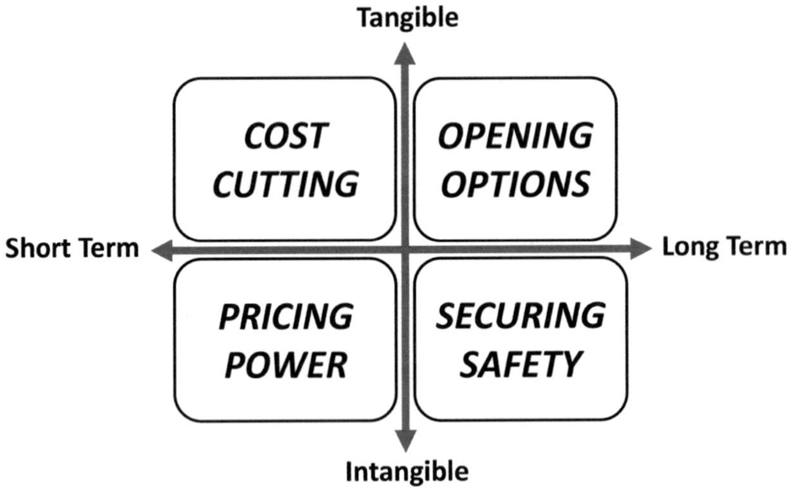

Figure 2.1 *Corporate benefits of sustainability*

2 BIG BUCKS IN BUILDING STAKEHOLDER INFLUENCE CAPACITY

Many hundreds of studies have empirically tested the business case (Barnett, Henriques & Husted, 2020). The literature is so vast that it has spawned a great many reviews. Margolis and Walsh (2003) tallied thirteen reviews since 1978, a number which has surely grown considerably two decades hence. In one of the earliest literature reviews, Ullmann (1985) described this body of research as "data in search of a theory." A dozen years later, Griffin and Mahon (1997) entitled their review "Twenty-Five Years of Incomparable Research." Roman, Hayibor, and Agle (1999) "repainted the portrait" they ascribed to Griffin and Mahon's (1997) critical study to recast it as more supportive of the business case, but Mahon and Griffin (1999) subsequently repainted that repaint to return the portrait to its original critical state. More recently, Orlitzky et al. (2003) performed a meta-analysis of the population of quantitative studies to date and found support for the business case. Margolis and Walsh (2003: 278), however, argued that any conclusion that the business case is now established because more empirical studies have been published in support of it than against it is "illusory."

Though the empirical testing is vast, the results cannot conclusively state that it does or does not pay to be sustainable. Rather, the literature evinces considerable variation: sometimes sustainability pays, sometimes it does not. Often lacking in this massive literature is the theoretical logic to explain this variation. Over the past several decades scholars have added myriad control variables to their studies to capture variation, but they have done so in an ad hoc fashion, leaving critics to contend that the end result is nothing more than a "mishmash" of variables (Rowley & Berman, 2000: 405).

McWilliams and Siegel (2001) constructed a supply and demand model of socially responsible activities such as sustainability that explained how size, level of diversification, R&D, advertising, government sales, consumer income, labor market conditions, and stage in the industry life cycle influenced the level of sustainability output by a given firm. Their "theory of the firm perspective" assumed, however, "that each firm makes optimal choices, which means that each produces at a profit-maximizing level of output" (McWilliams & Siegel, 2001: 125). Using this logic, sustainability must be an almost universally wise investment, considering it is already an "almost universal practice" (Dressel, 2003: 1). Support for the business case is an assumption of the model, since each firm only makes optimal choices—if sustainability did not maximize profit, then firms would not engage in it. Thus, offering an economic rationale for why firms supply sustainability (because there is profitable demand for its supply) fails to explain why or even acknowledge that some firms might earn negative financial returns from sustainability activities.

Accounting for R&D as a predictor of returns elicits an interesting research comparison on the link between organizational learning and innovation. One of the fundamental issues in the literature on innovation is why so many firms invest in basic R&D even though the fruits of such efforts are public goods. The prevailing logic for several decades was that basic R&D was primarily the territory of well-diversified firms, since such firms can capture a larger share of these otherwise public benefits (Nelson, 1959). Cohen and Levinthal (1990: 128) introduced the absorptive capacity construct, defined as "the ability of a firm to recognize the value of new, external information, assimilate it, and apply it to commercial ends." This construct shifted innovation research away from a quest to elucidate the structural conditions that produce spending on basic research, towards a quest to gain a deeper understanding of how basic research can serve as a form of organizational learning that mediates and moderates financial returns to R&D. Although costly R&D activities can increase social welfare by generating public knowledge, absorptive capacity helps explain how such activities can benefit the sponsoring firm and how they vary across firms and time. In effect, the construct of absorptive capacity solidified what could be called "the business case for basic R&D" by demonstrating the contingent link between R&D and corporate financial performance (CFP).

As Lane, Koka, and Pathak declared, "Absorptive capacity is one of the most important constructs to emerge in organizational research over the past decades" (2002: Ml). It clarified the cumulative and path-dependent nature of learning, arguing that the stronger the base in learning, the greater the payoff to future investments in learning: "Prior knowledge permits the assimilation and exploitation of new knowledge. ... Accumulating absorptive capacity in one period will permit its more efficient accumulation in the next" (Cohen & Levinthal, 1990: 135–136). Without absorptive capacity, new knowledge has no context, no way to associate and embed. It is analogous to soil; its presence is required for a seed to grow, and the richer the soil, the greater the growth. An extensive body of theoretical and empirical research now attests that some firms have more absorptive capacity than others and so can transform a unit of investment in learning into greater financial gains (Zahra & George, 2002). Therefore, the business case for basic R&D is contingent (on absorptive capacity), not universal.

The relationship between CSR and CFP is similar to the connection between learning and innovation as addressed in the absorptive capacity literature. One of the fundamental issues in the sustainability literature is to explain why so many firms devote resources to sustainability given that the benefits are public and the costs private. The long-standing assumption of the business case (normative and agency issues aside) has been that firms will increase investment in sustainability if they can capture more of its private benefits. Based on this assumption, researchers have sought to clarify the structural conditions under which firms might receive private gains from CSR and sustainability. While we have insight regarding why firms supply it (McWilliams & Siegel, 2001), the literature lacked a theoretical framework to explain heterogeneous returns to sustainability (Rowley & Berman, 2000).

To fill this void, Barnett (2007) introduced the construct of stakeholder influence capacity: the ability of a firm to identify, act on, and profit from opportunities to improve stakeholder relationships through CSR. Similar to how a firm can notice, assimilate, and exploit new knowledge depending on its prior knowledge, the ability of a firm to notice and profitably exploit opportunities to improve stakeholder relations through sustainability depends on its prior stakeholder relationships. The basic premise is that stakeholders draw from their prior knowledge of a firm when they assess the implications of new information generated by that firm's sustainability activities. In short, the actions of a firm and the responses by its stakeholders regarding sustainability are path dependent such that different firms obtain different results from sustainability, depending on their unique histories. Stakeholder influence capacity is therefore an umbrella construct that accounts for those factors that forge this history, influencing how stakeholders react to a firm's sustainability initiatives, thereby charting boundary conditions for the range of profitable opportunities.

If a firm's CSR activity is to alter its relationship with a stakeholder, that stakeholder must notice, interpret, and act on the information conveyed by this activity. The stakeholder influence capacity construct augments interest-based (Frooman, 1999) and identity-based (Rowley & Moldoveanu, 2003) views of stakeholder action by pointing out that the way a stakeholder will interpret and react to a noticed act of sustainability are influenced by the history of the focal firm. The path-dependent nature of stakeholder relations means that a given investment in sustainability may provoke different stakeholder reactions and yield different financial results for different firms at different points in time. Moreover, a firm's history affects the degree to which it will be presented with sustainability investment opportunities, be aware of such opportunities and be willing and able to exploit them. Therefore, the stakeholder influence capacity construct points out that lack of investment in stakeholder relationship building can limit the scope of future profitable sustainability opportunities. So just like absorptive capacity solidified "the business case for basic R&D" by demonstrating the contingent link between R&D and CFP, stakeholder influence capacity solidifies what could be called the "business case for sustainability" by linking sustainability and CFP.

Barnett and Salomon (2012) found empirical support for stakeholder influence capacity (SIC) by demonstrating a U-shaped relationship between a firm's social and financial performance. These findings suggest that firms should view sustainability as a long-term investment in creating the capacity to influence stakeholders; though it may not pay to be good now, it may pay to be good later, once adequate capacity is built. If a firm has little ability or desire to build such a capacity, then sustainability initiatives will prove to be poor financial investments. However, if a firm can build such capacity, it may find that it is very profitable to do so.

3 PROFITING FROM PLATFORMS AND SAVING WITH SAFETY NETS

Stakeholder influence capacity takes time to build. Firms lacking in SIC have not gained adequate stakeholder trust so are unable to profit from the resulting stakeholder favor. However, firms who make long-term investments in sustainability may gain ample SIC to profit. Thus, it can pay to be good to society, for those firms that stick with it. If stakeholders view the firm as a good corporate citizen, one concerned about the plight of the planet over time, not just as an opportunist, then the resulting improvement in stakeholder relationships can benefit the firm by providing it with greater upside opportunities and buffering it from downside losses (Fombrun, Gardberg & Barnett, 2000).

3.1 Opening Options

Traditionally, corporate investments are evaluated by calculating the net present value (NPV) of their projected cash flows. A careful analysis of projected cash flows of sustainability projects, using traditional techniques of valuation, often leads to the decision to forego such investments (McWilliams & Siegel, 2001). Unfortunately, the NPV approach fails to consider the value of strategic flexibility that certain investments create. This flexibility can be analyzed using the concept of real options, which refers to select investments, resources, and capabilities that provide the decision maker with "the ability to select an outcome only if it is favorable" (McGrath, 1997: 975). Such options are valuable because they can expose the holder to unfolding and upwardly unbounded market opportunities while limiting downside outcomes (Bookstaber, 1981; Bowman & Hurry, 1993; Sanchez, 1993).

Many options are based on financial instruments and stock options that were actively traded in organized exchanges. The theory of options pricing has revolutionized financial markets by clarifying when options are mispriced, thereby helping to identify profitable opportunities (Black & Scholes, 1973; Merton, 1973). To date there are many kinds of options. For example, landlords often give their tenants an option to buy the leased property at a specified price during the period of the lease agreement. The tenant can then later decide whether to purchase the property depending on their financial situation, other available properties, and general macroeconomic conditions.

In contrast to financial options, which are based on financial assets, real options depend on operating assets (Kogut, 1991). Options quite simply confer "preferential access to future opportunities" (Bowman & Hurry, 1993: 762). Real options include both the option to undertake activities or to acquire resources (Sanchez, 1993). They allow a person or a firm to defer a decision to commit resources until after the nature of an uncertain environment has revealed itself. If future conditions turn out to be poor, then decision makers can stop investment; if conditions turn out positively, investment may continue.

In financial markets, call options give the holder the right to buy a specific security within a certain time frame at a given price. This price is referred to as the strike or exercise price. Put options give the holder the right to sell a specific security within a certain time at the exercise price. If the market value of the underlying security is greater than the exercise price, then a call option has a positive value, while the put option is worthless. If the market value is less than the exercise price, then the call option is worthless, but the put option would have a positive value. The value of a call option may be defined as:

$$W = (S_t - E, 0) \tag{2.1}$$

where W is the value of the option, S_t is the value of the underlying security at a time t, and E is the exercise price — the price at which the underlying security may be bought under the terms of the option contract (Kogut, 1991: 23). Most pricing models do not specify an exact price for the option, but rather set the bounds on what the price of an option should be. Black and Scholes (1973) and Merton (1973) significantly advanced the theory of option pricing by specifying that the value of an option is a function of five variables: the value of the underlying security, the exercise price, the time to exercise, the risk-free interest rate, and the volatility of the underlying security.

Real options may be similarly conceived, except they are based on investment projects, rather than securities. According to Kogut (1991), the value of a real option may be defined as:

$$W = (V - P, 0) \tag{2.2}$$

where W is the value of the real option, V is the value of the underlying project, and P is the equivalent of the strike price or the cost of undertaking a project. The real option limits the firm's losses to W by allowing it to defer decisions until more information is available. If that information favors a future investment, that investment, equivalent to P, is undertaken. The method for the valuation of real options can vary from highly quantitative approaches applied to capital budgeting decisions (Trigeorgis, 1993) to more qualitative approaches (Bowman and Hurry, 1993; McGrath, 1997; Sanchez, 1993).

Real options logic can be applied to decisions involving resource allocation within the firm (Bowman & Hurry, 1993). Some investments provide the firm with the opportunity to continue or discontinue further investment, contributing to its strategic flexibility. Theorists have applied the real options logic to joint ventures (Chi, 2000; Kogut, 1991), technology investment (McGrath, 1997), research and development (Paxson, 2001), entrepreneurial failure (McGrath, 1999), and global manufacturing (Kogut & Kulatilaka, 1994). Others have even argued that strategy itself may be perceived as a portfolio of real options (Bowman & Hurry, 1993; Luehrman, 1998; Sanchez, 1993).

Given that sustainability often involves future opportunities, corporate sustainability can be analyzed from a real options perspective. In its broadest sense, CSR refers to "the firm's consideration of, and response to, issues beyond the narrow economic, technical, and legal requirements of the firm ... (to) accomplish social benefits along with the traditional economic gains which the firm seeks" (Davis, 1973). Corporate sustainability is an important component of CSR, as it is a form of investment (McWilliams & Siegel, 2001) that creates "opportunities to expand and grow in the future" (Kogut, 1991: 21). A firm's response to corporate sustainability may be proactive or reactive (Clarkson, 1995), although it is the proactive forms of corporate sustainability—as in, corporate activity that exceeds compliance with legal requirements (McWilliams & Siegel, 2001)—that we are especially interested in.

Real corporate sustainability options can be divided into two kinds: those that generate direct versus indirect benefits (Burke & Logsdon, 1996). Direct benefits derive from the creation of new products and services, generating rents that are captured by the firm. Indirect benefits include the development of firm-specific assets that are of value to the firm but require further steps to capture the rent potential of these assets.

In the case of real corporate sustainability options with direct benefits, corporate sustainability may act as a vehicle for innovation by providing the opportunity to test a product or service before launching it to a wider public (Kanter, 1999). For example, in the early 1990s, every flooring manufacturer was oblivious to corporate sustainability until Ray Anderson, the CEO of Interface, changed the landscape. Anderson recognized the waste problem and sought to address it long before his competitors by starting a movement to make firms more aware of and responsible for their environmental impacts. Influenced by Paul Hawken's (1993) book, *The Ecology of Commerce*, Anderson recounted the story of the overshoot and collapse of the reindeer of St. Matthew Island as a metaphor for the Earth as well as humankind

(Anderson, 2009). Interface began its journey by setting appropriate targets and accurately assessing environmental performance to become a world leader in industrial ecology. Anderson employed a collaborative stakeholder engagement process to incorporate the perspectives of employees, customers, designers, academics, and engineers in the circularization of Interface's manufacturing process. The collaborative approach resulted not only in waste savings that were then invested in subsequent environmental initiatives, but also an open approach to sharing what they learned from this journey with competitors and other industries (Anderson, 2009).

By solving a problem relevant to a specific group, corporate sustainability investment enables the firm to develop goods and services on a small scale. A corporate sustainability option then provides the firm with the flexibility to decide whether to continue investment on a larger scale or to withhold further investment. In this case, the real option is similar to that generally created by R&D and technology investments (McGrath, 1997; Paxson, 2001). In fact, corporate sustainability has a close relationship to R&D. An example of such a relationship is an organic, pesticide-free product which simultaneously speaks to the innovative organic methods employed by farmers as well as the product innovation developed by the natural food retailer (McWilliams and Siegel, 2000). McGrath (1997) provides an interesting example of the decision to invest in pollution control technology, which illustrates how this kind of real corporate sustainability option can be valued.

However, many real corporate sustainability options are not so easily valued because their benefits are less tangible. In this case, corporate sustainability projects rely on the indirect benefits generated from the goodwill of corporate sustainability investments within the community and among consumers to provide strategic flexibility. Corporate sustainability investment creates the option, but not the obligation, for the firm to call upon stakeholders for required resources, such as in the formation of a new venture (Fombrun & Shanley, 1990; Starr & MacMillan, 1990).

3.2 Securing Safety

Possibly the most dramatic instances where proactive corporate sustainability creates the option to call upon the support and resources of stakeholders occur in times of crisis. For example, Johnson & Johnson's reaction to the Tylenol poisoning crisis is an illustration of corporate sustainability as a real option. In response to the poisoning of some Extra-Strength Tylenol products, in September 1982, Johnson & Johnson immediately withdrew its entire inventory of Tylenol from supermarket and drugstore shelves around the world. The recall decision was the price or cost of the option—the firm lost nearly \$100 million in 1982. As a result of this decision, the company obtained strategic flexibility. It could choose to discard the product because of its damaged image or rescue the image of the product. When a technical solution to the problem was found and it was determined that the product could be distributed safely, Johnson & Johnson decided to reintroduce Extra-Strength Tylenol and undertook a successful marketing campaign. By February 1983, Tylenol had regained 65 percent of its original sales within nine weeks of the reintroduction (Siomkos, 1992). The ability to reintroduce the Extra-Strength Tylenol was largely due to the trust generated among consumers by the quick reaction of the company to the crisis. This provided the firm with a strategic flexibility it would otherwise not have enjoyed.

An interesting case to compare with Johnson & Johnson's response to the Tylenol poisoning is the *Exxon Valdez* incident. On March 22, 1989, the oil tanker, *Exxon Valdez*, struck a reef in Prince William Sound. The resulting oil spill caused the death of more than 6,000 otters and 750,000 seabirds. The proximate cause of the accident was the intoxicated ship captain who turned the helm over to the third mate who was not licensed to steer a tanker in those waters (Hosmer, 1998). However, this cause must be located within the organizational context at Exxon. By 1988, Exxon had just finished a significant downsizing of its workforce from 145,000 employees in 1986 to around 100,000 employees in 1988. This was in response to a dramatic decline in oil prices from $32.00 per barrel in 1981 to $12.00 per barrel in 1986. As a result of this reduction in the workforce, many officers, like the third mate, were routinely asked to perform functions for which they were not licensed. In addition, the firm had eliminated the emergency response crew and much of the equipment that could have contained the spill within five hours. The *Exxon Valdez* spill was not contained for 59 hours (Hosmer, 1998).

The decision to eliminate the emergency response team as well as to use the emergency response equipment for other purposes was a decision that eliminated strategic flexibility. In other words, it eliminated a real option. The investment cost for equipment and crew was a real cost, which in essence amounted to the purchase of a real option. By eliminating the crew and equipment, Exxon saved the cost of the option, but lost the flexibility to respond to unexpected events such as the intoxication of the captain. As a result, the savings left the firm exposed to a downside business risk valued at more than $8.7 billion in terms of clean-up costs and criminal fines (Hosmer, 1998).

The price of a corporate sustainability option is the cost of its development ("W" in equation 2.2). In terms of the Johnson & Johnson case, the development of the option involved the recall of the product. In the Exxon case, the cost of the option foregone was the cost of maintaining the security teams and equipment. The price of the corporate sustainability option is related to all the capital, intermediate goods, and labor involved in its creation (McWilliams & Siegel, 2001). Once the development of the corporate sustainability option was completed, an asset was created (V). This asset consists of the right to exploit the resources, such as goodwill or trust, created by the asset. Exercise of the corporate sustainability option then involves taking further action or making additional investments and in this way capture the goodwill created by the option (P).

The value of the corporate sustainability option, like other real options, depends on five variables: the value of the underlying project, the exercise price, the time to maturity, the risk-free interest rate, and the uncertainty or volatility of the returns making up the underlying project (Copeland, 2001; Luehrman, 1998). From a strategic point of view, if the value of the corporate sustainability option is greater than its price, the firm should acquire the option; otherwise, it should not.

The first variable to determine the value of a real corporate sustainability option is the expected value of revenues from the project's operations and the second is the value of the underlying project (McGrath, 1997; Sanchez, 1993). The expected value of revenues from corporate sustainability depends on the demand for it. This is determined by the price of the good with corporate sustainability attributes, the cost of advertising to increase the visibility of corporate sustainability attributes, the level of consumers' disposable income, and the price of substitute goods (McWilliams & Siegel, 2001). Consumer tastes and demographics also affect the demand for corporate sustainability, but their impact is complex and not easily determined.

The value of the underlying project may arise from the access it offers to resources such as financial, human, or social capital, which can be useful in a number of activities such as launching new ventures (Starr and MacMillan, 1990), or attracting qualified employees (Turban & Greening, 1997). The value of the underlying project can also depend on the costs avoided through the real corporate sustainability option. For example, the value of the real option foregone in the *Exxon Valdez* case is a function of the penalties, liability, and risk to reputation that could have been avoided by obtaining a real option through an investment in emergency response personnel and equipment (Fombrun et al., 2000).

Currently, the methods for the value measurement of the underlying project are ad hoc. Many of these methods, such as avoidable costs, hedonic pricing, travel costs, contingent valuation, and social discount rates, are commonly used in the field of cost–benefit analysis (Mishan, 1988). Given the state-of-the-art in the field, the use of specific methods varies greatly from project to project.

The exercise price of a corporate sustainability option refers to additional investments made by the firm to extract the value created by the corporate sustainability option. In the Johnson & Johnson case, the exercise price was the cost of the marketing campaign to reintroduce Extra-Strength Tylenol to the market.

The timing of the exercise of a real corporate sustainability option is also a critical variable that affects its value. Generally speaking, the longer one can defer the exercise of a real option, the more valuable that option will be; unless the asset value decays rapidly with time or there exists the threat of competitive preemption, in which case the option is more valuable if it can be exercised earlier (Bowman & Hurry, 1993; Sanchez, 1993). Returning to the Johnson & Johnson case, the former strength of the Tylenol brand would have deteriorated rapidly (given the tremendous competition in the market for pain relievers at the time) if the company had not acted quickly to take advantage of the goodwill it created in its response to the poisoning.

The risk-free interest rate is not widely discussed in the real options literature, although it is mentioned as a necessary element in the valuation of real options (Copeland, 2001; Luehrman, 1998). The risk-free rate is usually measured as the return on short-maturity U.S. treasury securities (Weston & Brigham, 1981). The higher the risk-free interest rate, the greater the value of an option (Bookstaber, 1981; Copeland, 2001). This relationship holds because the exercise price is paid in the future. As the risk-free interest rate increases, the present value of the exercise price decreases, thus increasing the value of the option itself.

Finally, the value of the corporate sustainability option rises when perceived environmental uncertainty increases (Bowman & Hurry, 1993; Sanchez, 1993). Increased uncertainty includes both the possibility of higher than expected and lower than expected returns on a project. Uncertainty refers to the variance of the expected value of the net revenues minus the costs of extracting benefits from the project (the exercise price). All factors that could increase either the variance in the expected value of net revenues or the variance in the exercise price will increase uncertainty and thus increase the value of the corporate sustainability option. As possible returns rise, the corporate sustainability option allows the decision maker to capture positive returns, while limiting the downside outcomes that may occur if those returns do not turn out as expected. Since the option limits the possible negative returns, the decision maker can capture the benefits of the increased variance in returns, thus increasing the value of the option as the variance of returns rises.

Uncertainty is also dependent upon certain boundary conditions, which affect the size and sustainability of rent streams from claims to underlying corporate sustainability assets. Boundary conditions also influence the costs of extracting the benefits from corporate sustainability investments. McGrath (1997) discusses the nature of these boundary conditions for technology options, many of which apply to corporate sustainability options. For example, stakeholders may either try to block the firm from accessing valuable resources or expropriate a portion of the firm's rent streams created by corporate sustainability options. Competitors may also try to match or imitate the benefits provided by corporate sustainability, thus reducing rents available to the firm. In each of these cases, the boundary conditions limit the rent streams and the variability of the underlying asset. As the variability decreases, the value of the real corporate sustainability option also decreases.

By only considering the conditions of supply (the cost of the option) and demand (the expected value of revenues) for proactive corporate sustainability, firms will undoubtedly underinvest in corporate sustainability projects. However, if the firm incorporates the value of the underlying project in terms of the access to resources it provides, the exercise price, the exercise timing of the option, the uncertainty of revenues and costs associated with the underlying project, and the risk-free interest rate into the valuation of the real corporate sustainability option, the firm will be able to determine more adequately the most profitable amount of corporate sustainability investment. Optimizing this amount of sustainability investment, as complex and subjective as the calculations can be, enables the firm to open up new options, as well as to build a safety net against losses.

Environmental issues such as energy security and climate change have increased the financial risk to firms (Henriques & Sadorsky, 2010). As a result, the safety-net benefits of corporate sustainability investments have become especially salient. Straightforward, technical aspects of environmental performance like pollution control and eco-efficiency can be implemented relatively quickly and efficiently, but more advanced environmental actions such as eco stewardship, business redefinition, and industrial ecosystems can be disruptive innovations (Sharma & Henriques, 2005). To make complex business cases here, managing risk becomes a very useful framework.

There are two kinds of risk associated with a firm's stock: systematic risk and unsystematic or business risk (Weston & Brigham, 1981). Systematic risk is the stock's correlation with the return of the stock market. Business risk "reflects the variation in a stock's return ascribable to firm-specific forces" (Amit & Wernerfelt, 1990: 521). Normally, business risk is irrelevant to financial theory because a diversified portfolio of securities can reduce or even eliminate business risk. However, a firm that successfully manages its business risk can provide above-normal returns to shareholders (Amit & Wernerfelt, 1990). As a result, Bettis (1983) argues that strategic management is essentially about business risk management.

A real options lens provides a sharper focus on the relationship of corporate sustainability to risk. First, real options by their nature deal with operating, rather than financial assets (Kogut, 1991). They are concerned with firm-specific risk rather than market-force risk. Similarly, real corporate sustainability options involve operating and strategic decisions by managers that are likely to have an impact on the business or unsystematic risk of the firm (Bowman, 1980). The real options logic of corporate sustainability thus shifts the interested party from the portfolio investor to the corporate manager.

Second, real options provide an important way for firms to manage business risk by reducing the downside risk of future investments (Bowman & Hurry, 1993; Miller & Reuer, 1996). Frequently, risk is conceptualized simply as the volatility of firm profitability and is measured as a variance in returns (Bromiley, 1991; Ruefli, Collins & Lacugna, 1999). However, considerable research indicates that managers only include the probability of loss, rather than the probability of gains, within their concept of risk (March & Shapira, 1987; Miller & Leiblein, 1996; Miller & Reuer, 1996), suggesting that the downside risk is especially relevant to firms and their managers. Corporate sustainability, like other real options, is also oriented toward downside risk—the containment of possible losses, rather than a concern with the variability of returns on the positive side. The focus on measures of the variance of accounting returns, common in the corporate sustainability-risk literature, is unrealistic given the real options nature of corporate sustainability with its focus on downside outcomes.

Lastly, a real corporate sustainability option explicitly includes a time dimension. The decision to invest in the corporate sustainability option is made before the investment could have a possible impact on business risk. This *ex ante* perspective is different from the focus on market risk and variance of accounting returns used in most corporate sustainability risk research, which is *ex post* in nature since it looks at historical returns. However, managers do not make decisions based on historical variability of returns, but on the perception of risk in the future (Bromiley, 1991; Ruefli et al., 1999). Given the nature of corporate social responsibility as a real option, we can hypothesize that the more proactive corporate sustainability projects are, the lower the *ex ante* downside business risk of the firm.

4 CONCLUSION

Firms can gain a myriad of near-term and long-term tangible and intangible benefits that build a business case for their sustainability initiatives. However, some business cases are easier to make than others. For the business case to succeed in spurring corporate sustainability initiatives beyond the low-hanging fruit that has already been largely exhausted, firms need to recognize the real option value that can be generated through sustainability initiatives that increase stakeholder influence capacity. These corporate sustainability real options can provide access to a range of new opportunities to increase revenue while safeguarding the firm from much of the downside risk.

BIBLIOGRAPHY

Abdelaziz, E. A., Saidur, R., & Mekhilef, S. 2011. A review on energy saving strategies in the industrial sector. Renewable and Sustainable Energy Reviews, 15(1): 150–168.

Amit, R., & Wernerfelt, B. 1990. Why do firms reduce business risk? Academy of Management Journal, 33(3): 520–533.

Anderson, R. C. 2009. *Confessions of a radical industrialist: Profits, people, purpose – doing business by respecting the earth.* McClelland & Stewart: Toronto, ON.

Bakan, J. 2006. The corporation. The pathological pursuit of profit and power. Society and Business Review, 1(3): 281–282.

Barnett, M. L. 2007. Stakeholder influence capacity and the variability of financial returns to corporate social responsibility. Academy of Management Review, 32(3): 794–816.

Barnett, M. L., Henriques, I., & Husted, B. W. 2020. Beyond good intentions: Designing CSR initiatives for greater social impact. Journal of Management, 46(6): 937–964.

Barnett, M. L., & Salomon, R. M. 2012. Does it pay to be really good? Addressing the shape of the relationship between social and financial performance. Strategic Management Journal, 33: 1304–1320.

Baumol, W. J. 1991. (Almost) perfect competition (contestability) and business ethics. In W. J. Baumol, and S. A. B. Blackman (Eds) *Perfect markets and easy virtue: business ethics and the invisible hand.* Blackwell Publishers: Cambridge, MA: 1–23.

Bettis, R. A. 1983. Modern financial theory, corporate strategy, and public policy: Three conundrums. Academy of Management Review, 8: 405–414.

Black, F., & Scholes, M. 1973. The pricing of options and corporate liabilities. Journal of Political Economy, 81: 637–659.

Bookstaber, R. M. 1981. *Option pricing and strategies in* investing. Addison-Wesley Publishing Company: Reading, MA.

Bowman, E. H. 1980. A risk/return paradox for strategic management. Sloan Management Review, 21(3): 17–31.

Bowman, E. H., & Hurry, D. 1993. Strategy through the option lens: An integrated view of resource investments and the incremental-choice process. Academy of Management Review, 18(4): 760–782.

Bromiley, P. 1991. Testing a causal model of corporate risk taking and responsibility. Academy of Management Journal, 34(1): 37–59.

Burke, L., & Logsdon, J. 1996. How corporate social responsibility pays off. Long Range Planning, 29: 495–502.

Carroll, A. B. 1979. A three-dimensional conceptual model of corporate social performance. Academy of Management Review, 4: 497–505.

Chi, T. 2000. Option to acquire or divest a joint venture. Strategic Management Journal, 21: 665–687.

Clarkson, M. B. E. 1995. A stakeholder framework for analyzing and evaluating corporate social responsibility. Academy of Management Review, 20(1): 92–117.

Cohen, W., & Levinthal, D. 1990. Absorptive capacity: A new perspective on learning and innovation. Administrative Science Quarterly, 35: 128–152.

Copeland, T. 2001. The real-options approach to capital allocation. Strategic Finance, 83(4): 33–37.

Davis, K. 1973. The case for and against business assumption of social responsibilities. Academy of Management Journal, 16: 312–322.

Delmas, M. 2018. *The green bundle: Pairing the market with the planet*. With David A. Colgan. Stanford University Press: Stanford, CA.
Delmas, M. A., & Gergaud, O. 2021. Sustainable practices and product quality: Is there value in eco-label certification? The case of wine. Ecological Economics, 183.
Dowell, G. W. S., & Muthulingam, S. 2017. Will firms go green if it pays? The impact of disruption, cost, and external factors on the adoption of environmental initiatives. Strategic Management Journal, 38(6): 1287–1304.
Dressel, C. 2003, August 18. For effective CSR campaigns, sincerity starts at home. *PR News*: 1–3.
Dutt, N., & King, A. A. 2014. The judgment of garbage: End-of-pipe treatment and waste reduction. Management Science, 60(7): 1812–1828.
Dyllick, T., & Hockerts, K. 2002. Beyond the business case for corporate sustainability. Business Strategy & the Environment, 11(2): 130–141.
Fink, S. 1986. *Crisis management*. American Management Association: New York, NY
Fombrun, C., Gardberg, N., & Barnett, M. 2000. Opportunity platforms and safety nets: Corporate citizenship and reputational risk. Business and Society Review, 105: 85–106.
Fombrun, C., & Shanley, M. 1990. What's in a name? Reputation building and corporate strategy. Academy of Management Review, 33(2): 233–258.
Friedman, M. 1962. *Capitalism and freedom*. University of Chicago Press: Chicago, IL.
Frooman, J. 1999. Stakeholder influence strategies. Academy of Management Review, 24: 191–205.
Griffin, J., & Mahon, J. 1997. The corporate social performance and corporate financial performance debate: Twenty-five years of incomparable research. Business and Society, 36: 5–31.
Hahn, T., Figge, F., Pinkse, J., & Preuss, L. 2010. Trade-offs in corporate sustainability: You can't have your cake and eat it. Business Strategy & the Environment, 19(4): 217–229.
Hart, S. L. 1995. A natural-resource-based view of the firm. Academy of Management Review, 20(4): 986–1014.
Hart, S. L., & Milstein, M. B. 2003. Creating sustainable value. Academy of Management Executive, 17(2): 56–67.
Hawken, P. 1993. *The ecology of commerce: A declaration of sustainability*. Harper Business: New York, NY.
Henriques, I., & Sadorsky, P. 1996. The determinants of an environmentally responsive firm: An empirical approach. Journal of Environmental Economics and Management, 30(3): 381–395.
Henriques, I., & Sadorsky, P. 1999. The relationship between environmental commitment and managerial perceptions of stakeholder importance. Academy of Management Journal, 42: 87–99.
Henriques, I., & Sadorsky, P. 2010. Can environmental sustainability be used to manage energy price risk? Energy Economics, 32(5): 1131–1138.
Herremans, I. M., Nazari, J. A., & Mahmoudian, F. 2016. Stakeholder relationships, engagement, and sustainability reporting. Journal of Business Ethics, 138(3): 417–435.
Hosmer, L. T. 1998. Lessons from the wreck of the Exxon Valdez: The need for imagination, empathy, and courage. Business Ethics Quarterly Special Issue No. 1: 109–122.

Hunt, C. B., & Auster, E. R. 1990. Proactive environmental management: Avoiding the toxic trap. Sloan Management Review, 31(2): 7–18.
Husted, B. W. 2005. Risk management, real options, and corporate social responsibility. Journal of Business Ethics, 60(2): 175–183.
Kanter, R. M. 1999. From spare change to real change. Harvard Business Review, 77(3): 122–132.
Kim, Y. H., Barber, N., & Kim, D. K. 2019. Sustainability research in the hotel industry: Past, present, and future. Journal of Hospitality Marketing & Management, 28(5): 576–620.
Kogut, B. 1991. Joint ventures and the option to expand and acquire. Management Science, 37(1): 19–33.
Kogut, B., & Kulatilaka, N. 1994. Operating flexibility, global manufacturing, and the option value of a multinational network. Management Science, 40(1): 123–139.
Lane, P., Koka, B., & Pathak, S. 2002. A thematic analysis and critical assessment of absorptive capacity research. Academy of Management Best Paper Proceedings, BPS: M1–M6.
Luehrman, T. A. 1998. Strategy as a Portfolio of Real Options, In J. Magretta (Ed) *Managing in the new economy*. Harvard Business School Press: Boston, MA: 91–111.
Mahon, J., & Griffin, J. 1999. Painting a portrait. Business and Society, 38: 126–133.
March, J. G., & Shapira, Z. 1987. Managerial perspectives on risk and risk taking. Management Science, 33(11): 1404–1418.
Margolis, J., & Walsh, J. 2003. Misery loves companies: Rethinking social initiatives by business. Administrative Science Quarterly, 48: 268–305.
McGrath, R. G. 1997. A real options logic for initiating technology positioning investments. Academy of Management Review, 22: 974–996.
McGrath, R. G. 1999. Falling forward: Real options reasoning and entrepreneurial failure. Academy of Management Review, 24(1): 13–30.
McWilliams, A., & Siegel, D. 2000. Corporate social responsibility and financial performance: Correlation or mis-specification? Strategic Management Journal, 21: 603–609.
McWilliams, A., & Siegel, D. 2001. Corporate social responsibility: A theory of the firm perspective. Academy of Management Review, 26: 117–127.
Merton, R. C. 1973. The theory of rational option pricing. Bell Journal of Economics, 4: 141–183.
Miller, K. D., & Leiblein, M. J. 1996. Corporate risk–return relationships: Returns variability versus downside risk. Academy of Management Journal, 39(1): 91–122.
Miller, K. D., & Reuer, J. J. 1996. Measuring organizational downside risk. Strategic Management Journal, 17: 671–691.
Mishan, E. J. 1988. *Cost–benefit analysis: An informal introduction*. Unwin Hyman: Boston, MA.
Mitchell, R. K., Agle, B. R., & Wood, D. J. 1997. Toward a theory of stakeholder identification and salience: Defining the principle of who and what really counts. Academy of Management Review, 22: 853–886.
Mitroff, I., Pauchant, T. C., & Shrivastava, P. 1989. Crisis, disaster, catastrophe: Are you ready? Security Management, 33(2): 101–108.
Nelson, R. 1959. The simple economics of basic research. Journal of Political Economy, 67: 297–306.

Nuttavuthisit, K., & Thogersen, J. 2017. The importance of consumer trust for the emergence of a market for green products: The case of organic food. Journal of Business Ethics, 140(2): 323–337.

Orlitzky, M., Schmidt, F., & Rynes, S. 2003. Corporate social and financial performance: A meta-analysis. Organization Studies, 24: 403–441.

Paxson, D. A. 2001. Introduction to Real R&D Options. R&D Management, 31(2): 109–113.

Porter, M. E., & Kramer, M. R. 2006. The link between competitive advantage and corporate social responsibility. Harvard Business Review, 84(12): 78–92.

Roman, R., Hayibor, S., & Agle, B. 1999. The relationship between financial and social performance: Repainting a portrait. Business and Society, 38: 109–125.

Roome, N. 1992. Developing environmental management systems. Business Strategy and the Environment, 1: 11–24.

Rowley, T., & Berman, S. 2000. A brand-new brand of corporate social performance. Business and Society, 39: 397–418.

Rowley, T., & Moldoveanu, M. 2003. When will stakeholder groups act? An interest and identity-based model of stakeholder group mobilization. Academy of Management Review, 28: 204–219.

Ruefli, T. W., Collins, J. M., & Lacugna, J. R. 1999. Risk measures in strategic management research: Auld lang syne? Strategic Management Journal, 20: 167–194.

Russo, M. V., & Fouts, P. A. 1997. A resource-based perspective on corporate environmental performance and profitability. Academy of Management Journal, 40: 534–559.

Sanchez, R. 1993. Strategic flexibility, firm organization, and managerial work in dynamic markets: a strategic-options perspective. Advances in Strategic Management, 9: 251–291.

Schäufele, I., & Hamm, U. 2017. Consumer perceptions, preferences and willingness-to-pay for wine with sustainability characteristics: A review. Journal of Cleaner Production, 147: 379–394.

Sharbrough, W. C., & Moody, J. W. 1995. Managing the media. Journal of Systems Management, 46(4): 4–11.

Sharma, S., & Henriques, I. 2005. Stakeholder influences on sustainability practices in the Canadian forest products industry. Strategic Management Journal, 26(2): 159–180.

Shrivastava, P., & Siomkos, G. 1989. Disaster containment strategies. Journal of Business Strategy, 105: 26–30.

Siomkos, G. J. 1992. Conceptual and methodological propositions for assessing responses to industrial crises. Review of Business, 13(4): 26–42.

Starr, J. A., & MacMillan, I. 1990. Resource cooptation via social contracting: Resource acquisition strategies for new ventures. Strategic Management Journal, 11: 79–92.

Stead, W. E., & Stead, J. G. 1995. An empirical investigation of sustainability strategy implementation in industrial organizations. In J. E. Post, D. Collins & M. Starik (Eds) *Research in corporate social performance and policy: Sustaining the natural environment—empirical studies on the interface between nature and organizations*, Supplement 1, JAI Press: Greenwich, CT: 43–66.

Stead, W. E., & Stead, J. G. 1996. *Management for a small planet* (2nd edn), Sage: Thousand Oaks, CA.

Trigeorgis, L. 1993. The nature of option interactions and the valuation of investments with multiple real options. Journal of Financial and Quantitative Analysis, 28(1): 1–20.

Turban, D. B., & Greening, D. W. 1997. Corporate social responsibility and organizational attractiveness to prospective employees. Academy of Management Journal, 40: 658–672.

Turner, D., & Stephenson, R. 1994. Managing media attention. Security Management, 38(12): 55–57.

Ullmann, A. 1985. Data in search of a theory: A critical examination of the relationship among social performance, social disclosure, and economic performance. Academy of Management Review, 10: 450–477.

Walmart Press Release. 2006. Wal-mart is taking the lead on environmental sustainability. Available at: https://corporate.walmart.com/newsroom/2006/03/02/wal-mart-is-taking-the-lead-on-environmental-sustainability. Accessed January 27, 2022.

Wartick, S. L., & Cochran, P. L. 1985. The evolution of the corporate social performance model. Academy of Management Review, 4: 758–769.

Weston, J. F., & Brigham, E. F. 1981. *Managerial finance*. Dryden Press: Hinsdale, IL.

Zahra, S., & George, G. 2002. Absorptive capacity: A review, reconceptualization, and extension. Academy of Management Review, 27: 185–203.

3. Sustaining society

INTRODUCTION

Corporate sustainability programs are now widespread. Their broad implementation has enabled firms to realize a myriad of benefits. But beyond the general notion of sustainability, it is important to understand the specific benefits that these programs can provide to society. In this chapter, we discuss the range of sustainability outcomes that corporate sustainability initiatives can create. We begin by outlining a typology of societal benefits and then we examine the ways in which corporate sustainability programs generate these benefits.

1 MAPPING OUT SOCIETAL WINS FROM CORPORATE SUSTAINABILITY

"Win–wins" are wonderful! Who wouldn't want to benefit as they are benefiting others? In Chapter 2, we mapped out the wins for firms from their sustainability initiatives, charting the range of tangible and intangible benefits that they can gain in the short term and over time. But what do the "wins" for society look like as firms profit from "win–win" outcomes via the business case for sustainability? In this chapter, we address the corresponding benefits for society, showing how corporate sustainability initiatives can help to advance sustainability in the near term and in the long run, in both tangible and intangible ways.

As a firm implements a sustainability initiative, some tangible benefits accrue almost immediately. If a firm installs a new technology to reduce pollutants, for example, the air near the plant may quickly become easier to breathe and the water safer to drink. However, broader ecosystem stabilization may take years to be realized. Thus, as shown in Figure 3.1, there is variation in the pace and tangibility of the benefits of corporate sustainability for society.

Short-term local benefits are the low-hanging fruit in this setting. Firms who ease the flow of effluents and roll back their environmental footprint can immediately and tangibly improve the cleanliness of the communities surrounding their plants. Studies of these sorts of benefits have looked at food waste (Devin & Richards, 2018), emissions (Chatterji, Levine & Toffel, 2009), and employee engagement (Flammer & Luo, 2017), for example.

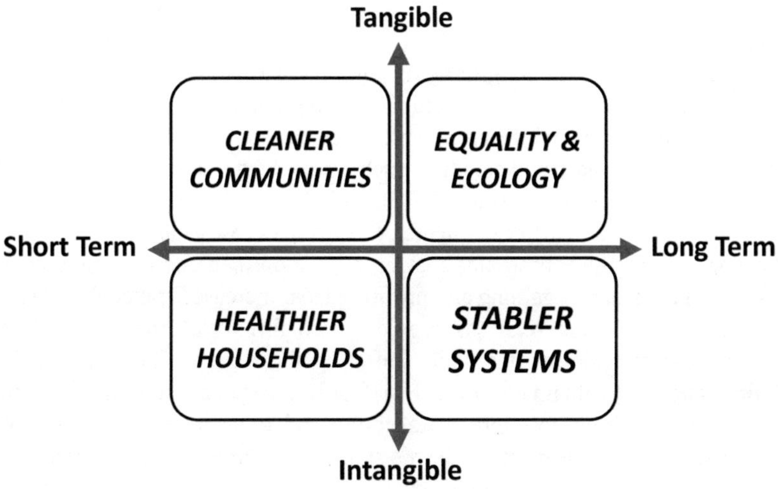

Figure 3.1 *Societal benefits of corporate sustainability*

Short-term benefits can also be more subjective. As firms engage in sustainability initiatives that reduce harm to their surrounding communities, those who live in those communities experience a better quality of life. Stress is multi-causal and may arise from environmental factors such as noise and a poor diet, as well as social factors related to income disparities (Greenberg, Carr & Summers, 2002; Pickett & Wilkinson, 2010). As firms undertake initiatives that reduce these and other stressors, residents of their local communities become healthier.

Benefits that extend beyond local communities take more time to unfold. It takes time to overcome economic and social inequality with collective and perhaps coordinated corporate initiatives to implement fair hiring practices and pay fair wages, as many have been seeking to accomplish for decades. It takes time to renew and rebuild forests and waterways and to regenerate endangered flora and fauna. But as firms' sustainability efforts compound, a more just economy, equitable society, and robust ecology can arise, with outcomes that can be measured in tangible ways (Hoffman, 2000; Laszlo & Zhexembayeva, 2017). Some of the United Nations' sustainable development goals like climate action, peace, justice, and strong institutions represent the objectives and social benefits that would fall in this quadrant. In each case, the benefit is the result of a combination of numerous initiatives and causes that are intertwined to create the intended objective over time.

Currently we face a variety of ongoing crises, such as devastating wildfires, extreme heat and droughts, massive flooding, violent clashes caused by economic and social injustice, and so on that threaten many societies in unpredictable ways. Over the long term, as corporate sustainability programs help to clean up communities, renew natural resources, and establish resilience, the broader systems in which firms are embedded can stabilize, thereby providing the benefit of at least withstanding such crises, if not suffering fewer such crises (Linnenluecke & Griffiths, 2010).

As we discussed in the prior chapter, the business case establishes that firms develop sustainability programs that promise these benefits to society as an instrumental means of gaining and profiting from increased stakeholder favor. Favorable stakeholder relations provide these firms with improved access to new market opportunities while buffering them from a myriad of risks. A firm's ability to obtain economic benefits from corporate sustainability thus depends on its ability to improve stakeholder relationships through corporate sustainability. This means that a firm's stakeholders must value corporate sustainability initiatives. For example, customers must be cognizant of and willing to pay a price premium for products and services with sustainability attributes. Similarly, corporate sustainability can benefit the firm via its employees if it is sufficiently valued by its employees to increase their loyalty to the firm and reduce turnover and recruiting costs. In the remainder of this chapter, we discuss the ways in which this drive to gain stakeholder favor shapes corporate sustainability initiatives and the resulting societal benefits.

2 CERTIFIABLE CONTRIBUTIONS TO CORPORATE SUSTAINABILITY

A good illustration of how firms gain valuable stakeholder favor through the provision of environmental benefits is through certifications with voluntary environmental programs (VEPs) (Henriques, Husted & Montiel, 2013). In recent years, a myriad of voluntary environmental programs (VEPs) have been implemented through which firms voluntarily reduced their polluting emissions. However, results from empirical research looking at the efficacy and performance implications of VEPs are mixed. For example, some scholars found a positive relationship between VEPs and environmental performance (Dasgupta, Hettige & Wheeler, 2000; Potoski & Prakash, 2005a), while others determined no relationship (Delmas, 2002; King, Lenox & Terlaak, 2005). These mixed results suggest that certifying with any VEP does not necessarily improve a firm's environmental impacts—rather, it is the VEP design that matters.

So, when does the adoption of a VEP generate positive environmental benefits that can protect the environment? The provision of environmental protection has two salient properties. First, once an investment has been made, the benefits of such an investment are non-excludable for all stakeholders. For example, if firm A were to change its processes to improve air quality, everyone benefits, including competitors. Second, the consumption of the benefits associated with improved air quality by a firm does not affect the consumption of other firms: that is, it is non-rival. Given the existence of these two characteristics, one would predict that the private provision of environmental protection would be undersupplied (McNutt, 2002). Since firm B cannot be excluded from securing the environmental benefits supplied by firm A, there is no incentive for firm B to pay the costs of undertaking such an investment. Environmental protection is, therefore, a public good whose benefits are both non-excludable and non-rival. Consequently, private provision (i.e., the market) will not be sufficient to meet demand, resulting in a market failure.

Then why would firms not simply mount their own individual campaigns to convince stakeholders that they are good environmental citizens? Unfortunately, asymmetric information is such that stakeholders cannot readily assess or monitor firms' environmental claims, creating credibility problems: The campaigns will, therefore, fail to convince stakeholders (Akerlof, 1970; Conroy, 2007). In this case, there is a need for an institution to be created that not only provides stakeholders with a credible reputational signal (Spence, 1973), but also allows firms, which are undertaking significant efforts, to claim the benefits of "club" membership based on substantive reductions in emissions, while shielding them from competitors who simply want to free-ride or certify symbolically.

A well-designed certifiable VEP, therefore, seeks to overcome the problem of asymmetric information by creating a credible brand that signals the commitment of participating firms to environmental stewardship, which stakeholders are otherwise unable to assess, and thereby confer on participants a credible environmental reputation—an intangible asset (Conroy, 2007; Klein & Leffler, 1981). Certified firms not only capture benefits from the program's certification (such as its reputation, the development of environmental management resources and capabilities, and improved environmental conduct), they also become distinguishable from non-certifiers. Unfortunately, poorly designed programs can create problems of adverse selection and attract managers of firms that wish to engage in greenwashing and free riding (Delmas & Montes-Sancho, 2010).

Club theory provides a way to compare the relative efficacy of different VEPs (Buchanan, 1965; Potoski & Prakash, 2005b). VEPs can differ significantly along several different dimensions, such as the requirements for membership, the environmental targets, provisions for third-party auditing, sanctioning mechanisms, and costs. We argue that the scheme will provide greater incentives for certifiers to invest more in improving their targeted environmental behavior, but only to the extent that a certifiable VEP is able to set more stringent targets and effectively exclude free riders (i.e., participants who obtain the benefits of initial certification and then fail to maintain compliance) from the benefits of the certification.

For a club to be successful, it must compel members to abide by club rules—in this case clear environmental targets—and deter free-riding. The two critical components to deter free-riding or symbolic adoption are third-party auditing and the existence of sanctions for members who do not abide by the VEP standards (Conroy, 2007; Prakash & Potoski, 2007). The pivotal element is coercion or the use of force. In a weak sense, sanctions can mean nothing more than the withdrawal of a certification. In a stronger sense, it can include the application of financial penalties.

The extent to which a VEP is more effective in reducing free riding (symbolic adoption) means a greater incentive for certifiers to invest more in order to improve their targeted behavior; such VEPs can thus induce higher levels of performance with respect to a given goal because certifiers are able to appropriate the benefits of their efforts by signaling their true environmental conduct. Free riding reduces the incentive of any agent to invest when the benefits of the effort are not fully appropriated by the investor (Samuelson, 1954).

A study comparing the efficacy of Clean Industry, a Mexican certification (Henriques, et al., 2013), with the well-known ISO 14001, found that Clean Industry had much more stringent standards and sanctions for failure to maintain compliance with the standard. Given these stricter standards and sanctions, they compared these certifications' impact on emissions. They discovered that certification with Clean Industry is related to higher levels of targeted and untargeted environmental performance (CO_2 emissions), while ISO 14001 showed no sign of improvement. So, there is evidence that sustainability programs like Clean Industry can significantly improve air quality; however, the programs must be designed properly.

3 THE UPS AND DOWNS OF REPUTATION AND REAL OPTIONS

Investing in sustainability involves risk. The initiatives may fail, the firm may suffer losses, not only financially but also reputationally, damaging valuable stakeholder relationships. Managers tend to be risk averse, principally viewing risk in terms of the potential for loss (March & Shapira, 1987). As they focus on potential losses from sustainability initiatives, however, managers may overlook the potential for gains from risk. Risk is bi-directional. As also discussed in the prior chapter, taking on the risk of investing in a sustainability initiative also means gaining exposure to the upside, which can be viewed and assessed as real options.

Thinking in these bi-directional terms can help firms justify riskier projects that offer greater potential for impact on sustainability. Any given initiative may fail, but each also offers potential to improve the firm's standing with its stakeholders. Thus, each stakeholder is a source of reputational risk to be managed through a firm's portfolio of sustainability initiatives (Fombrun, Gardberg & Barnett, 2000).

Consider giant retailer Wal-Mart. Investors applaud its profitability and customers welcome its quality at a low-price ethic. However, communities and the media often deplore the arrival of a new Wal-Mart store due to its negative impact on existing retail businesses. To counter negative sentiments and build reputational capital, Wal-Mart has developed an extensive portfolio of citizenship activities that target its key stakeholders. These initiatives seem to be effective from a business case perspective, as evidenced by Wal-Mart's tremendous market value.

Corporate sustainability is an integral part of a cycle through which companies generate reputational capital, manage reputational risk, and enhance performance. Companies invest in sustainability activities that generate reputational capital. In turn, stocks of reputational capital serve a twofold purpose. On the one hand, reputational capital serves as a platform from which future opportunities may spring. On the other hand, reputational capital safeguards the existing assets of the firm, serving as a buffer against loss (Fombrun et al., 2000).

Effective sustainability programs heighten stakeholder support that savvy firms can utilize to enact new opportunities that have large upside potential, yet limited downside risk. J. P. Morgan serves as a case in point: In the early 1990s, Morgan's portfolio of sustainability activities included community development programs, charitable grants, volunteering, and donations. These programs contributed to the large stock of reputational capital the company enjoyed, particularly in its New York home base. In 1991, when several large non-profit organizations in New York City needed an underwriter, they turned to J. P. Morgan. The bank underwrote a $20 million financing package for the National Audubon Society in New York City, as well as another $54 million for the renovation of Manhattan's Guggenheim Museum. In short, Morgan realized the potential to capitalize on an untapped source of synergy between its line activities and its sustainability activities. To do so, the bank created a not-for-profit group to market its asset and liability management services to nonprofit agencies and assist philanthropists in structuring trusts and foundations. This resulted in the group quickly becoming a large profit center for the bank (Fombrun, 1996).

Sustainability programs, like those of J. P. Morgan, create the potential for gains by increasing the real options available to a company (Myers, 1977). The premise is simple: corporate sustainability creates reputational capital and provides a platform from which other opportunities may spring. The supportive social relationships that a company builds through its sustainability programs today put it in a more favorable position to take advantage of opportunities that emerge tomorrow. In contrast, companies who fail to invest in corporate sustainability today may lack the relationships and reputational capital they need to exploit emerging opportunities tomorrow. In this way, Morgan's sustainability programs can be viewed as platform investments from which new paths for growth arise. These platform investments derive value not from direct income creation, but from indirectly creating potential for future gains. Therefore, corporate sustainability programs are comparable to R&D and training: they are platform investments whose value partly lies in unlocking future growth opportunities for companies. This perspective helps to make the business case for riskier sustainability initiatives that offer more benefits to society yet may not pass muster by standard NPV calculations.

Furthermore, sustainability programs are boundary-spanning activities that sensitize employees to environmental conditions and help companies adapt to changing circumstances (Katz & Kahn, 1978). "Hands on" corporate volunteerism and community development typically expose employees to the diverse needs and perspectives of multiple constituencies, thereby fostering increased awareness and understanding of stakeholders and their expectations. Some companies treat community involvement as a "leadership laboratory." Through "action learning," managers develop "a broader repertoire of cultural, relational, and self-leadership competencies" (Bartell, Saavedra & Van Dyne, 1999). Through community involvement, employees learn valuable information about the environment that enhances the company's adaptability. In turn, personal understanding increases corporate opportunities for profit making, and makes it more likely the company can capitalize on those opportunities.

4 BACK TO THE FUTURE: BETTER BUSINESS MODELS

Whereas focusing on the upside potential for improved stakeholder relations can drive firms to take on risky sustainability initiatives that offer more long-term benefits to society, developing innovative business models to implement these initiatives can increase their ability to garner stakeholder favor and lessen the risk that they will fail for either the firm or society. Recently, new business models have laid out path-breaking ways to improve social inclusion. For example, Greyston Bakery is generating significant social benefits through innovative product and service capacity as they attempt to restore dignity to the previously unemployed in a needy community. Greyston flips the well-established model of heavy screening and selective hiring of employees on its head, turning instead to open hiring practices and shifting their focus from screening to training. Open hiring is not for every firm, and those firms who do succeed at it face many implementation challenges. However, if done right, it creates ample value for both business and society (Pirson & Livne-Tarandach, 2020).

Social innovation and experimentation have stood at the heart of CSR from the beginning as businesspeople sought to solve social problems faced by their employees and communities. Take the case of company welfare programs, which began in the German states in the first half of the nineteenth century (Hilger, 1998). These programs focused on health insurance, housing, and company stores. The Ruhr industrial elite became prominent with their coal, iron, and then steel production starting in 1850. They had a very significant influence on the process of nation building in Germany due to their relationships with Otto von Bismarck, the country's first chancellor (Spencer, 1979). In addition, ties were strengthened by a significant number of business executives drawn from the public sector. The social welfare programs developed by the Ruhr business elite served not only to attract labor, but also to "demonstrate social responsibility and thereby deflect criticism of industrial capitalism," which was at the time too focused on the "reckless pursuit of profit" (Spencer, 1979: 48).

Of special note is the social welfare program developed by Alfred Krupp. It began with a health insurance plan for workers as early as 1836 and was then modified in 1853 (McCreary, 1968). This early health insurance program included a pension for permanently disabled workers. In 1885, a workers' pension fund was established with a 1.5 percent wage contribution (one-third paid by the company). The company's contributions were subsequently raised to match the worker's contribution. In 1890, Krupp provided office workers with similar coverage. Starting in 1877, Krupp subsidized the cost of life insurance by employees. Even when insurance programs were legally mandated by the government, Friedrich Alfred (Fritz) Krupp continued to grant benefits beyond the legal requirements. Krupp also developed funds to provide care for those workers and dependents who fell between the cracks of the legally mandated programs (McCreary, 1968).

Beyond this early form of health insurance, the company built housing for single workers in 1856. In 1865, Krupp initially supported and then purchased a cooperative in 1868. McCreary (1968) found that the cooperative differed significantly from the U.S. or U.K. company store, because the price of goods was actually lower than in the city stores, due to subsidized administrative and other costs. Workers paid cash for all purchases, avoiding the situation found in the British and U.S. company stores, where workers were paid with coupons only valid in company stores. Alfred Krupp built a hospital in 1866 in response to the cholera epidemic. In the 1860s, supplemental health benefits included the workers' dependents.

Between 1870 and 1874, the company built 3,200 apartments for workers (McCreary, 1968: 36). Disability and retirement programs were developed in 1885 for all workers. Later work accommodations were made for disabled employees and subsidized life insurance was inaugurated. In 1892, Fritz Krupp began building apartments for retirees where they could live the rest of their lives rent free. In 1896, a convalescent home was built to provide care for employees with long-term illnesses. Other programs included the construction of a casino, gardens, schools for home economics, a library, and scholarships for specialized technical training.

Krupp and the Ruhr industrialists were not alone in Prussia, and later, Germany. The Berlin firm of Siemens and Halske introduced profit sharing, yearly bonuses, and a company party shortly after its founding in 1847. In 1872, Siemens started a pension fund (Kastl & Moore, 2010), which, if run for one year, was estimated to cost the same amount of "profits that would be lost if Siemen's workforce were to go on strike for 2 weeks—a strike of average duration in that time period in Germany" (Kastl & Moore, 2010: 322). It was concluded that the investment made economic sense.

The welfare programs developed by Krupp and the Ruhr industrialists later served as the model Bismarck used for Germany as a whole. Bismarck's social welfare plan consisted of three prongs: (1) the Health Insurance Law of 1883, (2) the Accident Insurance Law of 1884, and (3) the Old Age and Invalidity Insurance Law of 1889 (Hilger, 1998). The Reichstag accepted the model because it was familiar to the business elite and was not seen as radical (McCreary, 1968; Spencer, 1979). This same social welfare program became part of the Rhenish model of capitalism found in Northern Europe which was subsequently exported in some form to much of the rest of the world. Clearly, there was a business case for corporate social welfare programs; however, only by solving real problems and creating impact were such programs able to serve as the blueprint for the modern welfare state.

5 CONCLUSION

The business case for corporate sustainability promises simultaneous benefits to both business and society. In this chapter, we mapped the promised benefits to society and the mechanisms through which firms produce them as they seek to benefit themselves. Without these positive tangible and intangible societal impacts, in the near term and especially in the long run, corporate sustainability programs are no more than greenwashing, providing marketing for firms but failing to help sustain society. To be effective in sustaining society, the pursuit of profit must drive firms to produce the promised benefits for society outlined in this chapter. Are firms fulfilling their promises? In the next section, we analyze the reality of corporate sustainability.

BIBLIOGRAPHY

Akerlof, G. 1970. The market for lemons: Quality uncertainty and the market mechanism. Quarterly Journal of Economics, 84: 488–500.

Barnett, M. L. 2020. Helping business help society: Overcoming barriers to corporate social innovation. Rutgers Business Review, 5(2): 137–144.

Barnett, M., Henriques, I., & Husted, B. W. 2020. Beyond good intentions: Designing CSR initiatives for greater social impact. Journal of Management, 46(6): 937–964.

Bartell, C. A., Saavedra, R., and Van Dyne, L. 1999. Learning to lead with a conscience through community involvement. Unpublished manuscript.

Bénabou, R., & Tirole, J. 2010. Individual and corporate social responsibility. Economica, 77(305): 1–19.

Bhattacharya, C. B., Korschun, D., & Sen, S. 2009. Strengthening stakeholder–company relationships through mutually beneficial corporate social responsibility initiatives. Journal of Business Ethics, 85(2): 257–272.

Buchanan, J. M. 1965. An economic theory of clubs. Economica, 32: 1–14.

Chatterji, A. K., Levine, D. I., & Toffel, M. W. 2009. How well do social ratings actually measure corporate social responsibility? Journal of Economics & Management Strategy, 18(1): 125–169.

Collins, K. L. 2004. Profitable gifts: A history of the Merck Mectizan donation program and its implications for international health. Perspectives in Biology and Medicine, 47(1): 100–109.

Conroy, M. E. 2007. *Branded! How the "certification revolution" is transforming global corporations*. New Society Publishers: Gabriola Island, Canada.

Dasgupta, S., Hettige, H., & Wheeler, D. 2000. What improves environmental compliance? Evidence from Mexican industry. Journal of Environmental Economics and Management, 39: 39–66.

Delmas, M. 2002. The diffusion of environmental management standards in Europe and in the United States: An institutional perspective. Policy Sciences, 35: 91–119.

Delmas, M., & Montes-Sancho, M. 2010. Voluntary agreements to improve environmental quality: Symbolic versus substantive cooperation. Strategic Management Journal, 31: 575–601.

Devin, B., & Richards, C. 2018. Food waste, power, and corporate social responsibility in the Australian food supply chain. Journal of Business Ethics, 150(1): 199–210.

Flammer, C., & Luo, J. 2017. Corporate social responsibility as an employee governance tool: Evidence from a quasi-experiment. Strategic Management Journal, 38(2): 163–183.

Fombrun, C. J. 1996. *Reputation: Realizing value from the corporate image*. Harvard Business School Press: Boston, MA.

Fombrun, C. J., Gardberg, N. A., & Barnett, M. L. 2000. Opportunity platforms and safety nets: Corporate citizenship and reputational risk. Business and Society Review, 105(1): 85–106.

Greenberg, N., Carr, J. A., & Summers, C. H. 2002. Causes and consequences of stress. Integrative and Comparative Biology, 42(3): 508–516.

Hahn, T., Figge, F., Pinkse, J., & Preuss, L. 2010. Trade-offs in corporate sustainability: You can't have your cake and eat it. Business Strategy and the Environment, 19(4): 217–229.

Hart, S. L. 1997. Beyond greening: Strategies for a sustainable world. Harvard Business Review, 75(1): 66–77.

Henriques, I., Husted, B. W., & Montiel, I. 2013. Spillover effects of voluntary environmental programs on greenhouse gas emissions: Lessons from Mexico. Journal of Policy Analysis and Management, 32(2): 296–322.

Hilger, S. 1998. Welfare policy in German big business after the First World War. Business History, 40(1): 50–76.

Hoffman, A. J. 2000. Integrating environmental and social issues into corporate practice. Environment: Science and Policy for Sustainable Development, 42(5): 22–33.

Husted, B. W. 2015. Corporate social responsibility practice from 1800–1914: Past initiatives and current debates. Business Ethics Quarterly, 25(1): 125–141.

Jamali, D., Lund-Thomsen, P., & Khara, N. 2017. CSR institutionalized myths in developing countries: An imminent threat of selective decoupling. Business & Society, 56: 454–486.

Kastl, J., & Moore, L. 2010. Wily welfare capitalist: Werner von Siemens and the pension plan. Cliometrica, 4: 321–348.

Katz, D., & Kahn, R. L. 1978. *The social psychology of organizations* (Vol. 2). Wiley: New York: 528.

Kesidou, E., & Demirel, P. 2012. On the drivers of eco-innovations: Empirical evidence from the UK. Research Policy, 41(5): 862–870.

King, A., Lenox, M., & Terlaak, A. 2005. The strategic use of decentralized institutions: Exploring certification with the ISO 14001 management standard. Academy of Management Journal, 48: 1091–1106.

Klein, B., & Leffler, K. B. 1981. The role of market forces in assuring contractual performance. Journal of Political Economics, 89: 615–641.

Laszlo, C., & Zhexembayeva, N. 2017. *Embedded sustainability: The next big competitive advantage*. Abingdon, U.K.: Routledge.

Linnenluecke, M., & Griffiths, A. 2010. Beyond adaptation: Resilience for business in light of climate change and weather extremes. Business & Society, 49(3): 477–511.

March, J. G., & Shapira, Z. 1987. Managerial perspectives on risk and risk taking. Management Science, 33(11): 1404–1418.

McCreary, E. C. 1968. Social welfare and business: The Krupp welfare program, 1860–1914. Business History Review, 42(1): 24–49.

McNutt, P. 2002. *The economics of public choice II*. Edward Elgar Publishing: Cheltenham, U.K. and Northampton, MA, U.S.A.

Myers, S. C. 1977. Determinants of corporate borrowing. Journal of Financial Economics, 5(2): 147–175.

Pfeffer, J., & Salancik, G. 2015. *External control of organizations—Resource dependence perspective*. Abingdon, U.K.: Routledge: 373–388.

Pickett, K. E., & Wilkinson, R. G. 2010. Inequality: An underacknowledged source of mental illness and distress. The British Journal of Psychiatry, 197(6): 426–428.

Pirson, M., & Livne-Tarandach, R. 2020. Restoring dignity with open hiring: Greyston Bakery and the recognition of value. Rutgers Business Review, 5(2): 236–247.

Potoski, M., & Prakash, A. 2005a. Covenants with weak swords: ISO 14001 and firms' environmental performance. Journal of Policy Analysis and Management, 24: 745–769.

Potoski, M., & Prakash, A. 2005b. Green clubs and voluntary governance: ISO 14001 and firms' regulatory compliance. American Journal of Political Science, 49: 235–248.

Prakash, A., & Potoski, M. 2007. Collective action through voluntary environmental programs: A club theory perspective. Policy Studies Journal, 35: 773–792.

Samuelson, P. A. 1954. The pure theory of public expenditures. Review of Economics and Statistics, 36: 387–389.
Spence, A. 1973. Job market signaling. Quarterly Journal of Economics, 87: 355–379.
Spencer, E. G. 1979. Rulers of the Ruhr: Leadership and authority in German big business before 1914. Business History Review, 53(1): 40–64.
Varadarajan, R. 2017. Innovating for sustainability: A framework for sustainable innovations and a model of sustainable innovations orientation. Journal of the Academy of Marketing Science, 45(1): 14–36.

PART II

The realities of corporate sustainability

4. Satisfying stakeholders shan't sustain society

Just do the right thing. Do what's good for society. Do what helps to sustain the planet. Simple as that, right? If only. It is difficult to get anyone, and especially for-profit corporations, to do anything that they believe goes against their self-interest. Even the most altruistic of firms, with limited resources and operating in competitive environments, prioritize initiatives that promise profits (Aguilera et al., 2007).

Fortunately, thousands of studies have demonstrated that firms can "do well by doing good." Under a variety of conditions, firms gain financial (Barnett & Salomon, 2012), reputational (Fombrun et al., 2000), and insurance-like benefits (Godfrey, 2005) from their good deeds. At a minimum, socially and environmentally responsible firms rarely suffer financial harm (Margolis & Walsh, 2003). Overall, there is a well-established "business case" showing that firms benefit from being good corporate citizens (Fombrun et al., 2000).

The business case is well established not only in the academic literature but also in practice. Firms commonly file sustainability reports alongside their financial reports and, therein, declare a positive relationship between the firm's success and its contributions to sustaining society. For example, in its 2019 Sustainability Progress Report—its 18th annual—UPS states:

> As part of UPS's enterprise-wide strategy, we are focused on four Strategic Growth Imperatives to drive business growth. These initiatives align with our sustainability priorities and include focused investments in areas that will create a more inclusive global economy. Here's how accomplishments in 2019 are generating value not only for our business, but for all of our stakeholders (p. 5).

In its June 2020 sustainability report, Amazon declared:

> At Amazon, we first began discussing the possibility of company-wide net zero commitments during a senior planning summit in 2016. We knew that to continue to be a relentlessly resilient and innovative business, we would need to deeply understand what is happening on our planet. We also knew that we would need to build and dedicate financial resources, intellectual capital, and change management work to creating the tools, data, and understanding about how to achieve these types of commitments (p. 4).

Despite so many major firms espousing the centrality of sustainability to their missions and declaring the many benefits gained from doing so, sustainability remains a problem and is worsening in many ways. For example, economic inequality is rising, as is the planet's temperature, and with it, the oceans. Ecological disasters are commonplace. Women and children continue to be sold into slavery. Diseases still kill thousands due to lack of access to vaccines or clean water. How can this still be?

The root of the problem is that both the academic literature and business practice have muddled serving powerful stakeholders with sustaining society. The two, though, are far from synonymous. While firms successfully honed their stakeholder management strategies, they failed to ameliorate the many severe problems that jeopardize society's sustainability. Instead, strong stakeholders benefit over society's sustainability from the extensive (and perhaps sincere) corporate interest in doing good.

1 MUDDLING STAKEHOLDERS AND SOCIETY

Aided by the clarity of purpose it provides managers (cf. Jensen, 2000), the notion that a firm should operate solely for the benefit of its shareholders has held sway for many decades. This position is famously represented by Friedman (1970), who decreed that the business of business is business and not to meddle in society's problems. Freeman (1984: 46) later countered that the firm's strategic imperative is to attend to the concerns of "any group or individual who can affect or is affected by the achievement of the organization's objectives." This stakeholder approach, or what is now generally deemed stakeholder theory, has "infiltrated the academic dialogue in management" (Harrison & Wicks, 2013: 97) and helped to spur legions of scholars as well as titans of industry to broadly discredit the shareholder model as "wrong," "a tragically flawed premise," "dreary and demeaning," "totally idiotic," and even "the dumbest idea in the world" (Denning, 2015).

Although they are commonly depicted as diametrically opposed, the shareholder and stakeholder perspectives both seek to maximize the profitability of the firm and differ only in the path prescribed to do so. Whereas Friedman (1970) was quick to dismiss spending on non-compulsory benefits for employees, suppliers, customers, and the like as tantamount to theft from the firm's owners, Freeman (1984) shone a favorable light on the benefits that can accrue to the firm from investing in its relationships with its various stakeholder groups. But the "Friedman–Freeman debate" (Freeman, 2008) comes to an amicable close whenever attending to stakeholder concerns helps the firm to improve its financial performance. Under such conditions, the only difference between the two is that Friedman views any stakeholder who favors a firm due to its social practices as misguided, whereas Freeman is pleased by the prospect of stakeholders making social demands of firms. Yet even Friedman would encourage rather than begrudge managers for seeking to capture any profit that sustainability can bring the firm.

Note that neither perspective is directly concerned with the sustainability of anything other than the firm's profits. Friedman was quite clear about his exclusive focus on firm profitability. But Freeman and his colleagues have not hidden the fact that the primary concern of stakeholder theory is also the welfare of the firm, not of society. For example, Freeman and Phillips (2002) declared, "first and foremost, stakeholder theory is about business and capitalism" (p. 340). Walsh (2005) thoroughly reviewed Freeman (1984) and two other core books about stakeholder theory (Phillips, 2003; Post, Preston & Sachs, 2002) and noted their lack of concern for social or even stakeholder welfare:

> ... make no mistake, he [Freeman] is not interested in serving stakeholders to satisfy their needs in any altruistic sense. (p. 428)

> ... stakeholder management ideas complement the neoclassical theory of the firm; they do not challenge it ... If we want to browbeat infidels and supplant the stockholder theory of the firm, then we must look elsewhere for relief. (p. 437)

Nevertheless, stakeholder theory underpins the management literature on the responsibilities of corporations. In fact, stakeholder theory is so consonant with this literature that, as Laplume, Sonpar, and Litz's (2008) systematic review noted, many have argued that stakeholder theory obviates and even supersedes the construct of corporate social responsibility (p. 1168). Wood (1991) framed stakeholder theory as a way of helping firms to think more concretely about their responsibilities to society, whereas Waddock and Graves (1997) described CSR as being composed of the firm's interactions with its various stakeholders. Argandoña (1998) combined the two perspectives into a single term: "the stakeholder theory of the social responsibility of business" (p. 1093). Freeman (2005) characterized CSR as superfluous, given stakeholder theory and its associated focus on the firm's responsibilities to a broad set of stakeholders, and Rowley and Berman (2000), a fortiori, suggested replacing the CSR construct with stakeholder theory.

Conflating or replacing the concept of corporate social responsibility with that of stakeholder management has led to a narrow interpretation of firms' obligations to sustaining society, one that seldom reaches beyond the interests of those stakeholders who have direct power over the firm. Some corporations have more resources than some countries, but even the largest cannot attend to all the demands of all its stakeholders, let alone all the challenges associated with sustaining society. Thus, stakeholder management becomes a matter of sorting out which competing stakeholder demands to address. Unfortunately, this sorting process tends to exclude significant engagement with the major challenges of sustainability from most firms' agendas.

Scholars have written extensively about how managers should decide which stakeholder demands to fulfill and which to ignore. Freeman's (1984) guidance was blunt, advising firms to focus on stakeholders who could jeopardize the firm's survival and to not "give in" (p. 149) to those who lack such power (see Walsh, 2005: 428). Phillips (2003) argued for a graduated approach: A firm ought to concern itself with a stakeholder issue only to the degree that the stakeholder affects the firm, while stakeholders without strong influence over the firm "should look elsewhere for relief" (p. 142). The most dominant perspective specifies three factors that underpin the triage process that managers use to determine whether a stakeholder "really counts": power, legitimacy, and urgency (Mitchell et al., 1997). Of those three factors, power dominates.

But what about those problems that lack an urgent push from powerful and legitimate stakeholders? Failing ecosystems cannot make demands of firms, so sustainability issues may fall to the wayside under the stakeholder model, along with other important social problems. For example, Walsh (2005) concluded that if managers are guided by stakeholder theory, a call by the Secretary-General of the United Nations for corporations to help in the fight against AIDS would go unheeded. Disasters in the natural environment would be ignored (Starik, 1995). The suffering of the impoverished, diseased, starving... if lacking power over firms, they "should look elsewhere for relief" (Phillips, 2003: 142).

Granted, stakeholders with power can act on behalf of those without power by pushing firms to address sustainability issues (Frooman, 1999). But the same problematic logic holds: Only the concerns of the most powerful, whether self-serving or in selective support of those without power, will gain managerial attention and perhaps firm resources. As prescribed by stakeholder theory, there is no direct access to the firm for those without power; the interface is via amply powerful stakeholders. Yet might this still be sufficient? Despite our ecosystem's impotence in directly making powerful demands, do firms have ample incentive to prioritize initiatives that sustain society as a means of managing their most powerful stakeholders? We next discuss this indirect path to sustainability.

2 CHARTING AN INDIRECT PATH TO SUSTAINABILITY

The stakeholder concept is often bemoaned as vague. Freeman's (1984) initial definition of a stakeholder as "any group or individual who can affect or is affected by the achievement of the firm's objectives" ruled little out (p. 46), as mostly anyone or anything has the potential to affect or be affected by any firm by at least some stretch of the imagination (Orts & Strudler, 2002). Others have since parsed stakeholders in many ways, particularly along the dimension of whether they can affect the firm or are affected by the firm. For example, Goodpaster (1991) categorized those who can affect the firm as strategic stakeholders, while those who are affected by the firm are deemed moral stakeholders.

Given the interest in establishing a business case, though, most scholars have focused on strategic stakeholders and parsed them according to the degree to which they could affect the firm (Mitchell et al., 1997). Those with direct influence on the firm are often characterized as primary stakeholders, whereas those with indirect influence are typically relegated to secondary stakeholder status (Carroll, 1979; Clarkson, 1995). Those who lack power, legitimacy, and urgency entirely are considered "nonstakeholders" (Mitchell et al., 1997: 873).

Empirical studies isolating the financial returns from serving different stakeholder groups have found the business case to hold for primary stakeholders—those whose support is necessary for a firm's survival—but the more secondary are stakeholders, the less likely is the firm to profit from serving them. Berman, Wicks, Kotha, and Jones (1999) found a positive relationship between return on assets and the level of support the firm provides its employees, as well as its level of concern for customers through the production of safer and higher quality goods. In contrast, the firm's support of diversity, safeguarding of the natural environment, and contributions to the broader community had no significant relationship with its return on assets. Hillman and Keim (2001) contrasted firm support for primary stakeholders with support of social issues and found the former to be positively related to financial performance, while the latter was negatively related. Although hypothesizing the opposite, Van der Laan, Van Ees, and Van Witteloostuijn (2008) also found empirical support for a positive relationship with financial performance for primary stakeholders and a negative relationship for secondary stakeholders. Thus, there is empirical validation that serving those who can directly affect the firm is profitable but extending the firm's actions beyond this powerful core group does not pay.

These findings seem to refute the validity of a business case for sustainability, as they show that the interests of firms and the welfare of broader society beyond primary stakeholders do not coincide and often conflict. However, such a conclusion is premature. Should there be a valid business case for sustainability, the same empirical results would prevail. By definition, secondary stakeholders and non-stakeholders lack an exchange relationship with the firm (Clarkson, 1995). Therefore, they are unable to directly reciprocate the firm's good deeds. Prior studies that isolated firms' efforts to advance social issues from their efforts to satisfy primary stakeholder interests found that the pursuit of social issues was not positively associated with firm profitability and often reduced it. However, all else being equal, when studies isolate the firm's efforts to aid non-primary stakeholders they find that as firms do more, they lose more, because non-primary stakeholders are unable to provide compensating revenues for the firm. Only primary stakeholders transact with the firm, so any returns to the firm must occur via these relationships. Simply put, a business case can only be made by focusing on those with whom the firm does business—its primary stakeholders.

The relationships between the firm and its secondary and non-stakeholders are akin to cost centers. Firms benefit from cost centers to the degree that they improve primary functions. If the performance of these primary functions is not considered, then investing more in a cost center appears to only generate more losses. For example, as a firm spends more on R&D or advertising, it may benefit from new product development and sales. But if R&D and advertising are assessed by themselves, then greater spending on either will seemingly lead to greater losses for the firm. To understand their true value, their effects on the firm's primary functions must be assessed. Does investing more in R&D and advertising help to create, build, and sell more innovative and marketable products? If so, then a business case can be established. Likewise, one cannot conclude that firms do not benefit from their efforts to sustain society unless the effects of these initiatives on primary stakeholder relationships are accounted for.

Prior conceptual studies have framed the business case in this way, arguing that a firm's contributions to society can increase the degree to which its primary stakeholders view the firm as a trustworthy, and so favored, party with which to transact. Although primary stakeholders do not receive the direct benefit of these acts, they might still respond in ways that benefit the firm:

> The business case for CSR implies that as stakeholders observe a firm's socially responsible behaviors, they will deem the firm a more favorable party with which to conduct their own transactions... Trust arises and relationships improve as stakeholders observe a firm's CSR activities, not as a consequence of a firm's use of direct influence tactics to capture their favor. (Barnett, 2007: 800)

Barnett (2007) argued that when firms respond to demands from their primary stakeholders, they are engaging in "direct influence tactics," not acts of social responsibility. Direct influence tactics are reciprocal, intended to maintain and improve relationships with powerful stakeholders through direct exchange. Such acts "are not necessarily focused on improving social welfare" and can "be instrumental in reducing a firm's contributions to social welfare" (p. 799). In contrast, CSR aims to improve social welfare rather than directly satisfy a stakeholder demand.

Empirical studies indicate that, contrary to direct influence tactics, CSR can help firms gain better access to key resources held by their primary stakeholders. For example, being a good corporate citizen can increase the desirability of firms to potential employees (Turban & Greening, 1997) and decrease constraints on firms' ability to acquire capital (Cheng, Ioannou & Serafeim, 2014). Thus, there exist both theoretical rationale and empirical support for the possibility of a business case for corporate sustainability that is distinct from the extant business case that focuses on responding to primary stakeholder demands.

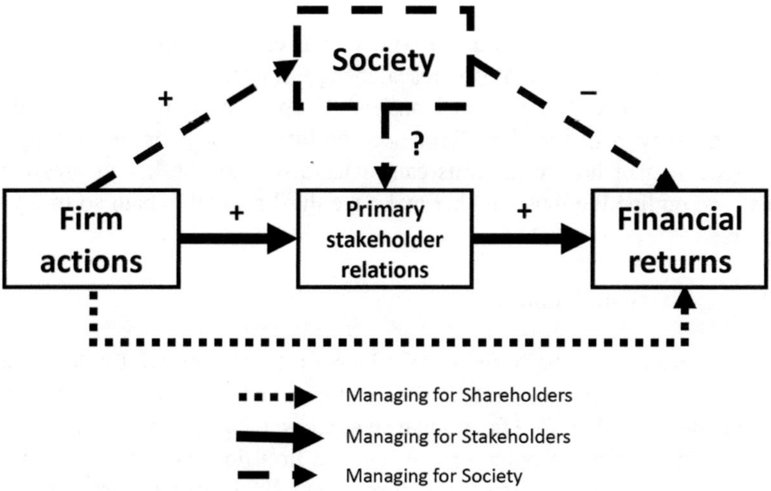

Figure 4.1 *Mapping the business case*

Figure 4.1 illustrates this indirect pathway to a business case. The dotted line in the lower part of the figure that links a firm's actions directly to its financial returns represents the traditional view that firms are managed solely for the benefit of their shareholders and are therefore obligated to take actions to maximize the firm's financial returns, unfettered by concern for others (cf. Friedman, 1970). The bold arrows through the center of the figure complicate this direct path to financial returns by introducing stakeholders as mediators. The positive signs reflect the findings of the literature on stakeholder theory that a firm's financial returns are enhanced through actions that improve its relationships with its primary stakeholders (cf. Freeman, 1984). The dashed arrows at the top of the figure illustrate the yet-more-complicated link between a firm's actions and its financial returns that we are addressing here.

Many studies have shown that a firm's efforts to benefit anyone other than its primary stakeholders tend to be financially detrimental for the firm (e.g., Hillman & Keim, 2001), which is why Figure 4.1 shows that firm sustainability actions lead to a decrease in financial returns. However, as previously argued, investments in sustainability can improve financial returns indirectly via their effects on primary stakeholder relations. The established business case literature has provided few insights into the validity of this indirect path to financial returns, so the figure labels this pathway with a question mark.

3 TENSIONS IN TRAVERSING THE INDIRECT PATH

To determine the conditions under which firms can serve their own interests through sustainability initiatives, researchers will need to move past ongoing efforts to correlate "various mishmashes" (Rowley & Berman, 2000: 405) of variables with financial performance and instead focus on developing an understanding of how well firms can manage several conflicting pressures. Next, we outline the tensions that make the third profitable path so tricky to traverse.

3.1 Giving or Taking?

The core premise of the business case is that a firm's powerful stakeholders will have greater trust in the firm if it engages in altruistic actions, and these stakeholders will therefore favor the firm as an exchange partner. Stakeholders still expect the firm to pursue profit, but the firm does not accrue goodwill from such self-serving pursuits (Godfrey et al., 2009). In fact, firms' actions that are perceived as self-serving can destroy trust (Varadarajan & Menon, 1988).

However, it may not be feasible for a stakeholder to categorize any particular action of a firm as entirely self- or other-serving, as even the most altruistic actions may have self-serving aspects to them (Glazer & Konrad, 1996). Because other-serving actions build trust while self-serving actions destroy it, these mixed motives must be accounted for when trying to understand how sustainability initiatives affect stakeholder relationships.

Corporate sustainability and other socially responsible activities can take many forms. Some initiatives are perceived as more altruistic than others, not just as altruistic or not (Ellen, Webb & Mohr, 2006). For example, firms often engage in cause-related marketing in which they may tie product sales to their contributions to a social or environmental cause, such as donating a percentage or flat amount from each item purchased to a charity that plants trees (Varadarajan & Menon, 1988). This benefits both the charity that advances sustainability and the firm. However, firms may also take a less transparently self-serving approach by directly donating to a charity independent of firm sales. Thus, there is a tension between the types of benefits firms may pursue:

the more a sustainability initiative directly benefits the firm, the less likely that initiative will improve the firm's relationships with its primary stakeholders.

3.2 Giving 'til it Hurts?

In his 2014 Lenten message, Pope Francis declared, "I distrust a charity that costs nothing and does not hurt" (Vatican, 2014). His comment suggests that sacrifice must be involved in an action for it to convey altruism and so earn trust. Symbolic adoption of an environmental cause does not signal a firm's concern for others as effectively as does substantively participating in an effort to resolve that same environmental problem.

The more difficult and costly a firm's effort to support an environmental cause, the more altruistic the firm is likely to be perceived, and the more stakeholder trust it will generate. Du, Bhattacharya, and Sen (2011) demonstrated the effects of having more "skin in the game" from a different perspective, showing that when consumers went beyond mere awareness of a firm's CSR effort and physically participated in it, they developed a more positive attitude toward the firm. This highlights a tension between burden and benefit: the less burdensome a sustainability initiative, the less likely it is to improve the firm's relationships with its primary stakeholders.

3.3 Giving Early?

When a firm increases employee pay or benefits, it is generally considered to be behaving in a socially responsible way. However, the context in which the action occurs can alter stakeholder perceptions about the degree to which the act may instead be self-serving. For example, in February 2015, Walmart announced that it would raise its minimum wage to U.S.$1.75 above the federal minimum wage and then by another U.S.$1 the following year. Whereas some saw this as an act of good corporate citizenship, others pointed out that Walmart did so under pressure. As a result, this socially responsible action engendered more skepticism than it likely would have had Walmart acted earlier:

> … you cannot deny the role of the United Food and Commercial Workers' campaign to organize Wal-Mart workers. "This is not an act of corporate benevolence," said Marc Perrone, president of UFCW, in a statement on the Wal-Mart announcement. "Walmart is responding directly to calls from workers and their allies to pay a living wage." In fact, the last time Wal-Mart faced significant labor unrest in 2006, it raised wages as a direct result, according to Federal Reserve minutes. It, like most businesses, makes changes that benefit workers only when its reputation is threatened, and poor publicity ensues. That means that worker voices play a powerful role in wage growth. (Dayen, 2015)

This suggests a tension between action and reaction. Though firms may not want to take the risk of being a first mover on controversial issues, the more time that a firm takes to respond to a sustainability challenge—particularly in the face of mounting pressure to act—the less likely a stakeholder is to perceive the eventual response as altruistic. Thus, any benefit from waiting can be offset by rising skepticism.

3.4 Giving Consistently?

Barnett (2007) theorized that firms suddenly becoming socially responsible are not believable. Stakeholders treat an unexpected act of goodwill with suspicion. A good act by a bad firm can actually backfire, harming trust between the firm and its stakeholders (Varadarajan & Menon, 1988). Barnett and Salomon (2012) empirically validated the importance of firm history, demonstrating that firms need an extensive record of social responsibility before they can profit from it.

The need to establish a consistent record of social and environmental involvement before being able to profit from it may apply not only at the firm level but also to specific initiatives. Although two firms may allocate the same overall level of funding and other resource commitments to sustainability, they may assemble very different portfolios. One firm might support many ad hoc projects, while another might focus on one or a few specific issues. For example, Google doles out a variety of grants each year, whereas McDonald's is closely associated with one charity, the Ronald McDonald House.

Firms face pressure to satisfy the demands of a wide range of stakeholders. Yet a firm's consistency in addressing a particular issue in depth and over time should provide its stakeholders with a greater indication that the firm is other-considering than would another firm's new or intermittent support of that same issue. That is, we expect that the less sustained a firm's sustainability initiatives are, the less likely are these initiatives to improve the firm's relationships with its primary stakeholders. This creates yet another tension, since taking on only a limited range of sustainability problems may require the firm to heed the demands of a smaller set of stakeholders, thus increasing the risk of failing to satisfy a larger set of stakeholders.

3.5 Giving and Gabbing?

Firms face a conundrum in publicizing their good deeds. A firm needs its primary stakeholders to be aware of its sustainability initiatives if it is to gain increased trust through them. Thus, it needs to publicize these acts. Yet, when a firm publicizes its good deeds, stakeholders may perceive the firm to be behaving in a self-serving way, and this may cause stakeholders to limit or even decrease their trust in the firm. As Du, Bhattacharya, and Sen (2010) noted, "While stakeholders claim they want to know about … good deeds … they also quickly become leery of the CSR motives when companies aggressively promote their CSR efforts" (p. 9). This suggests that the more that a firm promotes a sustainability initiative, the less likely is that initiative to improve the firm's relationships with its primary stakeholders. Thus, another tension faced in profiting from sustainability initiatives is in finding ways to make good deeds known without appearing self-serving.

4 HOMING IN ON THE HURDLES OF PROFITING FROM SUSTAINABILITY

Firms build valuable trust with their primary stakeholders by demonstrating their concern for the plight of others. The resulting improved relationships with key resource holders benefit the firm in a myriad of ways, thereby producing the "win–win" outcomes that are the defining characteristic of the popular business case (cf. Porter & Van der Linde, 1995). Yet despite the popularity of the business case in both theory and practice, it is inherently challenging for a sustainability initiative to be simultaneously self- and other-serving. There are tensions in trying to align what are fundamentally opposing outcomes.

As firms publicize the ways that they benefit from their sustainability initiatives, they may harm their ability to continue to gain such benefits. Yet this co-mingling of social and corporate benefits is common in CSR and sustainability reporting. Consider the 2014 report from Cisco mentioned at the start of this chapter. Cisco's CEO states that the firm is proud of its contributions to improving society and the environment, but the report also notes that these contributions benefit the firm by improving its stakeholder relationships and generating long-term value. CEO Howard Schultz similarly introduces Starbucks' (2014) Global Responsibility Report by writing, "I am proud that Starbucks not only achieved another year of record financial performance, but we did so while doing more for our people and the communities we serve than at any time in our history" (p. 1).

Firms' returns from sustainability initiatives are likely to be affected by the way they publicize these efforts. Because other-serving and self-serving actions have offsetting effects on stakeholder trust, firms may be able to improve their returns by downplaying the private benefits and instead focusing their messaging on the gains these initiatives create for society. For example, describing sustainability as an investment rather than as an act of goodwill may harm a firm's ability to build stakeholder trust. However, at least one stakeholder group, investors, may view a firm's declaration of profiting from its sustainability investments as further assurance that the firm is fulfilling its fiduciary responsibility, which serves to increase trust in the firm.

The more that a stakeholder perceives a firm's actions as self-serving, the less likely the firm will be able to gain the trust of the stakeholder (Varadarajan & Menon, 1988). Firms must publicize their sustainability initiatives to create awareness, yet "tooting one's own horn" can appear self-serving to the very stakeholders it is hoping to impress. Thus, it may be best to specify how these actions bring about sustainability, not profitability, when advertising them. Moreover, third-party recognition and publicity are more likely to foment stakeholder trust than self-promotion.

The earlier figure also illustrates that both the established business case (which focuses on how firms may profit by managing in the interests of stakeholders) and the revised business case (which, as outlined herein, looks at how firms may profit by managing in the interests of society) are premised on gaining favor with primary stakeholders. Where they differ is in how firms gain this favor. The established business case argues that firms maintain the most stakeholder favor by prioritizing the needs of their most powerful, legitimate, and urgent stakeholders (Mitchell et al., 1997). However, in a business case for sustainability, the reverse may hold true. By investing in sustainability without facing immediate pressure to do so, the firm is better able to demonstrate to its primary stakeholders that it is other-serving, and so gain their favor. If the firm faces urgent pressure from its powerful stakeholders to become more sustainable, then the response may be perceived as self-serving and result in a loss of favor with primary stakeholders.

Power and trust thus interact in determining the degree to which corporate sustainability affects stakeholder favor, but exactly how remains unclear. A firm's relationships with its primary stakeholders is a function of how it deals with the demands these stakeholders make of the firm to take on specific issues, as well as how these stakeholders react to its decisions to take on or ignore other issues without such pressure. Given limited time, attention, and resources, firms must be selective in their pursuit of sustainability and other causes. The calculus involved in rationing the firm's resources must include more than just power, legitimacy, and urgency if it is to determine the most optimal way to manage primary stakeholder relations. Perhaps the firm best advances its own interests by dealing with a sustainability issue before, rather than after, it becomes a stakeholder demand. However, any given firm faces a mix of issues vying for its limited resources, many of which are championed by powerful stakeholders.

A firm can increase its financial returns not only by increasing its revenues but also by decreasing its costs. Perceptions that a firm has willingly taken on a significant burden in its efforts to better society are helpful in convincing stakeholders of the firm's trustworthiness. Thus, firms may gain valuable stakeholder favor by committing more resources to sustainability initiatives. However, greater spending, all else equal, simply means greater difficulty in turning a profit. Therefore, profit-seeking firms must manage spending on sustainability in a way that allows them to gain the most benefit at the lowest cost.

Barnett and Salomon (2012) acknowledged the countervailing force of costs on returns to CSR and called for research on the efficiency by which firms can produce stakeholder favor through CSR. Some firms may have to spend considerably more than others, and perhaps more than they can recover through improved stakeholder favor, to convince their primary stakeholders that their firm is other-considering. Firms' efficiency in running social initiatives has not been well accounted for. Some firms may be able to mount a campaign to, say, end homelessness in their local community or increase high school graduation rates, at lower cost than others. Overall, a firm's efficiency at producing stakeholder favor through sustainability initiatives should be accounted for and improved.

5 AN INDIRECT PATH TO NOWHERE

Firms have incentive to invest in sustainability, but optimizing returns is a complex undertaking, fraught with counterposing pressures. Examining these tensions, we can see that a sustainability initiative is more likely to improve primary stakeholder relationships and so benefit the firm if it entails self-sacrifice, is costly to the firm, occurs in advance of calls for such action, is a sustained effort, and is not self-promoted. Perversely, then, the better aligned a sustainability initiative is with a firm's self-interest—be that because it is cheaper, easier, or less risky to undertake—then the less that initiative may be capable of advancing the firm's self-interest. That is, the pursuit of self-interest through corporate sustainability can be self-defeating. Yet firms can and often do find ways to manage these tensions so they can profit from their sustainability initiatives, as shown across thousands of studies.

But what about the benefits to society? Might they also be difficult to achieve? Studies have seldom confirmed the presumed benefits to society. The thousands of studies that have sought to explain if (e.g., Orlitzky, Schmidt & Rynes, 2003), how (e.g., Peloza & Shang, 2011), and when (e.g., Grewatsch & Kleindienst, 2017) it "pays to be good" have done so without giving due heed to how much "good" has actually been produced.

As Margolis and Walsh (2003: 289) lamented, "Although the financial effects of corporate social performance have been extensively studied, little is known about any other consequences of corporate social initiatives." Blowfield (2007: 683) later asserted that "we know most about CSR's impact on business itself and the benefits for business, and least about how CSR affects the major societal issues it was intended to tackle." More recently, Wood (2010: 76), who, like Margolis and Walsh (2003), focused on the closely related concept of corporate social performance (CSP), argued that social impact continues to be overlooked: "The whole idea of CSP is to discern and assess the impacts of business-society relationships. Now it is time to shift the focus away from how CSP affects the firm, and towards how the firm's CSP affects stakeholders and society."

But not every study has completely ignored the public good produced by corporate social and environmental initiatives. The CSR literature began about 50 years ago (Wood, 2010), and "the theme of improving society was certainly in the mind of early theorists and practitioners" (Carroll & Shabana, 2010: 91). Though several reviews have rightfully criticized the well-established literature's predominant focus on firm financial performance, they have not closely analyzed what those studies that have looked beyond financial performance have revealed over time. Moreover, many years have passed since many of these calls to look beyond financial performance were made and, in that time, thousands more studies have been published. In the face of rising public expectations and mounting scholarly calls for change, the literature may have advanced, so we will take a closer look.

The literature is massive. Searching the fields of business, management, ethics, economics, and environmental studies from 1968 to 2018, we found 6,254 articles published on the performance implications of CSR; 5,788 of these were published in the last decade. Clearly, much work has been done. To make analysis manageable, we focused only on the most cited articles published in the last decade. To structure our analysis, we adapt the logic model, a tool rooted in the development studies literature (Ebrahim & Rangan, 2014; Rogers, 2008; Weiss, 1972). The logic model illustrates that inputs feed into activities that result in immediate outputs, leading to medium- to long-term outcomes that have impacts on communities and ecosystems. This model has been adapted to examine the social performance of non-profit organizations, philanthropy, and social enterprises (Ebrahim & Rangan, 2014). So, we adapt it to assess how far the literature has come in assessing impact.

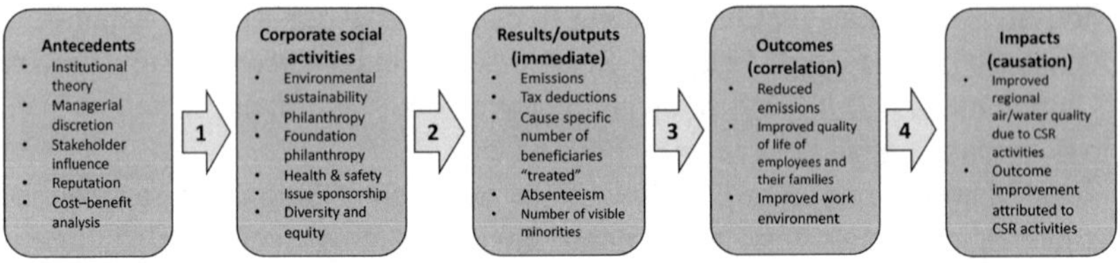

Figure 4.2 A CSR logic model

Figure 4.2 presents our logic model. It contains four categories: (a) CSR activities; (b) immediate outputs from CSR activities, such as tax deductions, number of beneficiaries served, emissions, or financial performance; (c) outcomes, defined as the change in the output, such as reduced emissions, improved work environment, or improved quality of life; and (d) impacts, defined as change in the output caused by the CSR activity (Khandker et al., 2010).

Category 1 studies analyzed CSR activity as the dependent variable. Papers looking at the impact of CEO political ideology (e.g., Chin, Hambrick & Trevino, 2013), ecological responsiveness (e.g., Hamann, Smith, Tashman & Marshall, 2017), greenwashing (e.g., Delmas & Burbano, 2011), CSR ratings (e.g., Bear, Rahman & Post, 2010), and political CSR (e.g., Scherer, Rasche, Palazzo & Spicer, 2016) on CSR activities are included in this category. Of the most-cited papers, 43 percent examined factors influencing CSR activities.

Composing Category 2, 51 percent had a result or output of a CSR activity as the dependent variable. Of these, 80 percent had financial performance as the dependent variable (e.g., Flammer, 2015). That is, the focus was on the business case for CSR rather than on the social output of the activity. In the seven papers that did not focus on financial performance, food waste (Devin & Richards, 2018), emissions (Chatterji, Levine & Toffel, 2009), employee engagement (Flammer & Luo, 2017), societal goals (Benabou & Tirole, 2010), stakeholder relations (Bhattacharya, Korschun & Sen, 2009), and environmental innovations (e.g., Kesidou & Demirel, 2012; Varadarajan, 2017) were the dependent variables.

Moving to Category 3, only four papers addressed the outcome of CSR activities. Jamali, Lund-Thomsen, and Khara (2017) examined whether CSR initiatives among small and medium-sized enterprises (SMEs) in an industrial cluster in India served the intended purpose of improving the quality of life of marginalized workers. They collected fieldwork data in the Jalandhar football manufacturing cluster. They interviewed marginalized workers to see work conditions from their perspective. Jamali et al. (2017: 480) found that "local SME manufacturers have circumvented local labor laws and outsourced the most labor-intensive aspects of football manufacturing—the stitching of footballs—to home-based locations," which led to deteriorating social outcomes for the stitchers.

Kitzmueller and Shimshack (2012) provided an economic perspective on CSR and its outcomes. The standard economic argument is that the market's invisible hand allows consumers and corporations to pursue their self-interests. Government only needs to intervene when there is a market failure, redistributing income and wealth via the tax system and regulations. Unfortunately, governments can fail to provide ample oversight, creating a void wherein citizens and corporations voluntarily undertake CSR activities beyond their legal and contractual obligations (Benabou & Tirole, 2010). Kitzmueller and Shimshack (2012) argue that more research is needed to determine the welfare properties of CSR. More specifically, questions relating to who, what, when, and how to measure changes in welfare need to be developed.

Drawing from economics, McWilliams and Siegel (2011) suggest hedonic pricing and contingent valuation techniques to measure the value of a CSR action to society. Firms can capture the value of providing such social goods through gains to reputation (Fombrun & Shanley, 1990). Finally, Devika, Jafarian, and Nourbakhsh (2014) propose a supply chain network design in which the focus is not solely on minimizing total costs or maximizing profit but includes environmental and social impacts. Here the social and ecological dimensions are quantified and embedded as distinct objectives along with total costs. This requires researchers to correctly model and provide initial values for the system being examined and to subjectively account for trade-offs between objectives.

Concerning the impact of CSR activities, the pipeline goes dry; no papers fit Category 4. Thus, these studies focused almost entirely on inputs and practices, with a handful addressing immediate outputs, often drawn from secondary data sources that take into account relative levels of corporate spending toward various social issues. This is consistent with Ebrahim and Rangan's (2014: 123) broader insight that "outcome measurement is less common and more difficult to do given that organizations have the most control over their immediate activities and outputs, whereas outcomes are often moderated by events beyond their organizational boundaries."

As a check on this lack of impact measures among highly cited papers, we performed an additional analysis of the 5,314 CSR–performance articles published in the past decade, using "social impact" as the keyword. The search returned twenty-four papers. Two were unavailable because they were published in obscure journals. Of the remaining twenty-two papers, only three evaluated and measured the social impact of the CSR activity. Sinha and Chaudhari (2018) examined the impact of a CSR program that develops special classes for weaker students. The study includes a pre- and post-test but no control group. Thus, it cannot determine what might have happened to students in the absence of the initiative. Loosemore and Bridgeman (2018) examined employee volunteering in schools. Like the Sinha and Chaudhari (2018) study, it includes an evaluation of students before, during, and after participation in the program but also fails to include a control group. Both studies allow the analyst to determine whether students attained educational goals but cannot infer causality. Luo, Kaul, and Seo (2018) examined the impact of corporate philanthropy on oil spills. In a rigorously designed study that used panel data to confidently infer causality, they theorized about adverse selection and moral hazard and found that philanthropy increases oil spills, which is not the intended result. Thus, after an extensive analysis of the thousands of studies populating the CSR–performance literature, we find that the literature has advanced, but we do not find a single study that adequately demonstrates that CSR initiatives have resolved the social problems they intended to address.

6 CONCLUSION

Do firms really do well by ensuring that society becomes more sustainable? In this chapter, we find cause for concern about the impact of the business case on sustainability. The amorphous nature of the stakeholder concept (cf. Orts & Strudler, 2002) has blurred the distinction between responding to stakeholder demands and acting in ways that substantively sustain broader society.

As portrayed in their reports, press releases, websites, and other public statements, businesses intend to do a tremendous amount of good for society through their countless sustainability initiatives. Yet the massive literature offers little evidence of the actual impact of these initiatives. The ever-growing field is evolving but still primarily assumes, rather than validates, that the myriad of sustainability initiatives that firms undertake generate the desired outcomes. Even when they have purported to focus on impact, business case studies have stopped short of doing so. For example, in their popular article that sought to explain social change by putting "the S back in corporate social responsibility," Aguilera et al. (2007: 841) developed a complex figure which shows the countless drivers of change in CSR. Yet the figure concludes with only a singular bold arrow connecting change in CSR to social change. The study simply presumes that CSR initiatives help society. Peloza and Shang (2011) reviewed the literature to determine how CSR creates value for stakeholders, but they focused on financial returns to the firm from improved stakeholder relationships, not on the benefits to stakeholders. Aguinis and Glavas (2012) tried clarifying "what we know and don't know about corporate social responsibility," the outcomes of CSR actions across different levels of analysis, yet no outcomes extended beyond the firm and its employees. Thus, the literature demonstrates at best that it can pay to intend to be good. To move beyond good intentions, one thing is abundantly clear: "Colleagues, we have a lot more work to do" (Wood, 2010: 76).

BIBLIOGRAPHY

Aguilera, R. V., Rupp, D. E., Williams, C. A., & Ganapathi, J. 2007. Putting the S back in corporate social responsibility: A multilevel theory of social change in organizations. Academy of Management Review, 32: 836–863.

Aguinis, H., & Glavas, A. 2012. What we know and don't know about corporate social responsibility: A review and research agenda. Journal of Management, 38(4): 932–968.

Argandoña, A. 1998. The stakeholder theory and the common good. Journal of Business Ethics, 17: 1093–1102.

Barnett, M. L. 2007. Stakeholder influence capacity and the variability of financial returns to corporate social responsibility. Academy of Management Review, 32: 794–816.

Barnett, M. L., & Salomon, R. M. 2012. Does it pay to be really good? Addressing the shape of the relationship between social and financial performance. Strategic Management Journal, 33: 1304–1320.

Bear, S., Rahman, N., & Post, C. 2010. The impact of board diversity and gender composition on corporate social responsibility and firm reputation. Journal of Business Ethics, 97(2): 207–221.

Benabou, R., & Tirole, J. 2010. Individual and corporate social responsibility. Economica, 77(305): 1–19.

Berman, S. L., Wicks, A. C., Kotha, S., & Jones, T. M. 1999. Does stakeholder orientation matter? The relationship between stakeholder management models and firm financial performance. Academy of Management Journal, 42: 488–506.

Bhattacharya, C. B., Korschun, D., & Sen, S. 2009. Strengthening stakeholder–company relationships through mutually beneficial corporate social responsibility initiatives. Journal of Business Ethics, 85: 257–272.

Blowfield, M. 2007. Reasons to be cheerful? What we know about CSR's impact. Third World Quarterly, 28(4): 683–695.

Carroll, A. B. 1979. A three-dimensional conceptual model of corporate performance. Academy of Management Review, 4: 497–505.

Carroll, A. B., & Shabana, K. M. 2010. The business case for corporate social responsibility: A review of concepts, research and practice. International Journal of Management Reviews, 12(1): 85–105.

Chatterji, A. K., Levine, D. I., & Toffel, M. W. 2009. How well do social ratings actually measure corporate social responsibility? Journal of Economics & Management Strategy, 18(1): 125–169.

Cheng, B., Ioannou, I., & Serafeim, G. 2014. Corporate social responsibility and access to finance. Strategic Management Journal, 35: 1–23.

Chin, M. K., Hambrick, D. C., & Trevino, L. K. 2013. Political ideologies of CEOs: The influence of executives' values on corporate social responsibility. Administrative Science Quarterly, 58(2): 197–232.

Cisco. 2014. Social responsibility report. Available at: www.cisco.com/assets/csr/pdf/CSR_Report_2014.pdf. Accessed January 27, 2022.

Clarkson, M. E. 1995. A stakeholder framework for analyzing and evaluating corporate social performance. Academy of Management Review, 20: 92–117.

Dayen, D. 2015, February 24. Scott Walker's economic mess: How worker wages were gutted in Wisconsin. Slate.com.

Delmas, M. A., & Burbano, V. C. 2011. The drivers of greenwashing. California Management Review, 54(1): 64–87.

Denning, S. 2015, February 5. Salesforce CEO slams world's dumbest idea. Forbes.com.

Devika, K., Jafarian, A., & Nourbakhsh, V. 2014. Designing a sustainable closed-loop supply chain network based on triple bottom line approach: A comparison of metaheuristics hybridization techniques. European Journal of Operational Research, 235(3): 594–615.

Devin, B., & Richards, C. 2018. Food waste, power, and corporate social responsibility in the Australian food supply chain. Journal of Business Ethics, 150(1): 199–210.

Du, S., Bhattacharya, C. B., & Sen, S. 2010. Maximizing business returns to corporate social responsibility (CSR): The role of CSR communication. International Journal of Management Reviews, 12: 8–19.

Du, S., Bhattacharya, C. B., & Sen, S. 2011. Corporate social responsibility and competitive advantage: Overcoming the trust barrier. Management Science, 57: 1528–1545.

Ebrahim, A., & Rangan, K. 2014. What impact: A framework for measuring the scale and scope of social performance. California Management Review, 56(3): 118–141.

Ellen, P. S., Webb, D. J., & Mohr, L. A. 2006. Building corporate associations: Consumer attributions for corporate socially responsible programs. Journal of the Academy of Marketing Science, 34: 147–157.

Flammer, C. 2015. Does corporate social responsibility lead to superior financial performance? A regression discontinuity approach. Management Science, 61: 2549–2568.

Flammer, C., & Luo, J. 2017. Corporate social responsibility as an employee governance tool: Evidence from a quasi-experiment. Strategic Management Journal, 38(2): 163–183.

Fombrun, C. J., Gardberg, N. A., & Barnett, M. L. 2000. Opportunity platforms and safety nets: Corporate citizenship and reputational risk. Business and Society Review, 105: 85–106.

Fombrun, C., & Shanley, M. 1990. What's in a name? Reputation building and corporate strategy. Academy of Management Journal, 33: 233–258.

Freeman, R. E. 1984. *Strategic management: A stakeholder perspective*. Pitman: Boston, MA.

Freeman, R. E. 2005. The development of stakeholder theory: An idiosyncratic approach. In K. G. Smith & M. A. Hitt (Eds) *Great minds in management: The process of theory development.* Oxford, U.K.: Oxford University Press: 417–435.

Freeman, R. E. 2008. Ending the so-called "Friedman–Freeman" debate. Business Ethics Quarterly, 18: 153–190.

Freeman, R. E., & Phillips, R. A. 2002. Stakeholder theory: A libertarian defense. Business Ethics Quarterly, 12: 331–349.

Friedman, M. 1970. The social responsibility of business is to increase its profits. New York Times Magazine, 13: 32–33.

Frooman, J. 1999. Stakeholder influence strategies. Academy of Management Review, 24: 191–205.

Glazer, A., & Konrad, K. A. 1996. A signaling explanation for charity. The American Economic Review, 86(4): 1019–1028.

Godfrey, P. C. 2005. The relationship between corporate philanthropy and shareholder wealth: A risk management perspective. Academy of Management Review, 30: 777–798.

Godfrey, P. C., Merrill, C. B., & Hansen, J. M. 2009. The relationship between corporate social responsibility and shareholder value: An empirical test of the risk management hypothesis. Strategic Management Journal, 30: 425–445.

Goodpaster, K. E. 1991. Business ethics and stakeholder analysis. Business Ethics Quarterly, 1: 53–73.

Grewatsch, S., & Kleindienst, I. 2017. When does it pay to be good? Moderators and mediators in the corporate sustainability–corporate financial performance relationship: A critical review. Journal of Business Ethics, 145(2): 383–416.

Hamann, R., Smith, J., Tashman, P., & Marshall, R. S. 2017. Why do SMEs go green? An analysis of wine firms in South Africa. Business & Society, 56(1): 23–56.

Harrison, J. S., & Wicks, A. C. 2013. Stakeholder theory, value, and firm performance. Business Ethics Quarterly, 23: 97–124.
Hillman, A. J., & Keim, G. D. 2001. Shareholder value, stakeholder management, and social issues: What's the bottom line? Strategic Management Journal, 22: 125–139.
Hoffmann, A. J. 2018. The next phase of business sustainability. Stanford Social Innovation Review, Spring: 34–39.
Jamali, D., Lund-Thomsen, P., & Khara, N. 2017. CSR institutionalized myths in developing countries: An imminent threat of selective decoupling. Business & Society, 56: 454–486.
Jensen, M. C. 2000. Value maximization and the corporate objective function. In M. Beer & N. Nohria (Eds) *Breaking the code of change*. Harvard Business School Press: Boston, MA: 37–57.
Kesidou, E., & Demirel, P. 2012. On the drivers of eco-innovations: Empirical evidence from the UK. Research Policy, 41(5): 862–870.
Khandker, S., Koolwal, G. B., & Samad, H. 2010. *Handbook on impact evaluation: Quantitative methods and practices*. The World Bank: Washington, D.C.
Kitzmueller, M., & Shimshack, J. 2012. Economic perspectives on corporate social responsibility. Journal of Economic Literature, 50(1): 51–84.
Laplume, A. O., Sonpar, K., & Litz, R. A. 2008. Stakeholder theory: Reviewing a theory that moves us. Journal of Management, 34: 1152–1189.
Loosemore, M., & Bridgeman, J. 2018. The social impact of construction industry schools-based corporate volunteering. Construction Management and Economics, 36(5): 243–258.
Luo, J., Kaul, A., & Seo, H. 2018. Winning us with trifles: Adverse selection in the use of philanthropy as insurance. Strategic Management Journal, 39(10): 2591–2617.
Margolis, J. D., & Walsh, J. P. 2003. Misery loves companies: Rethinking social initiatives by business. Administrative Science Quarterly, 48: 268–305.
McWilliams, A., & Siegel, D. S. 2011. Creating and capturing value: Strategic corporate social responsibility, resource-based theory, and sustainable competitive advantage. Journal of Management, 37(5): 1480–1495.
Mitchell, R. K., Agle, B. R., & Wood, D. J. 1997. Toward a theory of stakeholder identification and salience: Defining the principle of who and what really counts. Academy of Management Review, 22: 853–886.
Orlitzky, M., Schmidt, F., & Rynes, S. 2003. Corporate social and financial performance: A meta-analysis. Organization Studies, 24: 403–441.
Orts, E. W., & Strudler, A. 2002. The ethical and environmental limits of stakeholder theory. Business Ethics Quarterly, 12: 215–233.
Peloza, J., & Shang, J. 2011. How can corporate social responsibility activities create value for stakeholders? A systematic review. Journal of Academy of Marketing Science, 39: 117–135
Phillips, R. 2003. *Stakeholder theory and organizational ethics*. Berrett-Koehler: San Francisco, CA.
Porter, M. E., & Van der Linde, C. 1995. Green and competitive: Ending the stalemate. Harvard Business Review, 73: 120–134.
Post, J. E., Preston, L. E., & Sachs, S. 2002. *Redefining the corporation: Stakeholder management and organizational wealth*. Stanford University Press: Stanford, CA.
Rogers, P. J. 2008. Using programme theory to evaluate complicated and complex actions of interactions. Evaluation, 14(1): 29–48.
Rowley, T., & Berman, S. 2000. A brand new brand of corporate social performance. Business & Society, 39: 397–418.

Scherer, A. G., Rasche, A., Palazzo, G., & Spicer, A. 2016. Managing for political corporate social responsibility: New challenges and directions for PCSR 2.0. Journal of Management Studies, 53(3): 273–298.

Sinha, S. N., & Chaudhari, T. 2018. Impact of CSR on learning outcomes. Management of Environmental Quality, 29(6): 1026–1041.

Starbucks, 2014. Global responsibility report. Available at: www.starbucks.com/responsibility/global-report. Accessed January 27, 2022.

Starik, M. 1995. Should trees have managerial standing? Toward stakeholder status for non-human nature. Journal of Business Ethics, 14: 207–217.

Turban, D. B., & Greening, D. W. 1997. Corporate social performance and organizational attractiveness to prospective employees. Academy of Management Journal, 40: 658–672.

Van der Laan, G., Van Ees, H., & Van Witteloostuijn, A. 2008. Corporate social and financial performance: An extended stakeholder theory, and empirical test with accounting measures. Journal of Business Ethics, 79: 299–310.

Varadarajan, P. R., & Menon, A. 1988. Cause-related marketing: A coalignment of marketing strategy and corporate philanthropy. The Journal of Marketing, 52: 58–74.

Varadarajan, R. 2017. Innovating for sustainability: A framework for sustainable innovations and a model of sustainable innovations orientation. Journal of the Academy of Marketing Science, 45(1): 14–36.

Vatican. 2014. Lenten message of our Holy Father Francis.

Waddock, S. A., & Graves, S. B. 1997. The corporate social performance-financial performance link. Strategic Management Journal, 18: 303–319.

Walsh, J. P. 2005. Book review essay: Taking stock of stakeholder management. Academy of Management Review, 30: 426–438.

Weiss, C. H. 1972. *Evaluation research: Methods for assessing program effectiveness*, Urban Institute Press: Washington, D.C.

Wood, D. J. 1991. Corporate social performance revisited. Academy of Management Review, 16: 691–718.

Wood, D. J. 2010. Measuring corporate social performance: A review. International Journal of Management Reviews, 12(1): 50–84.

5. Baked-in biases of the business case

The central mechanism of any business case is money. Without it, firms wither and die. So, firms generally take part in acts they think increase income and stop doing things they think decrease it. If there is a change in where big bucks abound, a change in firm behavior eventually follows. Firms change as best they are able so that they can comport with changing market demands. In 1802, for instance, DuPont made black powder. Around 1902, DuPont recognized that chemicals made more money than black powder and so it became a chemical company. By 2002, DuPont was also manufacturing food products, fibers, and more. As this suggests, a firm will grow fruit or shift to manufacturing fruit-shaped toilet brushes (it's a real thing somehow; just look it up on the ever-evolving Amazon website) if there's more money to be made in the latter.

Accordingly, if firms believe that being more sustainable makes more money, then firms become more sustainable; that's the essence of the business case for sustainability. However, if firms believe that being less sustainable is more profitable, then firms will do more environmental harm. That, we must acknowledge, is also the essence of the business case. Therefore, to understand the degree to which a firm will take action to help sustain society or take self-serving actions that harm society, we must follow the money. This entails sorting out what stakeholders—those who control a firm's critical resources—demand of firms.

In this chapter, we sort out the sorts of sustainability initiatives that firms tend to undertake when seeking to satisfy stakeholders. We begin by addressing stakeholder preferences and their willingness to pay for sustainable goods and services. Thereafter, we show how these stakeholder preferences and actions shape the sorts of sustainability initiatives that firms pursue, driving firms toward simple victories and a focus on technology and consumption.

1 PUTTING THEIR MONEY WHERE THEIR MOUTHS ARE?

Market measures indicate that there is broad stakeholder support for corporate sustainability. Many studies show that firms who engage in more responsible business practices tend to outperform those that are less responsible over time (Barnett & Salomon, 2006, 2012). The returns are significant enough that firms maintain such practices even through economic downturns (Barnett,

Darnall & Husted, 2015). However, the types of corporate initiatives that please stakeholders and thereby generate favorable market returns may not provide optimal solutions to society's sustainability problems (Barnett, 2019). Thus, it is important to clarify the sorts of sustainability initiatives that are rewarded.

What sorts of sustainability initiatives do stakeholders favor? The answer depends on individual attitudes toward sustainability. Within the field of environmental psychology, significant effort has been devoted to uncovering the nature of environmental attitudes. Broadly, the literature conceptualizes pro-environmental attitudes along a single scale, with the anthropocentric and ecocentric environmental paradigms reflecting the polar extremes of these attitudes (Brown, 1995; Purser, Park & Montuori, 1995). Anthropocentric approaches to the natural environment place human beings at the center of the model. Environmental management models are typically anthropocentric and assume that humans are in some sense above nature (Purser et al., 1995). Ecocentric approaches place the natural environment at the center of concern. Here, humans and nature are given equal importance, which is why ecocentrism is often considered to be "radically egalitarian" in that both "rivers and lakes, as well as animals and humans, would be conceived of as possessing intrinsic value" (Brown, 1995: 193).

The marketing literature has examined how environmental attitudes are manifested among consumers. Shrum, McCarty, and Lowrey (1995) found that people who consider themselves to be opinion leaders, early adopters of new products, or careful shoppers are more likely to buy green. Other marketing studies have focused on consumer preferences for products with ecologically friendly packaging and post-consumer recycling. Schwepker and Cornwell (1991) tied these preferences to a more nuanced set of environmental attitudes, finding that knowledge of ecological problems and the perceived ability of the person to create positive change were key predictors of purchases of ecologically packaged goods.

Studies of consumer attitudes, however, may not closely track with actual marketplace behavior. For instance, preferences for sustainable processes and products can falter if the price is too high. Economists thus focus on willingness to pay (WTP) for environmental outcomes (e.g., Johnston & Duke, 2009; Kotchen & Reiling, 2000). In Mexico, for example, several studies examined the willingness of households to pay for clean and reliable water resources (Ojeda, Mayer & Solomon, 2008; Vasquez, Mozumder, Hernández & Berrens, 2009). These studies tend to focus on public goods, not consumer goods (Anderson & Hansen, 2004; Sammer & Wustenhagen, 2006). Because we can observe actual prices and purchases, the more complicated WTP method is not always relevant when studying consumer goods. Yet, it can be difficult to value environmental attributes that are bundled into consumer goods, so WTP valuations can be useful for product attributes that are not directly observable.

Although the literature confirms the link between environmental attitudes and green purchase decisions (Anderson & Hansen, 2004; Blaney, Bennett, Louviere & Morrison, 2001; Sammer & Wustenhagen, 2006), it fails to demonstrate that these attitudes lead to a higher WTP. By contrast, the literature testing how environmentally oriented products elicit higher marginal WTP has ignored environmental attitudes. Husted et al. (2014) sought to bridge this gap by combining improved empirical methods to estimate marginal WTP with greater attention to the role of environmental attitudes when purchasing in an emerging market like Mexico. The premium that consumers are willing to pay for environmental goods is a behavioral intention (Ajzen, 2001; Ajzen & Driver, 1992) that relates to "the amount of effort a person exerts to perform a behavior" (Cordano & Frieze, 2000: 628). Thus, the magnitude of the premium reflects the amount of effort a person makes to reward a product attribute, such as an environmental certification (Bagozzi, 1992). Based on a conjoint analysis of marginal WTP on a survey of 301 Mexican furniture consumers, Husted et al. (2014) found that, as attitudes became more pro-environmental, middle-class consumers demonstrated a willingness to pay a price premium for environmentally certified wood products.

How do these environmental attitudes relate to a consumer's willingness to pay a premium for eco-friendly product attributes? Generally speaking, consumers with low pro-environmental (anthropocentric) attitudes are less likely to pay a premium for products with environmental attributes because of their optimism in technology's ability to overcome environmental problems. On the other hand, consumers with high pro-environmental (eco-centric) attitudes view the quality of the environment as vital to human well-being (Gladwin, Kennelly & Krause, 1995), believing that economic growth must occur sustainably in a way that does not undermine the ability of future generations to meet their needs (World Commission on Environment & Development, 1987). In this sense, environmental attributes of products are seen as an investment that ultimately serves human needs. Correspondingly, there should be an increasing willingness to pay for such attributes.

Of particular importance in this literature is the New Environmental Paradigm (NEP) (Dunlap & Van Liere, 1978). In contrast to the dominant social paradigm, which assumes that nature exists for human benefit, the NEP posits that humans are embedded in an interconnected web of ecological relationships and subject to biological constraints, rather than masters who preside over a landscape of unlimited resources (Jermier, 2008). In their work, Husted et al. (2014) build on the NEP scale to argue that there are four underlying factors affecting consumers' marginal WTP for green product attributes in a non-linear way: human interference with nature, equity and development issues, humans and economy over nature, and duties to non-humans. La Trobe and Acott (2000) found that these factors may be unrelated for some people, while for others they were viewed as related. Such ambivalence (Priester & Petty, 1996) tends to hinder increases in marginal WTP. However, it has been found to attenuate the relationship between attitudes and individual behavior (Conner et al., 2003). As attitude structures become more highly integrated and less ambivalent, the relationship among the underlying dimensions can increase their strength in non-linear ways (Priester & Petty, 1996). At intermediate levels of NEP, which tends to be characterized by inconsistency and ambivalence, Husted et al. (2014) posit that the impact of an incremental increase in pro-environmental attitudes on marginal WTP will be attenuated. However, at the extreme end of pro-environmental attitudes, nature substitutes human well-being as the priority and takes precedence over economic growth. At high levels of NEP (where the underlying factors become more integrated), attitudes widely support the notion that the economy should serve the health of ecosystems (Gladwin et al., 1995; Purser et al., 1995). Hence, the overall impact of an integrated and consistent pro-environmental attitude structure will be to create more than proportional increases in willingness to pay.

As more and more people realize that climate change and sustainability are important problems, the ability of organizations to provide sustainable products and services that address these challenges could break through what Gifford (2011) calls the general psychological barriers to behavior change – namely, limited cognition (e.g., ignorance, environmental numbness, uncertainty, optimism bias), ideologies (e.g., worldviews, technosalvation, system justification), comparison with others (e.g., social comparison, social norms and networks, perceived inequity), sunk costs (e.g., financial investments, conflicting values, behavioral momentum or habits), discredence (e.g., mistrust, denial), limited behavior (tokenism, rebound effect) and perceived risks (e.g., functional, physical, financial, social, psychological, temporal). As in other behavioral situations that were strongly resistant to change such as smoking and using safety belts, successful sustainable products are those that break down these psychological barriers by using "appropriately targeted messages, effective leadership, improved technical knowledge, equitable policies, enabling infrastructure, the development of norms, the setting of reasonable goals, in-your-face feedback, the spreading of social norms through social networks, and appropriate personal rewards" (Gifford, 2011: 298). Attitudes of consumers matter and changing these attitudes to incentivize businesses to produce more sustainable products, let alone meet today's sustainability challenges, will take time.

2 SUPPLYING THE SUSTAINABILITY THAT STAKEHOLDERS DEMAND

How do stakeholder preferences and willingness to pay (as outlined above) shape the types of sustainability initiatives that firms tend to undertake? We next outline three sustainability biases that result from firms' efforts to satisfy their stakeholders: simple victories, technological solutions, and consumption.

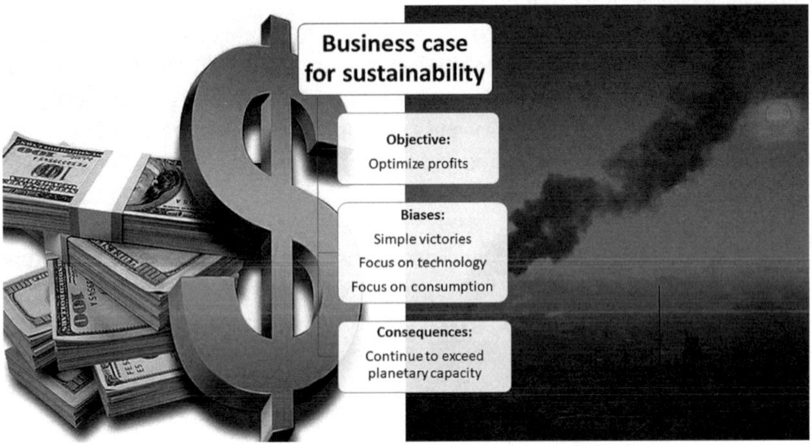

Figure 5.1 *The business case for sustainability*

2.1 Focus on Simple Victories

The business case emphasizes profit maximization as the primary goal of organizations, portraying sustainability as an investment rather than a responsibility (Dyllick & Hockerts, 2002; Porter & Kramer, 2006). This prioritization of profit significantly narrows the scope of environmental initiatives that corporations voluntarily undertake. Under a "win–win" paradigm (see Chapter 2), the environment is only provided the opportunity to "win" if and whenever corporations are first able to craft a financially viable "win" for themselves (Hahn et al., 2010). Where they perceive ample financial incentive to take on environmental issues and even to pioneer innovative solutions, corporations will develop green capabilities that enable them to outcompete their rivals (Hart, 1995; Russo & Fouts, 1997). But such opportunities only materialize where there is a "market for virtue" that rewards corporations for delivering green products and services to customers (Vogel, 2007). To attract customers, however, green products must also provide improved functionalities or aesthetics on top of environmental benefits (Olsen et al., 2014). Thus, "win–win" opportunities arise for only a subset of environmental issues.

Unending shareholder calls to increase quarterly profits have incentivized managers to adopt investments that result in immediate returns. Such investments, however, tend to be low-hanging fruit with limited long-term impacts. Tensions between the long-term versus short-term impacts (Slawinski & Bansal, 2015) and across economic, environmental, and social consequences require stakeholders to co-create the knowledge necessary to bridge these tensions that sustainability entails. Unfortunately, short-termism reduces the likelihood of doing so.

For some environmental issues, building a business case is relatively easy. For example, low-carbon products tend to be more energy efficient, so even consumers unconcerned about the environment purchase them to lower their energy bills. But for other important environmental issues (e.g., biodiversity conservation), building a business case is difficult or impossible. Except for a small segment of environmentally conscious consumers (White, Hardisty & Habib, 2019), most people do not recognize the direct benefits from buying a product that aids biodiversity, thus hindering the growth of biodiversity-friendly products on the market. On top of that, many other important environmental issues (such as ocean pollution, climate change, and habitat loss) lack a clear business case, provoking only a limited amount of corporate action.

Even those environmental issues that are amenable to a business case regularly fail to provoke corporate action. The same business case logic that can lead corporations to invest in the environment can also lead them to avoid making economically disadvantageous trade-offs (Hahn et al., 2010). If, for example, a corporation can choose between a project with a large financial return and a small environmental benefit, or one with a small financial return but a large environmental benefit, the business case prioritizes the project with the largest financial return. Both projects are win–win scenarios, but by following a business case rationale, corporations invariably put economic objectives above environmental objectives (Hahn et al., 2014). In short, society gets the short end of the stick.

Business case thinking can result in investments that benefit the environment, but it puts a strong financial constraint on the types of investments that are considered worthy of pursuit. Bound in this profit-prioritizing straitjacket, corporations target only a narrow range of consumer-facing environmental issues (Hahn et al., 2014). Thus, the business case paradigm renders corporate sustainability incapable of tackling the enormity of environmental crises that require more significant actions.

2.2 Focus on Technological Solutions

To make a business case, a corporation must not only uncover relevant market demand for an environmental initiative, but also develop the means to fulfill this demand cost effectively. This biases corporations toward techno-innovations because such innovations can help reduce operating costs (Sharfman & Fernando, 2008), minimize waste (Sam, Khanna & Innes, 2009), and reduce input requirements (Delmas & Pekovic, 2015) while creating new entrepreneurial opportunities (Cohen & Winn, 2007), opening new revenue streams through patents (Marin & Lotti, 2017), expanding to new markets (Beise & Rennings, 2005), and finding unique sources of competitive advantage (Shrivastava, 1995). The emphasis on techno-centric approaches is so dominant in corporate sustainability that it is often used synonymously with changes in products, technologies, and processes (Nidumolu, Prahalad & Rangaswami, 2009). Whether by promoting remote sensing technology as the ultimate solution to halt illegal logging or switching to hydrogen fuel cell electric vehicles for decarbonizing our transportation systems, the business case heavily relies on technological breakthroughs for sustainability solutions.

Unfortunately, technological innovations are inherently limited in their capacities to transform socio-ecological systems. Firstly, technological innovations are often riddled with unintended environmental consequences (Alexander & Rutherford, 2019; Carey et al., 2012; Tenner, 1997) that can give rise to new types of environmental problems. For example, electronic vehicles (EVs) help reduce transport-related carbon footprints, but they exacerbate soil toxicity through battery production involving “dirty” minerals such as cobalt and other rare-earth minerals (Arshi, Vahidi & Zhao, 2018). Similarly, switching from traditional to renewable sources of energy requires installation of switchgears in transmission grids. This installation process is associated with the leakage of sulphur hexafluoride (SF_6), a gas with a much higher global warming potential than CO_2. Windmill blades, for instance, are built to withstand hurricane force winds, but are hard to recycle and are quickly piling up in landfills (Martin, 2020).

Secondly, the positive effects of technological innovations on the environment, in the context of energy efficiency, are often offset by increased consumption. This rebound effect, known as Jevons’s paradox (Jevons, 1865), is largely ignored in corporate sustainability discourse. Precise assessment of the extent of this rebound effect and determination of its underlying mechanisms are empirically difficult to untangle, but there is ample evidence to suggest that this effect is not negligible and warrants consideration as we explore alternative approaches to sustainability (Munyon, Bowen & Holcombe, 2018; Sorrell, 2009).

Thirdly, there is often a significant timelag between a technological breakthrough and its deployment and mass commercialization. This time lag varies across industries and regions, with a recent study in the energy sector finding that its typical range is twenty to seventy years (Gross et al., 2018). This time frame is not at all proportionate to the urgency with which environmental problems must be addressed. Hence, while technological innovations are critically important for addressing environmental problems, it is also equally important to be cognizant of their limitations. The business case for corporate sustainability motivates corporations to push for technology-based solutions that are inherently limited in their abilities to address environmental problems within a short time frame.

2.3 Focus on Consumption

The business case paradigm dismisses limits to growth and fails to constrain consumption (Martin & Kemper, 2012). Sure, corporate sustainability programs promote green consumerism rather than sustainable consumption (Akenji, 2014). But it is ironic that the 1992 Rio Earth Summit, which brought corporate sustainability to prominence, identified unsustainable levels of consumption as a fundamental threat to sustainability rather than pinpointing the real problem—the patterns of production. Green products are weak solutions because they only increase eco-efficiency and initiate peripheral changes (Hobson, 2002; Jackson & Senker, 2011). In contrast, strong approaches would seek systemic changes to enable sustainable production–consumption systems (Lebel & Lorek, 2008). Such systems would discourage hyper-consumption (Albinsson, Wolf & Kopf, 2010) and promote a sufficiency paradigm (Fuchs & Lorek, 2005). Green consumerism can indeed nudge a small subset of consumers to make environmentally friendly purchases (Schwartz, Loewenstein & Agüero-Gaete, 2020), but it mistakenly places the consumer as the most salient agent in bringing about required changes in the production–consumption system to avert environmental crises (Akenji, 2014).

A shift away from consumerism—green or otherwise—is critical now that every year more people are entering the middle class in the most populous regions of the world. Within a five-year period (2007 to 2012), the total footprint from Chinese households increased by 19 percent; notably, three-quarters of this increase was due to growing consumption among the urban middle class and the rich (Wiedenhofer et al., 2017). Globally, it is estimated that within the next decade, middle class spending will grow from about $37 trillion in 2017 to $64 trillion, mostly driven by increased consumption in emerging economies (European Commission, 2020). This will inevitably put severe pressure on the natural environment due in large part to the business case paradigm falsely promising consumers that they can offset via green product purchases.

The result of this pressure? An adverse environmental impact created by an affluence of excessive consumption (Chertow, 2000). In the end, the "win–win" approach will not help to develop sustainable production–consumption systems.

3 CONCLUSION

Under a free market ethos, corporations have come to view sustainability initiatives as any other business investment (McWilliams & Siegel, 2000), seeking to find and exploit "win–win" opportunities that enable them to profit from addressing environmental problems. A business case paradigm dominates corporate approaches to sustainability issues (Salzmann, 2005), where the market rewards such activities and punishes their absence. Currently, most of the world's largest corporations now devote significant resources to sustainability programs (Eccles, Ioannou & Serafeim, 2014).

Yet the environment continues to degrade (Barnosky et al., 2012; IPBES, 2019; IPCC, 2018), with tropical deforestation expanding on a massive scale (Lambin et al., 2018; van der Ven et al., 2018), oceans choking with plastic residuals (Avio et al., 2017), and increasing soil toxicity (Loska et al., 2004). Even though corporate sustainability programs commonly note the problem of excessive greenhouse gas emissions (Morgan, 2019), half of all CO_2 emissions since the industrial revolution have occurred within the last three decades (Lindsey, 2020). In fact, according to the Climate Accountability Institute, the twenty largest oil, gas, and coal firms were responsible for 35 percent of all worldwide fossil fuel-related emissions from 1965 to 2018.

In this chapter, we explained how pursuing only those sustainability initiatives that are profitable creates biased behaviors that fail to adequately sustain society. The business case for corporate sustainability reduces environmental initiatives to those that focus on near-term, firm-level, self-interest. Such a perspective mitigates against a more holistic understanding of the production, distribution, and consumption of their products or services on ecosystems (Whiteman, Walker & Perego, 2013). That is, the message that firms are getting from stakeholders is that simple sustainability solutions that focus on technology and consumerism will suffice (Barnett, Cashore, Henriques, Husted, Panwar & Pinkse, 2021). But for those stakeholders who can see beyond this short-sighted approach to sustainability, is there a better way to influence corporate sustainability practices? In the next chapter we address the prospects for the digital age to give greater influence to those stakeholder voices demanding greater corporate accountability for environmental impacts.

BIBLIOGRAPHY

Ajzen, I. 2001. Nature and operation of attitudes. Annual Review of Psychology, 52: 27–58.

Ajzen, I., & Driver, B. 1992. Contingent value measurement: On the nature and meaning of willingness to pay. Journal of Consumer Psychology, 1(4): 297–316.

Akenji, L. 2014. Consumer scapegoatism and limits to green consumerism. Journal of Cleaner Production, 63: 13–23.

Albinsson, P. A., Wolf, M., & Kopf, D. A. 2010. Anti-consumption in East Germany: Consumer resistance to hyperconsumption. Journal of Consumer Behaviour, 9(6): 412–425.

Alexander, S., & Rutherford, J. 2019. A critique of techno-optimism: Efficiency without sufficiency is lost. In A. Kalfagianni et al. (Eds) *Routledge handbook of global sustainability governance*. Routledge: Abingdon, U.K. Accessed January 27, 2022, Routledge Handbooks Online.

Anderson, R., & Hansen, E. 2004. The impact of environmental certification on preferences for wood furniture: A conjoint analysis approach. Forest Products Journal, 54(3): 42–50.

Arshi P. S., Vahidi, E., & Zhao, F. 2018. Behind the scenes of clean energy: The environmental footprint of rare earth products. ACS Sustainable Chemistry & Engineering, 6(3): 3311–3320.

Avio, C. G., Gorbi, S., & Regoli, F. 2017. Plastics and microplastics in the oceans: From emerging pollutants to emerged threat. Marine Environmental Research, 128: 2–11.

Bagozzi, R. 1992. The self-regulation of attitudes, intentions, and behavior. Social Psychology Quarterly, 55(2): 178–204.

Barnett, M. L. 2019. The business case for corporate social responsibility. Business & Society, 58(1): 167–190.

Barnett, M. L., Cashore, B., Henriques, I., Husted, B. W., Panwar, R., & Pinske, J. 2021. Reorient the business case for corporate sustainability. Stanford Social Innovation Review, Summer 2021: 35–39.

Barnett, M. L., Darnall, N., & Husted, B. W. 2015. Sustainability strategy in constrained economic times. Long Range Planning, 48(2): 63–68.

Barnett, M. L. & Salomon, R. M. 2006. Beyond dichotomy: The curvilinear relationship between social responsibility and financial performance. Strategic Management Journal, 27: 1101–1122.

Barnett, M. L., & Salomon, R. M. 2012. Does it pay to be really good? Addressing the shape of the relationship between social and financial performance. Strategic Management Journal, 33: 1304–1320.

Barnosky, A. D., Hadly, E. A., (nineteen others), & Smith, A. B. 2012. Approaching a state shift in Earth's biosphere. Nature, 486(7401): 52–58.

Beise, M., & Rennings, K. 2005. Lead markets and regulation: a framework for analyzing the international diffusion of environmental innovations. Ecological Economics, 52(1): 5–17.

Blaney, R., Bennett, J., Louviere, J., & Morrison, M. 2001. Green product choice. In J. Bennett, & R. Blamey (Eds) *The choice modeling approach to environmental valuation*. Edward Elgar Publishing: Cheltenham, U.K. and Northampton, MA, U.S.A.: 115–130.

Brown, C. 1995. Anthropocentrism and ecocentrism: The quest for a new worldview. Midwest Quarterly (Pittsburg), 36(2): 191–202.

Carey, M., French, A., & O'Brien, E. 2012. Unintended effects of technology on climate change adaptation: An historical analysis of water conflicts below Andean glaciers. Journal of Historical Geography, 38(2): 181–191.

Chertow, M. R. 2000. The IPAT equation and its variants. Journal of Industrial Ecology, 4(4): 13–29.

Cohen, B., & Winn, M. I. 2007. Market imperfections, opportunity, and sustainable entrepreneurship. Journal of Business Venturing, 22(1): 29–49.

Conner, M., Povey, R., Sparks, P., James, R., & Shepherd, R. 2003. Moderating role of attitudinal ambivalence within the theory of planned behavior. British Journal of Social Psychology, 42(1): 75–94.

Cordano, M., & Frieze, I. 2000. Pollution reduction preferences of U.S. environmental managers: Applying Ajzen's theory of planned behavior. Academy of Management Journal, 43(4): 626–641.

Delmas, M. A., & Pekovic, S. 2015. Resource efficiency strategies and market conditions. Long Range Planning, 48(2): 80–94.

Dunlap, R., & Van Liere, K. 1978. The new environmental paradigm: A proposed measuring instrument and preliminary results. The Journal of Environmental Education, 9(4): 10–19.

Dyllick, T. & Hockerts, K. 2002. Beyond the business case for corporate sustainability. Business Strategy & the Environment, 11(2): 130–141.

Eccles, R. G., Ioannou, I., & Serafeim, G. 2014. The impact of corporate sustainability on organizational processes and performance. Management Science, 60(11): 2835–2857.

European Commission. 2020. Developments and forecasts of growing consumerism. Available at: https://ec.europa.eu/knowledge4policy/foresight/topic/growing-consumerism/more-developments-relevant-growing-consumerism-en. Accessed January 27, 2022.

Fuchs, D. A., & Lorek, S. 2005. Sustainable consumption governance: A history of promises and failures. Journal of Consumer Policy, 28(3): 261–288.

Gifford, R. 2011. The dragons of inaction: Psychological barriers that limit climate change mitigation and adaptation. American Psychologist, 66(4): 290–302.

Gladwin, T., Kennelly, J., & Krause, T. 1995. Shifting paradigms for sustainable development: Implications for management theory and research. Academy of Management Review, 20(4): 874–907.

Gross, R., Hanna, R., Gambhir, A., Heptonstall, P., & Speirs, J. 2018. How long does innovation and commercialisation in the energy sectors take? Historical case studies of the timescale from invention to widespread commercialisation in energy supply and end use technology. Energy Policy, 123: 682–699.

Hahn, T., Figge, F., Pinkse, J., & Preuss, L. 2010. Trade-offs in corporate sustainability: You can't have your cake and eat it. Business Strategy & the Environment, 19(4): 217–229.

Hahn, T., Preuss, L., Pinkse, J., & Figge, F. 2014. Cognitive frames in corporate sustainability: Managerial sensemaking with paradoxical and business case frames. Academy of Management Review, 39(4): 463–487.

Hart, S. L. 1995. A natural-resource-based view of the firm. Academy of Management Review, 20(4): 986–1014.

Hobson, K. 2002. Competing discourses of sustainable consumption: Does the 'rationalisation of lifestyles' make sense? Environmental Politics, 11(2): 95–120.

Husted, B. W., Russo, M. V., Basurto-Meza, C. E. B., & Tilleman, S. G. 2014. An exploratory study of environmental attitudes and the willingness to pay for environmental certification in Mexico. Journal of Business Research, 67(5): 891–899.

IPBES 2019. Intergovernmental Science-Policy Platform on Biodiversity and Ecosystem Services (IPBES). New York, United Nations General Assembly.

IPCC 2018. Special Report: Global warming of 1.5°C. World Meteorological Organization, United Nations: Geneva, Switzerland.

Jackson, T., & Senker, P. 2011. Prosperity without growth: Economics for a finite planet. Energy & Environment, 22(7): 1013–1016.

Jermier, J. 2008. Exploring deep subjectivity in sociology and organizational studies: The contributions of William Catton and Riley Dunlap on paradigm change. Organization & Environment, 21(4): 460–470.

Jevons, W. S. 1865. *The coal question*. MacMillan: London.

Johnston, R., & Duke, J. 2009. Willingness to pay for land preservation across states and jurisdictional scale: Implications for benefit transfer. Land Economics, 85(2): 217–237.

Kotchen, M., & Reiling, S. 2000. Environmental attitudes, motivations, and contingent valuation of nonuse values: A case study involving endangered species. Ecological Economics, 32(1): 93–107.

Lambin, E., Gibbs, H., (thirteen others) & Walker, N. 2018. The role of supply-chain initiatives in reducing deforestation. Nature Climate Change, 8: 109–116.

La Trobe, H. L., & Acott, T. G. 2000. A modified NEP/DSP environmental attitudes scale. The Journal of Environmental Education, 32(1): 12–20.

Lebel, L., & Lorek, S. 2008. Enabling sustainable production-consumption systems. Annual Review of Environment and Resources, 33: 241–275.

Lepere, M., & Eckhardt, G. 2020. Why we can't shop our way to sustainability. Stanford Social Innovation Review, July 16. Available at: https://ssir.org/articles/entry/why_we_cant_shop_our_way_to_sustainability. Accessed January 27, 2022.

Lindsey, R. 2020. Climate Change: Atmospheric Carbon Dioxide, ClimateWatch Magazine. Available at: www.climate.gov/news-features/understanding-climate/climate-change-atmospheric-carbon-dioxide. Accessed January 27, 2022.

Loska, K., Wiechuła, D., & Korus, I. 2004. Metal contamination of farming soils affected by industry. Environment International, 30(2): 159–165.

Marin, G., & Lotti, F. 2017. Productivity effects of eco-innovations using data on eco-patents. Industrial and Corporate Change, 26(1): 125–148.

Martin, C. 2020, February 5. Wind turbine blades can't be recycled, so they're piling up in landfills. *Bloomberg Green*. Available at: www.bloomberg.com/news/features/2020-02-05/wind-turbine-blades-can-t-be-recycled-so-they-re-piling-up-in-landfills. Accessed January 27, 2022.

Martin, R., & Kemper, A. 2012. Saving the planet: A tale of two strategies. Harvard Business Review (April): 48–56.

McWilliams, A., & Siegel, D. 2000. Corporate social responsibility and financial performance: Correlation or misspecification? Strategic Management Journal, 21(5): 603–609.

Morgan, B. 2019, August 26. 101 Companies committed to reducing their carbon footprint. *Forbes*. Available at: www.forbes.com/sites/blakemorgan/2019/08/26/101-companies-committed-to-reducing-their-carbon-footprint/#3b7c9993260b. Accessed January 27, 2022.

Munyon, V. V., Bowen, W. M., & Holcombe, J. 2018. Vehicle fuel economy and vehicle miles traveled: An empirical investigation of Jevons' Paradox. Energy Research & Social Science, 38: 19–27.

Nidumolu, R., Prahalad, C. K. & Rangaswami, M. R. 2009. Why sustainability is now the key driver of innovation. Harvard Business Review, 87(9): 56–64.

Ojeda, M., Mayer, A., & Solomon, B. 2008. Economic valuation of environmental services sustained by water flows in the Yaqui River Delta. Ecological Economics, 65(1): 155–166.

Olsen, M. C., Slotegraaf, R. J., & Chandukala, S. R. 2014. Green claims and message frames: How green new products change brand attitude. Journal of Marketing, 78(5): 119–137.

Porter, M. E., & Kramer, M. R. 2006. The link between competitive advantage and corporate social responsibility. Harvard Business Review, 84(12): 78–92.

Priester, J. R., & Petty, R. E. 1996. The gradual threshold model of ambivalence: Relating the positive and negative bases of attitudes to subjective ambivalence. Journal of Personality and Social Psychology, 71(3): 431–449.

Purser, R., Park, C., & Montuori, A. 1995. Limits to anthropocentrism: Toward an ecocentric organization paradigm? Academy of Management Review, 20(4): 1053–1089.

Russo, M. V., & Fouts, P. A. 1997. A resource-based perspective on corporate environmental performance and profitability. Academy of Management Journal, 40: 534–559.

Salzmann, O. 2005. The business case for corporate sustainability: Literature review and research options. European Management Journal, 23(1): 27–36.

Sam, A. G., Khanna, M., & Innes, R. 2009. Voluntary pollution reduction programs, environmental management, and environmental performance: An empirical study. Land Economics, 85(4): 692–711.

Sammer, K., & Wustenhagen, R. 2006. The influence of eco-labeling on consumer behavior—Results of discrete choice analysis for washing machines. Business Strategy and the Environment, 15(3): 185–199.

Schwartz, D., Loewenstein, G., & Agüero-Gaete, L. 2020. Encouraging pro-environmental behaviour through green identity labelling. Nature Sustainability, 3: 746–752.

Schwepker, C., & Cornwell, T. 1991. An examination of ecologically concerned consumers and their intention to purchase ecologically. Journal of Public Policy & Marketing, 10(2): 77–101.

Sharfman, M. P., & Fernando, C. S. 2008. Environmental risk management and the cost of capital. Strategic Management Journal, 29(6): 569–592.

Shrivastava, P. 1995. Environmental technologies and competitive advantage. Strategic Management Journal, 16(S1): 183–200.

Shrum, L. J., McCarty, J. A., & Lowrey, T. M. 1995. Buyer characteristics of the green consumer and their implications for advertising strategy. Journal of Advertising, 14(2): 71–82.

Slawinski, N., & Bansal, P. 2015. Short on time: Intertemporal tensions in business sustainability. Organization Science, 26(2): 531–549.

Sorrell, S. 2009. Jevons' Paradox revisited: The evidence for backfire from improved energy efficiency. Energy Policy, 37(4): 1456–1469.

Tenner, E. 1997. *Why things bite back: Technology and the revenge of unintended consequences*. Vintage Books: New York, NY.

Van der Ven, H., Rothacker, C., & Cashore, B. 2018. Do eco-labels prevent deforestation? Lessons from non-state market driven governance in the soy, palm oil, and cocoa sectors. Global Environmental Change, 52: 141–151.

Vasquez, W. F., Mozumder, P., Hernández, J., & Berrens, R. 2009. Willingness to pay for safe drinking water: Evidence from Parral, Mexico. Journal of Environmental Management, 90(11): 3391–3400.

Vogel, D. 2007. *The market for virtue: The potential and limits of corporate social responsibility*. Brookings Institution Press: Washington, D.C.

White, K., Hardisty, D. J., & Habib, R. 2019. The elusive green consumer. Harvard Business Review (July–August): 124–133.

Whiteman, G., Walker, B., & Perego, P. 2013. Planetary boundaries: Ecological foundations for corporate sustainability. Journal of Management Studies, 50(2): 307–336.

Wiedenhofer, D., Guan, D., Liu, Z., et al. 2017. Unequal household carbon footprints in China. Nature Climate Change, 7: 75–80.

World Commission on Environment & Development 1987. *Our common future*. Oxford University Press: Oxford, U.K.

6. Digital detours are dubious

Should a firm invest in production methods that reduce its greenhouse gas emissions? Should it demand that its supplies come only from sustainable sources? Should it take back and recycle all that it sells? A firm's answers to, and even awareness of, questions such as these are influenced by its stakeholders, who place voluminous demands upon the company to address a myriad of issues. These demands compete for the firm's limited resources and can counter managerial preferences, driving firms to advance issues that they otherwise would have overlooked or even opposed. For example, under intense pressure from Greenpeace, Shell famously made a costly decision to reverse its desired plan to dump the Brent Spar oil platform at sea.

At least since Barnard's (1938) *The Functions of the Executive*, management scholars have acknowledged that stakeholders influence firm behavior. Subsequently, the literature has focused on two questions: When will stakeholders act? And how will they do so? The first question was addressed in terms of the economic interests and social identities of stakeholder groups (Rowley & Moldoveanu, 2003). The second was studied by examining the balance of power in firm–stakeholder relationships, resulting in specific strategies (Frooman, 1999; Rowley, 1997), such as withholding (e.g., boycotts) and usage (i.e., providing resources with strings attached).

The arrival of the digital age, though, challenges established approaches to when and how stakeholders act. The massive increase in information available and the breadth and specialization of outlets through which it now flows have affected stakeholder perceptions of when their interests and identities need to be protected or could be advanced through efforts to influence firm behavior. For example, protests against the Dakota Access Pipeline achieved national visibility and support through millions of views on Facebook despite their remote location (Sotille, 2016). Moreover, the new structure and overwhelming flow of information in the digital age have altered the use of firm–stakeholder power relationships and strategies. Secondary stakeholders can now exert direct influence over firms (Jurgens et al., 2016), and firms can now more easily disguise their counterinfluence efforts, such as Walmart co-opting bloggers to appear as stakeholders spreading favorable views of the firm's labor practices (Barbaro, 2006).

In this chapter, we investigate how the digital age has affected stakeholder influence over firm behavior. Will the tools of the digital age increase public concern for corporate sustainability and drive more substantive corporate sustainability practices? Many predicted that with the increased ease of information sharing it brings, the digital age would empower stakeholders (e.g., Esty, 2004) and enable everyday people to change the world (Aaker & Smith, 2010). Anecdotes posted on Twitter, Facebook, and other social media platforms have sparked changes not only in firm behavior but also political rule (Allcott & Gentzkow, 2017), such as the Arab Spring of 2011 (Bruns, Highfield & Burgess, 2013). But scholars have yet to explore the aggregate effects of the digital age on stakeholder influence over corporate practices. What happens when we look beyond individual efforts to the broader context in which stakeholder influence efforts play out?

We analyze stakeholder influence from a cognitive perspective to understand how the significant changes in the quantity and quality of information in the digital age affect when and how stakeholders decide to act. Specifically, we show that the ways in which stakeholders filter information shape what they notice and how they make sense of it, thereby affecting when they start to exert influence over firms. Moreover, we show that sensegiving efforts conducted via social media shape how stakeholders—both individually and in concert with other stakeholders—frame issues and affect their decision in exerting influence over firms.

Overall, our analysis suggests that the methods that rational stakeholders use to cope with the overwhelming cognitive complexity of the digital age have retarded rather than reinforced or redoubled their influence over firm behavior. Although more want to see improvements in corporate sustainability, and it is now easier for stakeholders to broadcast their perspectives and demands, the resulting cacophony has made it harder to be heard by those they seek to influence. Moreover, the veracity of the voluminous and oft-competing stakeholder claims has become more difficult to discern (Walker, 2014). In this context, although stakeholders are now more likely to be exposed to new information from a wider variety of sources (Flaxman, Goel & Rao, 2016), they have become more selective in how they, and the digital information intermediaries (e.g., Facebook and Google) they explicitly and implicitly rely upon, process this information (Bozdag, 2013; Pariser, 2011). This leads to greater political and cultural polarization (Schmidt et al., 2017; Sunstein, 2017). As a result, firm–stakeholder relations have become more inertial, despite the many calls to action that saturate social media. Needless to say, stakeholders sometimes exert significant influence on firms, as various "tweetstorms" have demonstrated (e.g., Goodman, 2014), but overall, firms appear to have maintained, if not gained, autonomy from stakeholder influence in the digital age.

We begin by reviewing the underlying assumptions of the stakeholder influence literature. Thereafter, we detail how information overload, social media, and other hallmarks of the digital age challenge extant understanding of how stakeholders influence firm behavior. Then we develop a revised framework grounded in cognitive theory to better describe stakeholder influence in the digital age, and we contrast its mechanisms with those of the pre-digital age. We conclude with a discussion of the theoretical and practical implications of this revised framework.

1 ACKNOWLEDGING THE ASSUMPTIONS OF STAKEHOLDER INFLUENCE

The central question underlying organization theory is this: Why do organizations act the way they do? (Hambrick & Mason, 1984). Scholars have contrasted theories of external control (Pfeffer & Salancik, 1978) with those of strategic choice (Child, 1972) to sort out the degree to which firms and their managers possess discretion (Hambrick & Finkelstein, 1987). Stakeholder theory bridges these perspectives by arguing that because they can affect firm performance, stakeholders influence firm behavior, but it is ultimately up to the firm's strategic decisions about how to respond to stakeholder demands (Freeman, 1984). Thus, what a firm does is a function of the degree to which it is influenced by its stakeholders.

Management scholars have expected the digital age to increase stakeholders' influence over what firms do. Coombs (1998: 289) argued that the ease of information sharing on the Internet would empower activists: "Now activists have a new weapon which can change the organization–stakeholder dynamic—the Internet. … [T]he Internet, when used effectively, can allow activist groups to become more powerful." Others have been more grandiose about their views. Pitt et al. (2002: 14), for instance, called the Internet a "social earthquake, perturbing the relationship between business and consumers" that "could be a cataclysmic event for some firms."

As flows of information swell into torrents in the digital age, stakeholders have not largely forced firms to become ever responsive to their demands (Gladwell, 2010). Even when stakeholder attacks blossom into full-fledged media firestorms, firms may carry on with little change and minimal lasting harm, leading some to conclude that social media outrage is often just "a tempest in a teacup" (Lamba, Malik & Pfeffer, 2015: 17). For example, the major social media outrage and months of intense demonstrations seeking to stop the Dakota Access Pipeline have done little to stop Energy Transfer Partners using it to transport oil (Meyer, 2017). In another case, the death of Cecil the lion in 2015 at the hands of a trophy hunter created highly publicized outrage, but Cecil's son was still killed by a trophy hunter in 2017, as part of a legal hunt organized by Richard Cooke Safaris (Brulliard & Bever, 2017). Despite the social media bashing United Airlines received over a series of gaffes related to poor customer service, United and other airlines are still finding ways to render flying even less comfortable (Bachman, 2017).

In this section, we review extant literature to assess its ability to explain stakeholder influence in the digital age. As we show, the literature on stakeholder influence has yet to grapple with the informational challenges that characterize the digital age.

1.1 Sources of Stakeholder Influence

Stakeholder influence refers to the capacity of stakeholders to affect the actions of firms. It can be exercised through control over resources, social movements, and private politics. Let us examine each of these sources of influence more closely.

Firms engage their primary stakeholders because of the resources they can provide the firm to accomplish its objectives (Barnard, 1938). It is this same need that firms have for resources that can then be used by stakeholders to influence firms (Frooman, 1999) and appropriate rents (Coff, 1999). As a result, resource dependence theory has proven to be an effective way of understanding stakeholder influence (Frooman, 1999; Pfeffer & Salancik, 1978). This theory postulates that power arises from the dependence of one organization on another for necessary resources, which include access to information (Coff, 1999), network position (Henisz, 2013; Rowley, 1997), technology, service, and talent, among many others (Harrison, Bosse & Phillips, 2010). Kassinis and Vafeas (2006) empirically validated this. Given the dependence of polluting industries on local resources, they found that the most polluting industries in the United States were susceptible to community pressure, which had a significant negative impact on plant emissions.

In contrast to primary stakeholders, secondary stakeholders lack control over resources that would give them the ability to exert direct power and so they must undertake collective action to influence firms (King, 2008a). Social movement theory seeks to explain the conditions under which collective action emerges among these secondary stakeholders (Soule, 2012). Secondary stakeholder groups are more likely to exert influence on firms when they share interests and identity (Rowley & Moldoveanu, 2003).

Once mobilized, stakeholders engage in private politics, by which they negotiate and lobby the firm to achieve their goals (Baron, 2001, 2009; Baron & Diermeier, 2007; King, 2008a). Private politics, although closely related to social movement theory, applies an economic lens by examining the interests of the actors to explain the micro-level strategic behavior of activists that will generate changes in the redistribution of firm resources.

When do these stakeholder influence efforts lead to changes in firm behavior? Firms face myriad stakeholder demands (Freeman, 1984), but prefer to maximize decision-making autonomy (Oliver, 1991; Pfeffer & Salancik, 1978), thus only acquiescing to the most pressing demands. Managerial perceptions play a vital role in determining which stakeholder demands are deemed to be the most pressing. Mitchell, Agle, and Wood (1997) argued that the likelihood of a firm responding to a stakeholder demand depends on the salience of the particular stakeholder which, in turn, depends on the power of the stakeholder as well as the legitimacy and urgency of their claims. In an empirical study, Eesley and Lenox (2006) found that legitimate and urgent requests by secondary stakeholders are more likely to receive positive responses from firms. Murillo-Luna, Garcés-Ayerbe, and Rivera-Torres (2008) similarly found that the greater the perception of stakeholder pressure, the greater the firm's response.

1.2 Stakeholder Influence Strategies and Tactics

Stakeholders rely on a variety of strategies to exert influence over firms. Typologies of stakeholder influence strategies have been developed based on two dimensions: firm power and stakeholder power (Frooman, 1999). Firm and stakeholder power stem from control over resources (Frooman, 1999) as well as from the centrality of the firm in a stakeholder network or the density of the stakeholder network (Rowley, 1997).

Where there is low interdependence between the firm and its stakeholders, the firm avoids pressure from its stakeholders, who will generally exert indirect pressure through allied stakeholders. Where there is high interdependence because of the firm's central location in a dense stakeholder network, the firm will negotiate with those stakeholders who deal directly with it by attaching strings to the use of resources. When the firm dominates because of its control over resources and central network position, stakeholders will attach strings to the use of resources through allies, while the firm will attempt to control the stakeholders. Finally, where stakeholder power prevails, stakeholders will act directly by withholding resources (such as employee strikes), and the firm will comply with the demands of stakeholders (in this case, employees). This power arises from dense networks where stakeholder interests converge, thus allowing stakeholders to "speak with a clear voice" (Mintzberg, 1983: 98, cited by Rowley, 1997: 903).

Secondary stakeholders (such as environmental NGOs) are more likely to use indirect strategies (such as boycotts through allied stakeholders such as consumers) and other forms of information provision (such as demonstrations) to draw the public and news media's attention to the specific issues they advocate (Feddersen & Gilligan, 2001). In this way, boycotts and demonstrations provide important information to consumers about products they care about. Here, the methods social movements use become much more relevant (King,

2008a). Sharma and Henriques (2005) found substantial evidence of the effectiveness of both withholding and usage strategies to foster sustainability practices among Canadian forest products firms. Zietsma and Winn (2008) focused on secondary stakeholders and discovered how their influence tactics change over time through issue raising, issue suppression, positioning, and solution seeking.

Although the literature on social movements is ample, the relationship of social movements to stakeholder influence on corporate behavior is just beginning to develop (Campbell, 2006; de Bakker & den Hond, 2008). Because social movements are often excluded from participating in legitimate channels of organizational change, protests become influential when targeting critical stakeholder group issues (i.e., groups that are highly interdependent with the firm such as labor and consumers) (King & Soule, 2007) or highly legitimate groups with compelling claims (McDonnell & King, 2013).

According to the political process model of social movements, the influence of stakeholders depends on three elements: (1) mobilizing structures such as formal organizations and interpersonal networks, (2) political opportunities such as changes in corporate leadership and industry competition, and (3) framing processes (King, 2008b). Framing processes are especially relevant because stakeholder influence can often be conceived as a kind of framing contest with the firm (Benford & Snow, 2000). Frames refer to "schemata of interpretation," which convert "what would otherwise be a meaningless aspect of the scene [or event] into something that is meaningful" (Goffman, 1974: 21). Thus, the ability of stakeholders to influence the firm largely resides in their ability to frame issues—that is, to construct meaning around an issue and thereby facilitate mobilization (King, 2008b).

1.3 Underlying Assumptions

Despite the abundance of literature on stakeholder influence, these papers do not consider informational issues to be problematic. Coff (1999) recognized that information access can represent an important resource for stakeholders, and Baron (2001, 2009; Baron & Diermeier, 2007) explicitly considered information asymmetry, as is the usual practice in microanalytic modeling. Feddersen and Gilligan (2001) analyzed the role of information in their model—in which activists provide information to consumers in markets with incomplete information—that influences firms to provide "credence goods," such as environmentally friendly manufacturing processes. But beyond these exceptions, this work largely assumes that information is completely symmetric and that the cognitive capacity of stakeholders is unlimited. Rarely are the bounded rationality of the actors and limitations to cognitive capacity considered in the stakeholder influence literature. While there are exceptions in the social movement theory (King & Soule, 2007), there has also been some neglect in determining the role of information (Benford & Snow, 2000). In general, actors are assumed to have the cognitive abilities to process information in an accurate and timely manner.

The neglect of information and the assumption of unlimited rationality on the part of actors result in poorly equipped models that are unable to deal with situations in which bounded rationality proves a significant constraint. Extant studies have tended to observe stakeholder influence efforts in isolation, without accounting for this broader context. We next describe the noisy context of the digital age and its effects on stakeholder influence.

2 ACCOUNTING FOR INFORMATION OVERLOAD

Social media platforms such as Facebook, YouTube, Twitter, Wikis, blogs, Flickr, World of Warcraft, and Second Life are Internet-based applications that allow the creation and exchange of user-generated content (Kaplan & Haenlein, 2010). In the digital age, information flows widely and rapidly across the World Wide Web via social media, which is the first mass medium that streams information without gatekeeping or filtering (Pang, Hassan & Chong, 2013). As a result, firms and their stakeholders now engage in real-time, direct, two-way public communication.

These changes in information flows have given rise to many business opportunities, including the creation of companies such as Amazon, Google, and Facebook that are now among the most valuable in the world. Entrepreneurs now use social media to interact with their customers and learn from them ways to create further business opportunities. For example, Fischer and Reuber (2011), using a qualitative analysis of twelve entrepreneurs, found that Twitter-based interaction helped entrepreneurs identify opportunities and create new ventures. They noted that the impacts of social media are not limited to marketing but are also a means of testing out ideas for creating stakeholder values.

However, this unfettered information sharing comes with additional challenges. With so many social media platforms broadcasting so much information, the result is information overload. This is not a new phenomenon—it has existed since the invention of the typewriter and increased after the introduction of the photocopier and digitization (Hemp, 2009). Digitization, though, has made the transfer of information nearly cost free. Via commonplace smartphones, we can send and receive masses of information from almost anywhere in the world at any time. As a result, stakeholders, and firms who want to seek influence, are being continuously flooded with information from a myriad of sources.

Over the past twenty years, the Internet has significantly increased the flow of information. In 1995, there were 35 million Internet users globally (0.6 percent of the world's population); by 2015 there were 2.8 billion Internet users—39 percent of the world's population (Meeker, 2015). In 1995, the market capitalization of the top fifteen Internet companies was $16.8 billion; by 2017 it was $3.6 trillion and growing (Meeker, 2015, 2017). Today, more than 30 billion pieces of content are shared on Facebook each month, while more than 500 million tweets are sent every day (Meeker, 2015).

With the proliferation of modern information technologies and search engines, accessing this vast trove of information has never been easier. Paradoxically though, it is now possible to "drown in information while remaining thirsty for knowledge" (Königer & Janowitz, 1995: 5). As Edmunds and Morris (2000: 22) noted, "although there is an abundance of information, it is often difficult to obtain useful and relevant information among the vast volumes of information which, at the very least, need to be scanned through to find the nuggets." Echoing this sentiment, Beasley et al. (2011), after assessing modern-day medical practice, described a context of "information chaos," encompassing information overload, information underload, information conflict, information scatter, and erroneous information.

Information now flows freely, unhindered by gatekeepers, but its quality and veracity has become more suspect as a result. In the past, information gatekeepers such as journalists and experts like academics, doctors, governments, and consultants would filter the raw information and dig further to verify the assertions, test the explanations, and collect other viewpoints to explain complex issues. The digital age, though, has opened the door to unfiltered information that may not just be inaccurate, but also malicious (Wallace, 2017). Even "fake news" or "alternative facts" cannot be ignored because they can manipulate public opinion (Allcott & Gentzkow, 2017).

Manipulation of information by interest groups has become increasingly organized and professional in its approach, earning itself the moniker of "astroturfing." Astroturfing is synthetic grassroots organizing by a front group which masks the true identities and interests being represented, for the purpose of transmitting unverifiable information to lobby their claims or challenge claims that go against their interests (Cho et al., 2011; Lyon & Maxwell, 2004; McNutt & Boland, 2007). Examples of astroturf organizations include ExxonMobil's funding of "think tanks" who spread false information about climate change science (Cho et al., 2011), the mining companies funding of "People for the West!" used to help maintain the public land acquisition of $5 per acre (Lyon & Maxwell, 2004), and Microsoft funding the "Americans for Technology Leadership" group to defend itself against an antitrust lawsuit (Monbiot, 2011). Though they sometimes backfire, such "grassroots for hire" (Walker, 2014) campaigns can create enough stakeholder confusion to stall or block influence efforts. The lack of gatekeeping and filtering on the World Wide Web requires information users to ask questions, validate assertions, and check sources (Wallace, 2017) before acting on the information—an added burden for which many are unprepared.

Beyond astroturfing, companies must also worry about the damage a lone disgruntled customer can do through social media. Indeed, Pang, Hassan, and Chong (2013: 97) argued that "social media platforms are increasingly becoming breeding grounds for organizational crises" that are often triggered online when users take to social media platforms (such as YouTube, Twitter, Facebook, and blogs) to air their grievances. As the negative word of mouth builds, focal organizations can quickly lose control of the conversation (Grégoire, Salle & Tripp, 2015). For example, in 2008, David Carroll was angry that his $3,500 guitar broke during a trip on United Airlines. He complained to the airline and filed a damage claim but to no avail. After nine months of frustration, he wrote the song "United Breaks Guitars" and posted a YouTube video depicting his experience while playing his song. The video went viral with more than 5 million views in less than one month (Blitzer, 2009). The airline subsequently contacted the customer and resolved his complaint but suffered public humiliation from substantial mainstream and digital media coverage in the meantime. More recently, a viral video of an elderly passenger being forcibly removed from a United flight created a media firestorm that significantly decreased United's market value and led to calls to alter the way the entire airline industry operates (Arco, 2017).

In sum, individuals worldwide can now instantaneously connect to each other, and to firms. Traditional media is no longer the sole gatekeeper of information or opinion. Rather, social media has disrupted traditional media by democratizing news and information (Wallace, 2017). With the click of a button, a person (or interest group) can join millions of others in voicing concern about a corporate practice or advancing a particular cause. However, as we explain next, cognitive processes prevent this free flow of information from translating into greater stakeholder influence over firm behavior.

3 REASSESSING STAKEHOLDER INFLUENCE IN THE DIGITAL AGE

Awash in information, when and how do stakeholders influence firm behavior? Figure 6.1 illustrates the cognitive processes involved in translating disclosure of new information about a firm into stakeholder action and changes in firm behavior.

To cope with overload, stakeholders filter information. The information they filter out tends to be what conflicts with their established views, while salient information tends to be that which is consistent with their identities

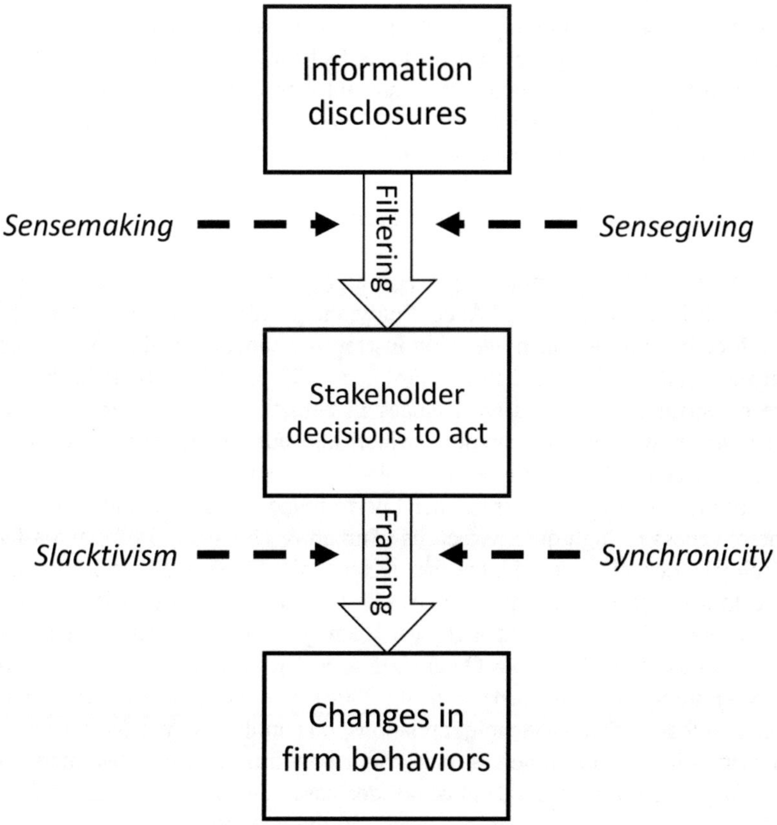

Figure 6.1 *Stakeholder influence in the digital age*

and economic interests. When they notice newly disclosed information, they make sense of it in ways that reinforce these established identities and interests. Further, by engaging in sensegiving efforts, which refer to the "processes by which strategic change is framed and disseminated to an organization's constituents" (Fiss & Zajac, 2006: 1173), managers shape stakeholder sensemaking of new information to favor their firms. Combining these factors limits the likelihood of stakeholders learning about information disclosures that may change their view on these firms and they are therefore motivated to act against them.

When new information does provoke stakeholder action, firms prioritize those demands they perceive to be the most pressing. Though mobilization is less costly in the digital age, synchronizing interests and efforts to enable collective action under a unified frame has become more difficult. Moreover, stakeholders now commonly engage in "slacktivism" in lieu of substantive action, further limiting the pressure firms feel toward change. Overall, these factors allow firms to retain significant autonomy despite the omnipresent potential of free-flowing information to empower stakeholders. Below, we explain these processes in more depth.

3.1 Cognitive Constraints on Control

As Emerson (1962: 32) noted, "power is a property of the social relation; it is not an attribute of the actor." Accordingly, the power to alter firm behavior is not directly held by stakeholders but instead is a function of the relationships between stakeholders and firms (Frooman, 1999). Information disclosures are powerful enough to drive changes in behavior if they alter the firm's relationship with its stakeholders, which depends on the firm's access to resources controlled by these stakeholders (Freeman, 1984). For example, because disclosure of corporate social performance metrics can alter a firm's attractiveness to high-quality recruits (Turban & Greening, 1997) and affect employee identification with the firm (Kim et al., 2010), such disclosures can lead to a revision of social practices (cf. Barnett, 2016). Likewise, because a corporate financial restatement can damage a firm's relationships with its investors (Cao, Myers & Omer, 2012), it can bring about executive and director turnover (Arthaud-Day et al., 2006). However, if new information has no effect on firm–stakeholder relations, it is unlikely to motivate a change in firm behavior. Prominent stories about how airlines treat customers and their baggage (Blitzer, 2009) have not decreased customer willingness to fly (Maidenberg, 2017), so have not produced the substantive change in airline practices that many stakeholders have called for (Bachman, 2017).

For newly disclosed information to actually change the relationship between a firm and its stakeholders, the stakeholders must first be aware of the information and interpret it; that is, notice and sensemake preceding action (Starbuck & Milliken, 1988; Weick, 1995). Yet extant stakeholder influence literature has paid little attention to these crucial steps (Barnett, 2014), instead focusing on the subsequent actions of both stakeholders and firms (e.g., Frooman, 1999; Rowley, 1997). Given the overwhelming quantity and questionable quality of information in the digital age, it is imperative to step back and account for these prior steps.

Like all people, stakeholders have limited fields of vision and will notice only a portion of their environments (Simon, 1947). High arousal tends to narrow attention, such that peripheral visual cues are less likely to be noticed (Kahneman, 1973). Though more information is available in the digital age, information overload further narrows one's field of vision, perversely leading to even less information being noticed (Bawden & Robinson, 2009). As Sparrow (1999: 144) described it:

> In coping with the volume of information (let alone its complexity and ambiguity) they begin to neglect large portions of it and try to "punctuate" its flow in predictable ways. This "punctuation" begins with omission, then greater tolerance of error, mis-cueing or mis-attributing the source of information, filtering its message, abstracting its meaning, attempting to use multiple channels to decode and transmit its content, and finally, through seeking escape!

When overwhelmed, people look for ways to simplify. They exclude portions of their environments from consideration and rely on heuristics to process what they do notice (March & Simon, 1958; Tversky & Kahneman, 1974). Rather than rationally revising their beliefs as new information is revealed, a firm's stakeholders rely on what they already know. In fact, the more complex the situation, the more one "searches for and relies on habitual and routine cues" (Sparrow, 1999: 145). For example, Jones, Felps, and Bigley (2007: 143) state:

> Culture helps people avoid information overload and make shared sense of (and take coordinated action in) complex and ambiguous situations. ... Taken-for-granted elements within the culture give rise to a sort of "automaticity" (e.g., Bargh & Ferguson, 2000) in the enactment of practices and routines in response to stakeholder issues and attributes.

Though people simplify in the face of information overload, they do not stop seeking information altogether. Rather, they narrow their search to information that confirms their prior beliefs (Wason, 1960). Given the volume and range of specialty media sources available in the digital age, it is now feasible and increasingly common for stakeholders to obtain their information only from confirming sources, thereby avoiding exposure to disconfirming information (Sunstein, 2001, 2017; Virag, 2008). New information that challenges one's established view may be overlooked, discounted, dismissed as fake news, or—no matter how well supported—actually reinforce the established view (Kolbert, 2017; Mercier & Sperber, 2017).

This simplification and automaticity render established viewpoints more inertial (Kolbert, 2017). Bakshy, Messing, and Adamic (2015) examined how 10.1 million U.S. Facebook users interacted with socially shared news. They found that there was, on average, less shared content and that individual choice further limited exposure to ideologically cross-cutting content. In fact, disclosing more scientific evidence to people backfires when this information does not reflect their worldviews or cultural values, instead making their views more extreme (Hoffman, 2015).

The process of filtering information has significant implications for stakeholder action. Action can be burdensome, and many stakeholders are unwilling to bear much of a burden. For example, though many consumers prefer firms to behave in ethical ways, only a small fraction are willing to take the actions necessary to reward or punish firms accordingly (Eckhardt, Belk & Devinney, 2010). The stakeholder influence literature argues, however, that stakeholders will act in spite of that burden when their economic interests or social identities are challenged (Rowley & Moldoveanu, 2003). Unfortunately, this literature pays minute attention to how stakeholders notice or assess such challenges.

Under information overload, stakeholders may overlook or misinterpret events that are of relevance to their economic or social interests. Selective exposure to social media exacerbates this problem. People ascribe partisan positions to media entities (Iyengar & Hahn, 2009), then filter their exposure to information based on whether these media entities are congruent with their personal beliefs (Stroud, 2008). In their efforts to manage information overload, the digital information intermediaries that have replaced the gatekeeping function of traditional media are explicitly and implicitly tailoring the information users receive based on what people want to hear. Algorithms now personalize information based on what users need and want and with whom they interact on social media (Bozdag, 2013). Information intermediaries such as Facebook and Google build user profiles using explicit methods whereby users customize the information source themselves by registering their interests or revealing demographic and locational information, and through implicit methods in which the system algorithm determines users' value-added information based on their activity on the Web (e.g., clickthroughs, browsing history, and time spent on a site) (Bozdag, 2013; Lu, 2007).

This explicit and implicit personalization amplifies cognitive biases. Sunstein (2001) argued that explicit personalization may lead individuals to avoid facts and opinions that contradict their beliefs and persuade them to join online groups that conform to their beliefs. This implicit personalization creates what Pariser (2011) calls the "filter bubble," in which information intermediaries filter out what they assume a user does not want to see (Bozdag, 2013). These filter bubbles decrease the ability of users to see the other side of an argument, thereby amplifying cognitive biases. Overall, the cognitive filtering process explains why stakeholders will be cognizant of and therefore confront the decision to act in only a fraction of the instances when firms behave in ways that conflict with their interests or identities (cf. Barnett, 2014).

When stakeholders do notice interest and identity challenges, social media influences how they respond. Social media makes communication among stakeholders less burdensome in the digital age (Grégoire, et al., 2015; Schurman, 2004), thus increasing the ease of mobilization. Distance no longer presents a significant barrier to communication, as stakeholders from across the globe can instantly share at no cost the information needed to organize protests, boycotts, and other forms of stakeholder action. For example, 25-year-old Anne Pruett, with nothing but her laptop, was able to successfully organize a large protest in San Francisco calling for Donald Trump to release his tax returns (Feuerherd, 2017).

Firms also make use of social media to intervene in the stakeholder influence process. Through the overt and covert use of sensegiving tactics (Gioia & Chittipeddi, 1991), firms influence the information stakeholders receive and how they make sense of it. The digital age has made it much less burdensome for firms to protect their interests by providing their own information to counter stakeholder concerns. Of course, the public may be skeptical of information from firms whose behaviors are being challenged, but the digital age has made it easier for firms to engage in astroturfing (Lyon & Maxwell, 2004; McNutt & Boland, 2007). Beyond issues of its biased bent, such information adds to the already overwhelming pool of information that stakeholders must digest.

Social media has not only made it less costly to mobilize for action but also less costly for stakeholder action. A stakeholder's range of available options when they feel that their interests or identities have been challenged now extends well beyond direct and indirect withholding and usage strategies. By using social media, stakeholders may now feel as if they have acted without altering their resource-wielding relationship with a firm or voicing concern directly to the firm. Social media allows "slacktivists" to perform token displays of action by retweeting a Twitter post or liking a Facebook comment. Thus, the meaning of stakeholder action has broadened in the digital age.

Even if a given stakeholder's chosen action is nominal, they still gain influence when they coordinate their efforts with other stakeholders. When there is a convergence of public opinion on highly salient issues, the necessary conditions to drive private policy becomes possible (Werner, 2012). The Police rock band put this more eloquently in the opening of their song "Synchronicity I": "With one breath/with one flow/you will know/synchronicity." Or, as an academic rock star noted in the same year, when stakeholders can "speak with a clear voice, the organization must typically follow suit with a consistent set of goals" (Mintzberg, 1983: 98). But achieving synchronicity—the convergence of interests, values, and objectives of diverse stakeholders—to gain such strength has become more difficult in the digital age. The sheer volume of "personalized action frames" (Bennett & Segerberg, 2013: 743) has made it difficult to synchronize into a committed, coherent, and persistent voice to bring about change (Kaplan, 2008).

Synchronicity can also be influenced by government intervention. The Chinese government, for example, is a leader in dampening social media synchronicity by using social media posts for strategic distraction. In the first large-scale empirical study of government posting disguised as ordinary people, King, Pan, and Roberts (2017) found that the Chinese regime follows two strategies. The first is passive, wherein the social media impersonators are told not to engage on controversial issues. The second is active, wherein they are told to stop discussions with the potential to enact collective action through active distraction and censorship.

Given the means of sharing information and the methods of coping with information overload in the digital age, information disclosure alone is often inadequate to alter the relationship between a firm and its stakeholders. Stakeholders cherry-pick information from the myriad interest- and identity-validating media sources now available, which allows them to "stick to their guns" even as disconfirming information is publicly disclosed (Hahn et al., 2014). Altering firm–stakeholder relations has become a matter of breaking through established mindsets and re-establishing new mental framing (Hahn et al., 2015). Though information is free-flowing, stakeholders must undertake an involved process to break the established frame and create a new framing around a particular issue (Dunbar, Garud & Raghuram, 1996). However, this is more difficult to do in the digital age now that it is easier to feed one's confirmation bias (Bozdag, 2013; Flaxman, et al., 2016; Pariser, 2011).

4 THE IMPLICATIONS OF STALLED STAKEHOLDER INFLUENCE

We argued above that the ceaseless flow of information imbuing the digital age with such promise has also created barriers to its effectiveness. We now have far too much of a good thing, and the methods of coping with digital information overload limit stakeholder influence over firm behavior. By looking beyond the ways in which social media amplifies a stakeholder's voice to account for the cacophony that results when anyone and everyone can command a microphone, we demonstrated that the cognitive mechanisms translating voluminous amounts of information disclosures into substantive stakeholder actions have become restrictive in creating much impact on firm behaviors.

Table 6.1 compares how the cognitive mechanisms involved in translating information disclosures into stakeholder influence over firm behavior functioned before and after the digital age. Before, the filtering of information was undertaken by gatekeepers that verified assertions, tested explanations, and expanded discussions by offering other viewpoints (Wallace, 2017). In the public arena, the information was then digested by stakeholders who attempted to frame and make sense of information to determine whether to mobilize or simply free ride on others, given that action is a costly endeavor (Olson, 1965). Sensegiving by firms was limited to a known, usually primary, set of stakeholders (Morsing & Schultz, 2006) on whom the firms were resource dependent. Consequently, two-way communication was infrequent. Efforts by stakeholders to pressure firms to change were only successful when political organizers were able to synchronize stakeholders to generate a committed, coherent, and persistent voice to influence firms (Bennett & Segerberg, 2013; Tilly, 2004).

Table 6.1 *The mechanisms of stakeholder influence before and after the digital age*

Mechanism	Pre-digital activity	Post-digital activity	Aggregate impact
Filtering	Professional gatekeepers curate across limited, broad media sources.	Unfiltered information flows across myriad narrow media sources.	Personal biases shape stakeholder media diet, reinforcing these biases.
Framing	Power, especially for secondary stakeholders, is a function of the ability to frame issues in ways that resonate.	Digital media has unleashed a torrent of personalized frames on issues.	Established frames are harder to break, which insulates firm–stakeholder relationships from change.
Sensemaking	Stakeholders interpret information in relation to their economic interests and social identities.	Media fragmentation and selective exposure limit likelihood of confronting interest- and identity-inconsistent information.	Extremes of information exposure produce threat-rigidity response or backlash, further reinforcing stakeholders' established view.
Sensegiving	Public relations efforts help firms to shape the narrative when managing crises.	Anonymity of Internet allows firms to covertly engage in countermovements, disguised as stakeholders.	Where successful, astroturfing further retards change in firm–stakeholder relations; where unsuccessful, it undermines the credibility of countermovements.
Slacktivism	Stakeholders who support a movement free-ride on the efforts of others if they deem the costs of action to be too high.	Costs of demonstrating support for a movement fall to nearly zero.	Slacktivism, or token displays of support, are now common, allowing firms to weather many social media firestorms.
Synchronicity	Political organizations generate commitment, coherence, and persistence of voice, and action to demand change (e.g., NGOs).	It is nearly costless to mobilize; almost anyone can organize large movements through social media.	The volume of customized efforts to act on various issues makes coherence, unity of purpose, and persistence hard to achieve.

Source: Reproduced from M. L. Barnett, I. Henriques & B. Husted, 2020. The rise and stall of stakeholder influence: How the digital age limits social control. Academy of Management Perspectives, 34(1): 48–64.

The digital age has blurred the distinction between primary and secondary stakeholders and may be rendering that distinction meaningless. Formerly, the key difference between the two was that primary stakeholders engaged in transactions with the firm whose survival depended to some extent on these primary stakeholders, while secondary stakeholders did not engage in transactions with the firm (Clarkson, 1995). Now, all stakeholder groups use the Internet and are influenced by or may participate in digital activism to one degree or another. For example, customers, one of the most important primary stakeholder groups, are often targeted by classic secondary stakeholders, such as NGO activists, to engage in boycotts. This indirect strategy has not only become more common today, but is also influencing potential future customers worldwide by providing secondary digital activists with as much or more influence than existing primary customer stakeholders. This suggests that the literature on stakeholder influence can no longer rely on the established binary distinction between primary and secondary stakeholders and must develop new stakeholder classifications that are more suited to the realities of the digital age.

The digital age has drastically eased the burden of information transmission, and this has unleashed a torrent of unfiltered and unverified information. Stakeholders must now verify the information themselves and, given human cognitive limitations (Mercier & Sperber, 2017), they favor sources of information that confirm their existing beliefs (Sunstein, 2017). Although digital media has increased two-way communication, the fragmentation of media and personalized frames allowed firms to overtly and covertly enter their frames into the sensemaking process, creating contentious framing contests (Kaplan, 2008) in an effort to dampen the movement or influence. Not only has the digital age made collective action nearly costless and effortless (Kristofferson, White & Peloza, 2014), it has also allowed such action frames to be posted anonymously. Together these features weaken commitment, lower coherence, and make it more difficult for organizers to synchronize the stakeholder actions that are necessary for firms to change their behavior.

As our review has shown, the literature acknowledges the central role of power in stakeholder influence on firms, as well as firm influence in response to and on stakeholders. The fight for stakeholder influence over firms creates power battles, with the winner gaining control of a firm's behavior regarding specific issues. But in the digital age, these battles play out differently. The digital age has lowered the costs of broadcasting concerns to and by the stakeholders on whom the firm is dependent. Thus, the digital age has democratized information and power by opening the firm to a host of stakeholders competing for managerial attention. Perversely, this dilutes rather than strengthens stakeholder influence in the aggregate.

Frooman (1999) sought to explain stakeholder influence by developing a typology of strategies based on relative power, due to control over resources. We have pushed these typologies into the digital age by embedding them in a broader context in which information can be empowering for individual stakeholders yet constraining in the aggregate. In a setting where information both helps and hinders, the ability to effectively manage this important resource has become a key source of power and so a determinant of stakeholder influence outcomes.

When taking this into account, we see that, in situations where neither the firm nor its stakeholders have much control over information (and are therefore unable to frame a focal issue effectively), stakeholder influence efforts tend to have little effect, allowing firms to escape deep scrutiny (Oliver, 1991). In circumstances where both a firm and its stakeholders can manage and frame information effectively, both truth and alternative facts can coexist, but that may also not push firms to change. For example, there exist parallel worlds regarding the human role in climate change in which both skeptics and advocates frame information yet talk past each other, speaking to their own constituencies but never breaking each other's frames (Hoffman, 2011). Rather than engaging in sensemaking, each side engages in unilateral sensegiving. Neither side can change the other's frame for understanding the problem. In this scenario too, firms tend to be able to weather the storm, as stakeholders lack the ability to transform information into power that exceeds the firm's influence.

Sometimes, firms can gain the upper hand relative to stakeholders, controlling information flows and the narrative. For example, some firms are skilled at challenging social media attacks, as Amy Brown did for Wendy's (Monllos, 2017), or can manipulate information through astroturfing, distracting attention by creating surrogates to send sympathetic messages via social media, as in the case of Peers, a supposedly grassroots organization that permits the sharing-economy Internet platforms like Lyft and Airbnb to thrive in a lax regulatory environment (Meronek, 2014). Such astroturfing facilitates the fragmentation of stakeholder networks so that they are unable to speak with a clear voice, again leaving firms with the discretion to behave as they wish relative to a given issue, rather than as stakeholders demand.

Finally, there are situations where stakeholder power prevails because of their collective ability to speak with a clear voice (Mintzberg, 1983). Here stakeholder networks are dense—not fragmented—allowing norms, values, and information to converge in a coherent way (Rowley, 1997). In situations where the firm lacks comparable abilities, it will acquiesce to stakeholder demands (Oliver, 1991). The key issue for stakeholder success is their ability to synchronize around a single narrative that expresses their expectations. Bank of America discovered the power of stakeholder synchronicity when it increased fees on accounts with small balances, affecting low-income customers. Initial protests by customers gained traction only when a graduate student launched an online petition and cut up her Bank of America cards on YouTube. This created a unified and compelling narrative, to which Bank of America eventually acquiesced (Jurgens et al., 2016; Shapira, 2011).

Overall, firms wish to maintain autonomy and so modify their behavior in response to external demands only as necessary (Pfeffer & Salancik, 1978). We have shown that these necessary conditions are infrequently met in the digital age, occurring primarily when the framing of the demands of myriad stakeholders can be synchronized, as this provides the power to force change. But synchronicity is difficult to achieve when the digital age produces an abundant amount of noise, allowing firm behavior to remain unchanged. The same elements that permit Internet activism across vast distances also create problems of fragmented control, decentralized decision making, and creating a collective identity (Bennett, 2003). But when stakeholders manage to develop a clear voice, a more sophisticated firm can counter that stakeholder influence by providing contrasting yet plausible frames, leading to stalemates, once again resulting in no change in firm behavior.

5 EXPLORING THE BOUNDARIES: PROXIMITY AND SIZE

Our analysis suggests that, in the aggregate, the digital age has not provided stakeholders with greater ability to force firms to be more sustainable. But our framework has only focused on distant stakeholders attempting to influence large public firms. What about small "mom & pop" firms dealing with local stakeholders? Might digital age effects be different for such cases? We next explore the implications of proximity and size for our framework.

Small firms do not have the resources to engage in astroturfing and counterattacks in social media in the same ways that a large corporation can. Hence, the likelihood that small firms will generate noise (misinformation, rumors, etc.) is lower than for large corporations. Moreover, in owner-managed firms, there is no agency problem. Mom & pop cannot act opportunistically with respect to themselves, nor do they need to be sensitive to the outrageous demands of shareholders. Instead, they may be extremely sensitive to customers and more so with respect to employees as well as neighbors (Darnall, Henriques & Sadorsky, 2010).

Geographic proximity captures the sense of community and defines small firm–community stakeholder relationships. Given proximity, there are additional opportunities and networks for communication that are not often available with digital communications. Thus, the model we have outlined for public corporations may not apply to the same extent to local firms, precisely because the local firm–stakeholder logic is different and richer than what occurs through social media.

However, this proximity and these networks existed before the digital age, and it is doubtful that it has done anything to amplify them. Rather, they may have stalled or even lessened in influence in the face of competing social media from afar. Thus, the promise of stakeholder influence in the digital age lies in the ability of stakeholders to influence distant firms by mobilizing dispersed stakeholders.

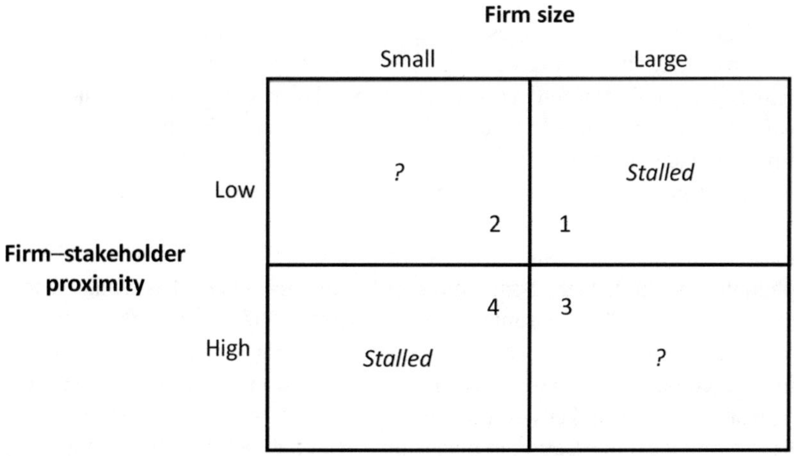

Figure 6.2 Aggregate change in stakeholder influence in the digital age

As shown in Figure 6.2, combining the dimensions of size and proximity creates four quadrants in which to further explore stakeholder influence over firm behavior in the digital age. Quadrant 1 involves large firms relating to distant stakeholders. This kind of influence was, in the aggregate, minimal before the digital transformation. Although there were cases of activism directed against large global companies, most stakeholders had little influence over what most firms did. Despite the promise of the digital age, this influence remains minimal in the aggregate. As we outlined, the cognitive processes inherent in coping with the excesses and oddities of the digital age have retarded stakeholder influence over firm behavior.

Quadrant 2 deals with the influence of stakeholders on small, distant firms. Most stakeholders are unaware of most small firms in distant locations and so hold little or no sway over their behaviors. It is unlikely that, say, a boutique bookstore in Austin will attract much attention from distant stakeholders in Boston, let alone face demands from them to alter their behaviors. However, the digital age may change this. It is now possible for the actions of small, local firms to reach national and international audiences quickly and without cost, such as the example of the Masterpiece Cakeshop in Lakewood, Colorado refusing to sell a wedding cake to a gay couple. If attacked, these small firms seem vulnerable, lacking the resources to independently respond. However, the digital age changes that, too. They could, in turn, mount a coordinated counterattack just as quickly and at no cost. Thus, the outcomes of stakeholder influence efforts on distant small firms in the digital age remain unclear, but it does seem that the dynamics of stakeholder influence do change in the digital age, which warrants further study. For example, how have small, independent firms adjusted their practices to deal with the possibility of online attacks? Perhaps the digital age has created a sort of "reputation commons problem" (King, Lenox & Barnett, 2002) across small firms in particular industries, whereby they now need to be concerned with events that happen at similar firms in distant locations.

Quadrant 3 again deals with large firms, but nearby ones. Major corporations, despite their size and resulting power, have long taken account of local concerns. For example, it is well known that the focus of CSR and philanthropy from large firms tends to be the city where it is headquartered (Galaskiewicz, 1997; Marquis, Glynn & David, 2007). These effects pre-date the digital transformation and exist because of the tightly connected networks in local communities, which permit the transmission of information about the firm and its social and environmental impacts. With small firms, which already have a rich local interaction in place, any social media interaction in the digital age would hardly contribute in changing stakeholder influence. However, the exploits of large firms in local communities can now be broadcast more easily. Social media campaigns can arise to shame large firms, for example, the campaign that Amazon faced regarding its opposition to further taxation in Seattle, or Facebook, Google, and other digital age titans continue to face in dealing with their impacts on Silicon Valley. Like quadrant 2, this quadrant is also worthy of further attention.

The fourth and final quadrant focuses on nearby small firms. This is where stakeholder influence is likely to be the highest. However, stakeholder influence was already high before the digital transformation. Social media has not increased stakeholder influence over their local firms; rather, fitting with our model, stakeholder influence has stalled.

6 CONCLUSION

Information about firm performance now flows freely in the digital age, while the costs of stakeholder mobilization and action in response to these ceaseless disclosures have declined precipitously, providing even secondary stakeholders the power to publicly pressure firms (Grégoire, et al., 2015). Thus, stakeholder influence on firm behavior should drastically increase, as is predicted (Coombs, 1998; Esty, 2004; Pitt et al., 2002) and often still expected (Jurgens et al., 2016). In short, we should have more power to pressure firms in becoming more sustainable.

Turns out, that's not the case. Although firms tend to be responsive to the myriad social media attacks they face today (e.g., Arco, 2017), the dawn of the digital age has not ushered in an era of widespread and substantive changes in firm behavior in response to stakeholder demands (cf. Gladwell, 2010). Social media firestorms may have gained a reach never before possible, but firms still maintain substantive autonomy (Lamba et al., 2015). As we have shown, the cognitive processes inherent in coping with the excesses and oddities of the digital age have served to retard stakeholder influence over firm behavior. Thus, stakeholders will not be our knights in shining armor for a corporate sustainability revolution.

BIBLIOGRAPHY

Aaker, J., & Smith, A. 2010. *The dragonfly effect*. John Wiley & Sons: New York.

Allcott, H., & Gentzkow, M. 2017. Social media and fake news in the 2016 election. Journal of Economic Perspectives, 31(2): 211–236.

Arco, M. 2017, April 11. Christie calls on feds to make big changes after United Airlines fiasco. NJ.com. Available at: www.nj.com/politics/index.ssf/2017/04/christie_calls_for_changes_after_man_forcibly_remo.html. Accessed April 11, 2017.

Arthaud-Day, M. L., Certo, S. T., Dalton, C. M., & Dalton, D. R. 2006. A changing of the guard: Executive and director turnover following corporate financial restatements. Academy of Management Journal, 49(6): 1119–1136.

Bachman, J. 2017, April 10. United is under fire for dragging a passenger off an overbooked flight. *Bloomberg*. Available at: www.bloomberg.com/news/articles/2017-04-10/united-s-forcible-removal-from-overbooked-flight-triggers-outrage. Accessed January 27, 2022.

Bakshy, E., Messing, S., & Adamic, L. A. 2015. Exposure to ideologically diverse news and opinion on Facebook. Science, 348(6239): 1130–1132.

Barbaro, M. 2006, March 7. Wal-Mart enlists bloggers in P.R. campaign. *New York Times*. Available at: www.nytimes.com/2006/03/07/technology/walmart-enlists-bloggersin-pr-campaign.html. Accessed January 27, 2022.

Bargh, J. A., & Ferguson, M. J. 2000. Beyond behaviorism: On the automaticity of higher mental processes. Psychological Bulletin, 126: 924–945.

Barnard, C. I. 1938. *The functions of the executive.* Harvard University Press: Cambridge, MA.

Barnett, M. L. 2014. Why stakeholders ignore firm misconduct: A cognitive view. Journal of Management, 40(3): 676–702.

Barnett, M. L. 2016. Mind: the gap – to advance CSR research, think about stakeholder cognition. Annals in Social Responsibility, 2(1): 4–17.

Barnett, M. L., Henriques, I., & Husted, B. 2020. The rise and stall of stakeholder influence: How the digital age limits social control. Academy of Management Perspectives, 34(1): 48–64.

Baron, D. P. 2001. Private politics, corporate social responsibility, and integrated strategy. Journal of Economics & Management Strategy, 10(1): 7–45.

Baron, D. P. 2009. A positive theory of moral management, social pressure, and corporate social performance. Journal of Economics & Management Strategy, 18(1): 7–43.

Baron, D. P., & Diermeier, D. 2007. Strategic activism and nonmarket strategy. Journal of Economics and Management Strategy, 16(3): 599–634.

Bawden, D., & Robinson, L. 2009. The dark side of information: Overload, anxiety and other paradoxes and pathologies. Journal of Information Science, 35(2): 180–191.

Beasley, J. W., Wetterneck, T. B., Temte, J., Lapin, J. A., Smith, P., Rivera-Rodriguez, A. J., & Karsh, B.-T. 2011. Information chaos in primary care: Implications for physician performance and patient safety. Journal of the American Board of Family Medicine, 24(6): 745–751.

Benford, R. D., & Snow, D. A. 2000. Framing processes and social movements: An overview and assessment. Annual Review of Sociology, 26(1): 611–639.

Bennett, W. L. 2003. Communicating global activism. Strengths and vulnerabilities of networked politics. Information, Communication & Society, 6(2): 143–168.

Bennett, W. L., & Segerberg, A. 2013. *The logic of connective action: Digital media and the personalization of contentious politics.* Cambridge University Press: Cambridge, U.K.

Blitzer, W. 2009, July 9. "United breaks guitars." The Situation Room. CNN. Available at: www.youtube.com/watch?v=-QDkR-Z-69Y. Accessed March 21, 2017.

Bozdag, E. 2013. Bias in algorithmic filtering and personalization. Ethics and Information Technology, 15(3): 209–227.

Brulliard, K., & Bever, L. 2017, July 20. Cecil the lion's son has "met the same fate"–killed in a trophy hunt in Zimbabwe, officials say. *Washington Post.* Available at: www.washingtonpost.com/news/animalia/wp/2017/07/20/cecil-the-lions-son-shot-dead-by-trophy-hunter-officials-say/. Accessed January 27, 2022.

Bruns, A., Highfield, T., & Burgess, J. 2013. The Arab Spring and social media audiences: English and Arabic Twitter users and their networks. American Behavioral Scientist, 57(7): 871–898.

Campbell, J. L. 2006. Institutional analysis and the paradox of corporate social responsibility. American Behavioral Scientist, 49(7): 925–938.

Cao, Y., Myers, L. A., & Omer, T. C. 2012. Does company reputation matter for financial reporting quality? Evidence from restatements. Contemporary Accounting Research, 29(3): 956–990.

Child, J. 1972. Organizational structure, environment and performance: The role of strategic choice. Sociology, 6(1): 1–22.

Cho, C. H., Martens, M. L., Kim, H., & Rodrigue, M. 2011. Astroturfing global warming: It isn't always greener on the other side of the fence. Journal of Business Ethics, 104(4): 571–587.

Clarkson, M. E. 1995. A stakeholder framework for analyzing and evaluating corporate social performance. Academy of Management Review, 20(1): 92–117.

Coff, R. W. 1999. When competitive advantage doesn't lead to performance: The resource-based view and stakeholder bargaining power. Organization Science, 10(2): 119–133.

Coombs, T. W. 1998. The internet as potential equalizer: New leverage for confronting social irresponsibility. Public Relations Review, 24(3): 289–303.

Darnall, N., Henriques, I., & Sadorsky, P. 2010. Adopting proactive environmental strategy: The influence of stakeholders and firm size. Journal of Management Studies, 47(6): 1072–1094.

de Bakker, F. G., & den Hond, F. 2008. Introducing the politics of stakeholder influence: A review essay. Business & Society, 47(1): 8–20.

Dunbar, R. L., Garud, R., & Raghuram, S. 1996. A frame for deframing in strategic analysis. Journal of Management Inquiry, 5(1): 23–34.

Eckhardt, G. M., Belk, R., & Devinney, T. M. 2010. Why don't consumers consume ethically? Journal of Consumer Behaviour, 9(6): 426–436.

Edmunds, A., & Morris, A. 2000. The problem of information overload in business organisations: A review of the literature. International Journal of Information Management, 20(1): 17–28.

Eesley, C., & Lenox, M. J. 2006. Firm responses to secondary stakeholder action. Strategic Management Journal, 27(8): 765–781.

Emerson, R. 1962. Power-dependence relations. American Sociological Review, 27(1): 31–41.

Esty, D. C. 2004. Environmental protection in the information age. New York University Law Review, 79(115): 115–211.

Feddersen, T. J., & Gilligan, T. W. 2001. Saints and markets: Activists and the supply of credence goods. Journal of Economics & Management Strategy, 10(1): 149–171.

Feuerherd, B. 2017, April 6. The unlikely organizers of the "Chicken Trump" tax march. NBC News Chicago. Available at: www.nbcchicago.com/news/national-international/Unlikely-Organizers-Chicken-Trump-Tax-March-418485653.html. Accessed April 10, 2017.

Fischer, E., & Reuber, A. R. 2011. Social interaction via new social media: (How) can interactions on Twitter affect effectual thinking and behavior? Journal of Business Venturing, 26(1): 1–18.

Fiss, P. C., & Zajac, E. J. 2006. The symbolic management of strategic change: Sensegiving via framing and decoupling. Academy of Management Journal, 49(6): 1173–1193.

Flaxman, S., Goel, S., & Rao, J. M. 2016. Filter bubbles, echo chambers, and online news consumption. Public Opinion Quarterly, 80: 298–320.

Freeman, R. E. 1984. *Strategic management: A stakeholder approach*. Pitman: Boston, MA.

Frooman, J. 1999. Stakeholder influence strategies. Academy of Management Review, 24: 191–205.

Galaskiewicz, J. 1997. An urban grants economy revisited: Corporate charitable contributions in the Twin Cities, 1979–81, 1987–89. Administrative Science Quarterly, 42(3): 445–471.

Gioia, D. A., & Chittipeddi, K. 1991. Sensemaking and sensegiving in strategic change initiation. Strategic Management Journal, 12(6): 433–448.

Gladwell, M. 2010, October 4. Small change: Why the revolution will not be tweeted. *The New Yorker*. Available at: www.newyorker.com/magazine/2010/10/04/small-change-malcolm-gladwell. Accessed January 27, 2022.

Goffman, E. 1974. *Frame analysis: An essay on the organization of experience*. Northeastern University Press: Boston, MA.

Goodman, M. 2014. Twitter storm forces Chimerix's hand in compassionate use request. Nature Biotechnology, 32: 503–504.

Grégoire, Y., Salle, A., & Tripp, T. M. 2015. Managing social media crises with your customers: The good, the bad, and the ugly. Business Horizons, 58(2): 173–182.

Hahn, T., Pinkse, J., Preuss, L., & Figge, F. 2014. Cognitive frames in corporate sustainability: Managerial sensemaking with paradoxical and business case frames. Academy of Management Review, 39(4): 463–487.

Hahn, T., Pinkse, J., Preuss, L., & Figge, F. 2015. Tensions in corporate sustainability: Towards an integrative framework. Journal of Business Ethics, 127(2): 297–316.

Hambrick, D. C., & Finkelstein, S. 1987. Managerial discretion: A bridge between polar views of organizational outcomes. Research in Organizational Behavior, 9: 369–406.

Hambrick, D. C., & Mason, P. A. 1984. Upper echelons: The organization as a reflection of its top managers. Academy of Management Review, 9(2): 193–206.

Harrison, J. S., Bosse, D. A., & Phillips, R. A. 2010. Managing for stakeholders, stakeholder utility functions, and competitive advantage. Strategic Management Journal, 31(1): 58–74.

Hemp, P. 2009. Death by information overload. Harvard Business Review, 87(9): 82–89.

Henisz, W. J. 2013. Preferences, structure, and influence: The engineering of consent. Global Strategy Journal, 3(4): 338–359.

Hoffman, A. J. 2011. The culture and discourse of climate skepticism. Strategic Organization, 9(1): 77–84.

Hoffman, A. J. 2015. *How culture shapes the climate change debate*. Stanford University Press: Stanford, CA.

Iyengar, S., & Hahn, K. S. 2009. Red media, blue media: Evidence of ideological selectivity in media use. *Journal of Communication*, 59(1): 19–39.

Jami, C. 2012. *Venus in arms*. CreateSpace Independent Publishing Platform: United States.

Jones, T. M., Felps, W., & Bigley, G. A., 2007. Ethical theory and stakeholder-related decisions: The role of stakeholder culture. Academy of Management Review, 32(1): 137–155.

Jurgens, M., Berthon, P., Edelman, L., & Pitt, L. 2016. Social media revolutions: The influence of secondary stakeholders. Business Horizons, 59(2): 129–136.

Kahneman, D. 1973. *Attention and effort*. Prentice Hall: Upper Saddle River, NJ.

Kaplan, A. M., & Haenlein, M. 2010. Users of the world, unite! The challenges and opportunities of social media. Business Horizons, 53(1): 59–68.

Kaplan, S. 2008. Framing contests: Strategy making under uncertainty. Organization Science, 19(5): 729–752.

Kassinis, G., & Vafeas, N. 2006. Stakeholder pressures and environmental performance. Academy of Management Review, 49(1): 145–159.

Kim, H., Lee, M., Lee, H., & Kim, N. 2010. Corporate social responsibility and employee–company identification. Journal of Business Ethics, 95(4): 557–569.

King, A., Lenox, M., & Barnett, M. 2002. Strategic responses to the reputation commons problem. In A. Hoffman and M. Ventresca (Eds) *Organizations, policy, and the natural environment: Institutional and strategic perspectives*. Stanford University Press: Stanford, CA: 393–406.

King, B. G. 2008a. A political mediation model of corporate response to social movement activism. Administrative Science Quarterly, 53(3): 395–421.

King, B. G. 2008b. A social movement perspective of stakeholder collective action and influence. Business & Society, 47(1): 21–49.

King, B. G., & McDonnell, M.-H. 2011, November 21. Case study – Delta Airlines boycott. *Financial Times*.
King, B. G., & Soule, S. 2007. Social movements as extra-institutional entrepreneurs: The effect of protests on stock price returns. Administrative Science Quarterly, 52(3): 413–442.
King, G., Pan, J., & Roberts, M. E. 2017. How the Chinese government fabricates social media posts for strategic distraction, not engaged argument. American Political Science Review, 111(3): 484–501.
Kolbert, E. 2017, February. Why facts don't change our minds: New discoveries about the human mind show the limitations of reason. *The New Yorker*. Available at: www.newyorker.com/magazine/2017/02/27/why-facts-dont-change-our-minds. Accessed January 27, 2022.
Königer, P., & Janowitz, K. 1995. Drowning in information, but thirsty for knowledge. International Journal of Information Management, 15(1): 5–16.
Kristofferson, K., White, K., & Peloza, J. 2014. The nature of slacktivism: How the social observability of an initial act of token support affects subsequent prosocial action. Journal of Consumer Research, 40(6): 1149–1166.
Lamba, H., Malik, M. M., & Pfeffer, J. 2015. A tempest in a teacup? Analyzing firestorms on Twitter. *Proceedings of the 2015 IEEE/ACM International conference on advances in social networks analysis and mining 2015* (pp. 17–24). ACM Press: New York.
Lu, Y. 2007. The human in human information acquisition: Understanding gatekeeping and proposing new directions in scholarship. Library and Information Science Research, 29(1): 103–123.
Lyon, T. P., & Maxwell, J. W. 2004. Astroturf: Interest group lobbying and corporate strategy. Journal of Economics and Management Strategy, 13(4): 561–597.
Maidenberg, M. 2017, July 18. United Airlines profit rises despite boycott threats over passenger treatment. *New York Times*. Available at: www.nytimes.com/2017/07/18/business/united-airlines-profit-earnings.html?mcubz=0. Accessed January 27, 2022.
March, J. G., & Simon, H. A. 1958. *Organizations*. John Wiley & Sons: New York.
Marquis, C., Glynn, M. A., & Davis, G. F. 2007. Community isomorphism and corporate social action. Academy of Management Review, 32(3): 925–945.
McDonnell, M. H., & King, B. 2013. Keeping up appearances: Reputational threat and impression management after social movement boycotts. Administrative Science Quarterly, 58(3): 387–419.
McNutt, J., & Boland, K. 2007. Astroturf, technology and the future of community mobilization: Implications for nonprofit theory. Journal of Sociology & Social Welfare, 34(3): 165–178.
Meeker, M. 2015. *2015 Internet Trends Report*. Kleiner, Perkins, Caufield and Byers. Available at: www.kpcb.com/internet-trends. Accessed July 28, 2017.
Meeker, M. 2017. *2017 Internet trends report.* Kleiner Perkins: Menlo Park, CA. Available at: www.kpcb.com/internet-trends. Accessed July 28, 2017.
Mercier, H., & Sperber, D. 2017. *The enigma of reason*. Harvard University Press: Cambridge, MA.
Meronek, T. 2014, April 20. Tech companies adopt astroturf to get their (wicked) way. *Truthout*. Available at: www.truth-out.org/news/item/23167-tech-companies-adopt-astroturf-to-get-their-wicked-way. Accessed April 15, 2017.
Meyer, R. 2017, June 9. Oil is flowing through the Dakota access pipeline. *The Atlantic*. Available at: www.theatlantic.com/science/archive/2017/06/oil-is-flowing-through-the-dakota-access-pipeline/529707/. Accessed January 27, 2022.

Mintzberg, H. 1983. *Power in and around organizations*. Prentice Hall: Englewood Cliffs, NJ.

Mitchell, R. K., Agle, B. R., & Wood, D. J. 1997. Toward a theory of stakeholder identification and salience: Defining the principle of who and what really counts. Academy of Management Review, 22(4): 853–886.

Mithas, S., Ramasubbu, N., & Sambamurthy, V. 2011. How information management capability influences firm performance. MIS Quarterly, 35(1): 237–256.

Monbiot, G. 2011, February 24. The need to protect the internet from "astroturfing" grows ever more urgent. *The Guardian*. Available at: www.theguardian.com/environment/georgemonbiot/2011/feb/23/need-to-protect-internet-from-astroturfing. Accessed January 27, 2022.

Monllos, K. 2017, March 2. Social media manager behind tweets that became Wendy's Super Bowl campaign is leaving the company. *Adweek*. Available at: www.adweek.com/brand-marketing/social-media-manager-behind-tweets-that-became-wendys-super-bowl-campaign-is-leaving-the-company/. Accessed April 18, 2017.

Morsing, M., & Schultz, M. 2006. Corporate social responsibility communication: Stakeholder information, response and involvement strategies. Business Ethics: A European Review, 15(October): 323–338.

Murillo-Luna, J. L., Garcés-Ayerbe, C., & Rivera-Torres, P. 2008. Why do patterns of environmental response differ? A stakeholders' pressure approach. Strategic Management Journal, 29(11): 1225–1240.

Oliver, C. 1991. Network relations and loss of organizational autonomy. Human Relations, 44(9): 943–961.

Olson, M. 1965. *The logic of collective action: Public goods and the theory of groups*. Harvard University Press: Cambridge, MA

Pang, A., Hassan, N. B. B. A., & Chong, A. C. Y. 2013. Negotiating crisis in the social media environment. Corporate Communications: An International Journal, 19(1): 96–118.

Pariser, E. 2011. *The filter bubble: What the internet is hiding from you*. Penguin Press: London.

Pfeffer, J., & Salancik, G. R. 1978. The external control of organizations: A resource dependence perspective. Academy of Management Review, 4(814): 521–532.

Pitt, L. F., Berthon, P. R., Watson, R. T., & Zinkhan, G. M. 2002. The internet and the birth of real consumer power. Business Horizons, 45(4): 7–14.

Rowley, T. J. 1997. Moving beyond dyadic ties: A network theory of stakeholder influences. Academy of Management Review, 22(4): 887–910.

Rowley, T. J., & Moldoveanu, M. 2003. When will stakeholder groups act? An interest- and identity-based model of stakeholder group mobilization. Academy of Management Review, 28(2): 204–219.

Schmidt, A. L., Zollo, F., Del Vicario, M., Bessi, A., Scala, A., Caldarelli, G., … Quattrociocchi, W. 2017. Anatomy of news consumption on Facebook. Proceedings of the National Academy of Sciences of the United States of America, 114(12): 3035–3039.

Schurman, R. 2004. Fighting "Frankenfoods": Industry opportunity structures and the efficacy of the anti-biotech movement in Western Europe. Social Problems, 51(2): 243–268.

Shapira, I. 2011, November 6. Grad Katchpole, who sparked Bank of America debit fee protest, needs a job. *Washington Post*. Available at: www.washingtonpost.com/local/art-grad-who-sparked-bofa-protest-could- use-some-cash-flow /2011/11/04/gIQA4uvMtM_story.html. Accessed January 27, 2022.

Sharma, S., & Henriques, I. 2005. Stakeholder influences on sustainability practices in the Canadian forest products industry. Strategic Management Journal, 26(2): 159–180.

Simon, H. A. 1947. *Administrative behavior*. Macmillan: New York.

Sotille, C. 2016, November 5. Dakota access pipeline fight watched on Facebook Live around the world. *NBC News*. Available at: www.nbcnews.com/storyline/dakota-pipeline-protests/dakota-access-pipeline-fight-watched-facebook-live-around-world-n678366. Accessed January 27, 2022.

Soule, S. A. 2012. Social movements and markets, industries, and firms. Organization Studies, 33(12): 1715–1733.

Sparrow, B. H. 1999. *Uncertain guardians: The news media as a political institution*. Johns Hopkins University Press: Baltimore, MD.

Starbuck, W. H., & Milliken, F. J. 1988. Challenger: Fine-tuning the odds until something breaks. Journal of Management Studies, 25(4): 319–340.

Stroud, N. J. 2008. Media use and political predispositions: Revisiting the concept of selective exposure. Political Behavior, 30(3): 341–366.

Sunstein, C. 2001. *Republic.com*. Princeton University Press: Princeton, NJ.

Sunstein, C. 2017. *#Republic: Divided democracy in the age of social media*. Princeton University Press: Princeton, NJ.

Tilly, C. 2004. *Social movements, 1768–2004*. Paradigm: Boulder, CO.

Turban, D. B., & Greening, D. W. 1997. Corporate social performance and organizational attractiveness to prospective employees. Academy of Management Journal, 40(3): 658–672.

Tversky, A., & Kahneman, D. 1974. Judgment under uncertainty: Heuristics and biases. Science, 185(4157): 1124–1131.

Virag, G. 2008. Playing for your own audience: Extremism in two-party elections. Journal of Public Economic Theory, 10: 891–922.

Walker, W. E. 2014. *Grassroots for hire*. Cambridge University Press: Cambridge, U.K.

Wallace, C. 2017, February 4. Scarecrows, watchdogs and strange bedfellows. *Toronto Star*, IN6–IN7.

Wallis, L. 2014, May 21. Why it pays to complain via Twitter. *BBC News*. Available at: www.bbc.com/news/business-27381699. Accessed January 27, 2022.

Wason, P. 1960. On the failure to eliminate hypotheses in a conceptual task. Quarterly Journal of Experimental Psychology, 12: 129–140.

Weick, K. E. 1995. *Sensemaking in organisations. Foundations for organisational science.* SAGE: Thousand Oaks, CA.

Werner, T. 2012. *Public forces and private politics in American big business*. Cambridge University Press: Cambridge, U.K.

Zietsma, C., & Winn, M. I. 2008. Building chains and directing flows: Strategies and tactics of mutual influence in stakeholder conflicts. Business & Society, 47(1): 68–101.

PART III

Getting good with government

7. Sussing out the scope of social control

It should come as no surprise that our planet and its people are in peril. Many have warned us for many years. For example, more than a century ago, Wallace (1903: 259) feared that, if left uncontrolled, we would kill the environment and ourselves, despite our ingenuity, scientific knowledge, and power:

> It is among those nations that claim to be the most civilized, those that profess to be guided by a knowledge of laws of nature, those that most glory in the advance of science, that we find the greatest apathy, the greatest recklessness, in continually rendering impure this all-important necessity of life …

How can we overcome the great apathy and recklessness that threatens the sustainability of our society? Well, sometimes you need power tools to get the job done. No matter how many neighbors gather and how earnest they may be in working with their bare hands, a town will not succeed in building substantial infrastructure such as a new school or road without heavy machinery. Likewise, no matter how many shoppers buy ethically, no matter how many recruits select employment based on a firm's sustainability practices, no matter how many suppliers shun irresponsible corporate buyers, we cannot build a sustainable society without substantive use of the heavy machinery of government.

As we explain in this chapter, stakeholders provide dispersed oversight of firms, and dispersed governance is weak governance (Jensen & Meckling, 1976), especially in the face of coordinated efforts across industries to counter stakeholder pressures. In contrast, government can bring centralized power to bear. Government has the access and authority necessary to force changes in individual and organizational behavior. As we explain in the next chapter of this book, the power of government can, of course, be misused. And it can sometimes do more harm than good, given its blunt force. But if we are to achieve a sustainable society, the central power of government is central to success. Without it, individuals, and the firms they compose, will not amply value or consistently undertake the hard work of achieving sustainability.

1 STAKEHOLDERS AS AGENTS OF SOCIAL CONTROL

Myriad laws ban specific types of firm misconduct, and criminal and civil courts provide a formal means of punishing violators. However, there are many acts of misconduct that, although they may impose harm on society, are not illegal or are impractical to control through legal proceedings. To fill this void, scholars in the burgeoning field of business and society began to study informal ways by which society might control firm behavior. As Jones (1982: 560) put it, "[T]he notion of 'social control of business,' defined as the means by which society directs business activity to useful ends ... is the core of the business and society field."

Freeman's (1984) stakeholder approach outlined the mechanisms that make business amenable to social control. He highlighted the relationships that exist between a firm and its various stakeholders—beyond just those who own shares of its stock—and argued that the strategic management of these relationships underpins firm performance. If its stakeholder relationships are weak, a firm will have difficulty attracting essential inputs and selling its outputs on favorable terms. Simply, if they are unhappy with a firm, "Customers stop buying products, shareholders sell their stock, employees withhold loyalty and best efforts" (Wood, 1991: 697), and so forth. But if these relationships are strong, the firm can gain competitive advantage (Jones, 1995). For example, firms that develop strong stakeholder relationships through socially responsible behaviors can better attract quality employees (Turban & Greening, 1997) and have easier access to foreign markets (Gardberg & Fombrun, 2006). Thus, the benefits reaped by courting stakeholder favor and the costs suffered by engendering their anger combine to form a profit motive—a "business case"—that logically drives firms to voluntarily behave responsibly and to avoid misconduct (Burke & Logsdon, 1996; Vogel, 2005).

Scholars have widely touted the "win–win" promise of the business case for both business and society (cf. Margolis & Walsh, 2003), while firms have widely proclaimed their support of its clear logic of enlightened self-interest (Hockerts, 2007). For example, Starbucks took out a full-page advertisement in *The New York Times* to proclaim, "High ideals don't have to conflict with the bottom line ... When we reached out through community programs, people bought more of our coffee. Values can actually enhance value, as revolutionary as that may sound ... Our shareholders think so, too." Walmart, though initially hesitant to engage, has come around to an appreciation of the business case, noting on its website: "At Walmart, we know that being an efficient and profitable business and being a good steward of the environment are goals that can work together."

Despite its deep entrenchment in business and academia, however, the business case is problematic. As we have shown thus far, it does not drive firms to engage in the range and scale of initiatives necessary to achieve sustainability. But does it at least help to limit the environmental harms that firms can and do cause? As we address in this chapter, the business case is not consistently effective at deterring misconduct. Though firms now broadly recognize the importance of maintaining favorable stakeholder relations, examples of misconduct continue, and those firms that engage in it may not always have reason to conclude that more misconduct would be detrimental to their self-interest. Consider BP. Though BP suffered severe punishment for its oil leak in the Gulf of Mexico, other oil firms have been leaking oil for decades without punishment. "The Niger Delta ... has endured the equivalent of the Exxon Valdez spill every year for 50 years by some estimates. The oil pours out nearly every week, and some swamps are long since lifeless" (Nossiter, 2010). ExxonMobil and Royal Dutch Shell, whose pipes were said to have leaked (Nossiter, 2010), recently set a string of record profits. Thus, the business case may be ineffective at deterring significant and recurring forms of misconduct.

How can examples of misconduct such as these persist in the face of widespread acceptance of the business case? By its own logic, the business case is a deterrent only to the degree that stakeholders present a credible threat of punishing those firms engaging in misconduct, thereby leading firms to conclude that misconduct would be too costly were it pursued. For example, when a firm decides to lower its costs of production through the socially irresponsible practice of exploiting child labor in its factories, it will only decide to stop such practices when stakeholders react by boycotting, leaving the employ of the firm, or terminating supply and distribution relationships. But, if firms engage in misconduct without engendering costly stakeholder punishment, then these firms may not learn to extinguish their bad behaviors.

In sum, the business case is only as effective a means of social control as those agents who underpin it—stakeholders. But how effective are stakeholders in this role? The next section focuses on the scope of the challenge stakeholders face in policing firm misconduct.

2 THE STAKEHOLDER AS SLIPSHOD SHERIFF

If stakeholders present a credible threat of punishing those firms that do too little to advance sustainability, then the business case is an effective form of corporate governance. Knowing the consequences of poor sustainability practices, firms would rationally conclude that impactful corporate sustainability programs are a good investment. Unfortunately, reality differs from this rational model. The threat of *ex post* settling up (cf. Fama, 1980) inadequately conditions firms to be consistently good corporate citizens, as evidenced by firms that have not ended their unsustainable practices even after being threatened with stakeholder punishment. For example, oil firms have caused great environmental destruction, yet have still profited greatly (e.g., ExxonMobil and Royal Dutch Shell).

The business case is only as effective a means of social control as those agents who underpin it—stakeholders. Unfortunately, stakeholders are not very effective agents of social control. Stakeholders undertake complex and cognitively demanding tasks when deciding to punish firms for their misconduct. To determine a punishment, a stakeholder must assess not only the characteristics of the act but also the character of the actor. As Godfrey (2005: 788) noted, firms accrue positive moral capital through philanthropy, and stakeholders account for this positive moral capital when weighing punishment:

> When bad acts occur, it is reasonable to assume that stakeholders invoke the cognitive template suggested by the mens rea doctrine to help determine appropriate sanctions. As stakeholders consider possible punishments and sanctions, positive moral capital acts as character evidence on behalf of the firm. Positive moral capital provides counterfactual evidence to mitigate assessments of a bad mind; it reduces the probability that the firm possessed the evil state of mind that justifies harsh sanctions. Positive moral capital encourages stakeholders to give the firm the benefit of the doubt regarding intentionality, knowledge, negligence, or recklessness.

Thus, when a firm engages in a bad act, the more positive moral capital it has accrued, the better it is protected from stakeholder sanction, since stakeholders account for this capital when imputing a sort of "culpability score" for the bad act (Godfrey, 2005: 788).

Barnett (2007a) argued that stakeholders account not only for a firm's past philanthropy but also for its overall corporate social performance (i.e., its historical record of socially responsible and irresponsible acts) when assessing a firm's character and deciding how to respond to its acts. Wood (1991: 693), who provides the most cited definition of corporate social performance, suggests the following means for assessing it:

> Thus, to assess a company's social performance, the researcher would examine the degree to which principles of social responsibility motivate actions taken on behalf of the company, the degree to which the firm makes use of socially responsive processes, the existence and nature of policies and programs designed to manage the firm's societal relationships, and the social impacts (i.e., observable outcomes) of the firm's actions, programs, and policies. In addition, the researcher would examine all these elements—principles, processes, and outcomes—in conjunction with each other to permit identification of analytically crucial but politically difficult results such as good outcomes from bad motives, bad outcomes from good motives, good motives but poor translation via processes, good process use but bad motives, and so on.

This is quite a burden to place on a researcher assessing even a single firm at a single point in time. Yet, as the literature acknowledges, stakeholders bear such a burden when deciding how to punish firms for misconduct. In fact, the process stakeholders undertake in punishing firms for misconduct is even more complex than the literature acknowledges. Before a stakeholder can assess the nature of misconduct and decide an appropriate punishment, that stakeholder must first notice that the act occurred. That is, events "must be bracketed from an amorphous stream of experience and be labeled as relevant before ongoing action can be focused on them" (Weick, Sutcliffe & Obstfeld, 2005: 415).

Is it correct to assume that stakeholders can successfully bear these burdens to consistently police firm misconduct? No. One of the foundational concepts of the modern management literature is that people have limited attention and so are boundedly rational in their decision making (Cyert & March, 1963; March & Simon, 1958; Simon, 1947). This significantly constrains a stakeholder's ability to notice, assess, and thereafter punish firm misconduct.

3 CORPORATE POLICING IS COMPLICATED

A person can focus their attention on only a portion of the unbounded environment, creating a limited field of vision (Simon, 1947). Stimuli falling outside this field of vision are unlikely to be noticed (James, 1890/1983; Kahneman, 1973). If a stakeholder is attending to other matters while a firm engages in an act of misconduct, that stakeholder may not notice the misconduct. But if it is noticed, the stakeholder then faces the challenge of making sense of what they have seen (Weick, 1995). For misconduct, this entails judging the act relative to the firm's history of good and bad acts (Barnett, 2007a; Godfrey, 2005) and considering the processes and policies in place (Wood, 1991). It is thus not a certainty but a probability that a stakeholder will even face the decision to punish a firm for its misconduct; the act may go unnoticed, or the firm may instead be given the benefit of the doubt. But even if a stakeholder is faced with the decision to punish a firm for misconduct, the stakeholder may choose to do nothing. They may believe that the punishment involves too much effort relative to other demands on their limited resources. Let's look at each step.

3.1 Noticing

Much falls outside one's field of vision. To which limited portion of our unlimited environment do we pay attention? Often, we look to others for guidance. People are likely to attend to something when directed to do so (Taylor & Fiske, 1975). For example, if someone shouts, "Hey, look over there!" you probably will. Things that direct our attention need not be surprising or fleeting, though. Organizations formally and informally direct the limited attention of their members through concrete and contextual structures that channel attention to those areas of the environment that support organizational goals (Ocasio, 1997). Thus, if a stakeholder is a member of an organization that seeks to address misconduct (such as a regulatory body or an NGO), then that stakeholder is more likely to be attentive to such misconduct. The more a stakeholder identifies with the organization's goals, the more attentive to such misconduct the stakeholder is likely to be (cf. Rowley & Moldoveanu, 2003). For those in its employ, organizations can formally direct their fields of vision for substantial periods of time through work duties that entail scanning particular areas of the environment.

More generally, people seek to use their limited attention to maximum benefit by selectively attending to those things that most fit with their goals and consequently ignoring those things that do not (Fiske & Taylor, 1991). For example, people are more likely to direct their attention to others upon whom their success depends, such as their superiors in the workplace (Porter & Roberts, 1976), crowding out attention to those of lesser instrumental value (Berscheid, Graziano, Monson & Dermer, 1976). Likewise, rivals pay closer attention to each other than to non-rivals (Ruscher & Fiske, 1990). Accordingly, if one's personal or professional interests are likely to be furthered by uncovering acts of misconduct, then one is more likely to look for them.

A stakeholder's self-interest need not be conceptualized as only an opportunity for personal and professional gain, however. It can include protecting oneself and one's community from harm. For example, a stakeholder who lives beside an oil pipeline is more likely to notice that the pipe is leaking oil than is a stakeholder who lives in another country (cf. Nossiter, 2010). In fact, since risk of loss tends to be more salient than opportunity for gain (Tversky & Kahneman, 1974), a stakeholder may be more likely to notice misconduct that threatens their self-interest and the interests of others they wish to safeguard than misconduct that might advance these interests. This does not imply that stakeholders will ignore all misconduct that does not help or threaten to hinder their interests. In fact, studies have demonstrated that people sometimes behave in self-sacrificial ways (e.g., Fiske, 1991; Kahneman, Knetsch & Thaler, 1986; Turillo et al., 2002). But even self-sacrificial stakeholders have limited fields of vision and so can notice only a portion of the environment wherein those events that they might deem to warrant their sacrifices occur.

Regardless of one's personal interests or tendencies toward self-sacrifice, stakeholders do not actively police most firms most of the time. It is impossible for a stakeholder to directly observe all firm actions at all points in time, even if all firms were completely transparent. Except for those issues in which they have particularly strong self-interest (or strong desire for self-sacrifice) and are able and willing to take on the burdensome duties of directly monitoring firm activities, most stakeholders become aware of most firm actions through an intermediary, typically the media (Deephouse, 2000).

The media make it easier for stakeholders to notice a firm's activities without having to directly monitor the firm, but the media cannot resolve stakeholders' limited field of vision. There are numerous media outlets pushing numerous stories from myriad perspectives, all vying for an audience. A stakeholder cannot attend to all media. So which media outlets are likely to fall within a stakeholder's field of vision?

People tend to seek out information that confirms their prior beliefs and ignore disconfirming information (Wason, 1960). This confirmation bias influences which media outlets are likely to fall within a stakeholder's field of vision. Media outlets vary, for example, in their political leanings (Groseclose & Milyo, 2005), and people prefer those media outlets that match their own political leanings (Mullainathan & Shleifer, 2005). Those with conservative political leanings often attend to different news sources than those with liberal political leanings (Bernhardt, Krasa & Polborn, 2008; Virag, 2008).

The news stories that one is likely to be exposed to depend on the media outlets one attends to. Coverage choices have been shown to vary, for example, with the political leanings of the media outlet (Baron, 2006; Patterson & Donsbach, 1996). Benediktsson (2010) found that the political ideology of newspapers significantly influenced their coverage of corporate scandals. Those with conservative political leanings, as evidenced by their political endorsements, were much less likely to cover incidents of high-profile accounting scandals than were those with liberal political leanings. Corporate ownership can also influence scandal reporting. Media owned by large corporations are prone to less negative coverage of business activity (Bagdikian, 2000). Overall, studies have uncovered a variety of persistent biases in media reporting about firm behavior and beyond (Baron, 2006).

Given the presence of more and more media outlets, the likelihood that any given act of misconduct will be covered by a media source has likely increased. However, the likelihood that any given stakeholder will encounter information that challenges their beliefs may have decreased, despite the abundance of information. Stakeholders now have access to so much belief-consistent information that media sources offering contrary evidence have difficulty crowding into a stakeholder's limited field of vision (Sunstein, 2001). With more media outlets customizing their content to compete for a niche in a crowded space, audience polarization and selective exposure to information continues to increase (Bernhardt et al., 2008; Virag, 2008).

If misconduct falls within a stakeholder's field of vision, it may still go unnoticed. People selectively perceive only a subset of the stimuli that fall within their fields of vision (Hambrick & Mason, 1984). Confronted with unbounded stimuli, people act as "cognitive misers" (Taylor, 1981) who tune out common and expected stimuli while conserving attention for stimuli that differ from expectations (Kiesler & Sproull, 1982). Even misconduct can fade into the background if commonplace. For example, bribery is more common yet is less likely to attract attention in countries with a high level of corruption (Lee, Oh & Eden, 2010; Mauro, 1998).

Lacking the cognitive capacity to independently assess all actions, people place actors into broad categories and assume similar attributes within these categories (Bruner, 1957). This conserves attention but produces stereotyping (Allport, 1954). When applied to firm misconduct, King, Lenox, and Barnett (2002) termed this a "reputation commons problem." Unable to observe all the practices of all firms, people presume that similar firms behave similarly. As a result, when a firm engages in misconduct, its entire industry may be "tarred by the same brush" (Barnett, 2007b; Yu et al., 2008). With suspicions raised, stakeholders direct their attention toward the entire industry, so any new acts of misconduct therein become highly salient. Barnett and King (2008) found this to hold in the chemical industry, for example, where, in the aftermath of Union Carbide's disaster in Bhopal, India, a sort of "chemophobia" (Gunningham, 1995: 72) arose in which stakeholders attended more closely to reports of chemical spills that might have received very limited attention previously. Similar patterns of heightened salience of previously ignored practices following crises can also be seen in responses to nuclear disasters, accounting scandals, and the bankruptcies of financial institutions.

Though one firm's misconduct can bring unwelcome attention to the previously overlooked misconduct of similar firms, it may benefit dissimilar firms. If a stakeholder's limited attention is directed toward the activity of one group, that attention is unavailable to focus elsewhere (Kahneman, 1973). As a result, a firm may benefit from a crisis in an unrelated area because stakeholder attention is less available to notice its misconduct.

In the media, where stakeholders tend to garner news of misconduct, there is evidence of significant events being crowded out when more newsworthy events coincide. Eisensee and Stromberg (2007) found that media coverage of the Olympic Games crowded out coverage of deadly natural disasters. Given limited capacity, events as extreme as terrorism can sometimes go uncovered (Delli Carpini & Williams, 1987: 60). However, some acts of misconduct receive scant media coverage even on a slow news day. The media choose which misconduct to cover not only by comparing it to other newsworthy events, but also based on the circumstances in which the misconduct occurs. As a result, two acts of misconduct may receive different amounts of media coverage even though both may cause similar amounts of social, environmental, and economic harm.

3.2 Assessing

When misconduct does make its way into a stakeholder's field of vision and is salient, the stakeholder next faces the task of assessing it. For example, if a stakeholder notices that a firm has suffered a chemical spill that led to an evacuation of the neighborhood surrounding one of its facilities, that stakeholder could interpret this as a minor and well-managed consequence of a complex production process or as a symptom of the firm's underlying disregard for public safety.

People tend to interpret the stimuli that they notice in ways that confirm their prior beliefs (Einhorn & Hogarth, 1986; Fazio & Williams, 1986; Pettigrew, 1979). This confirmation bias creates path dependence in a stakeholder's assessment of misconduct; how one assesses it depends upon what one already thinks of the firm. Some scholars have addressed this when theorizing about how stakeholders infer firms' social actions. Barnett (2007a) argued that stakeholders view a firm's actions relative to its history. A firm with a good reputation can improve its stakeholder relations through CSR because its stakeholders believe the act to be genuine, but a firm with a poor reputation may be unable to obtain the same benefits from the same act of CSR because its stakeholders discount or disbelieve the action. Barnett and Salomon (2012) found empirical support that firms with different histories of social performance do indeed earn different financial returns from CSR. Fombrun et al. (2000) and Godfrey (2005) argued that because of their different histories, firms vary not only in the financial returns they might accrue from CSR but also in the harm they might suffer from misconduct. Fombrun et al. (2000) theorized that by engaging in corporate citizenship activities, firms build reputational capital that improves stakeholder relations in good times and buffers them from stakeholder attacks during crises. Godfrey (2005) framed reputational capital as chits a firm accrues from its good deeds that are cashed in to offset damage during crises. That is, stakeholders interpret misconduct relative to a firm's stock of goodwill, and this creates, as Godfrey, Merrill, and Hansen (2009) affirm, a sort of insurance for firms with more socially favorable histories that better protects them from stakeholder punishment.

Though the literature demonstrates that, indeed, history matters in acts of misconduct, the argument is made at too high a level to adequately explain the effect of the confirmation bias on variation in stakeholder assessment of misconduct. Though a firm may accrue a favorable reputation, individual stakeholders may hold negative views of the firm, and vice versa. Thus, to explain how a firm's history affects how a stakeholder makes sense of its misconduct, the firm's overall reputation must be parsed into the views held by individual stakeholders. In parsing the reputation construct, Barnett, Jermier, and Lafferty (2006) term a stakeholder's view of a firm as an "image." As with overall reputation, a stakeholder's image of a firm is based on its history; the more favorable this record, the more favorable the stakeholder's image of the firm, and vice versa. As a stakeholder attends to different aspects of a firm over time, however, their image of the firm will vary. As a result, a stakeholder's image of a firm will change as they assess an act of misconduct committed by that firm.

As previously noted, misconduct must stand out against a noisy background of other stimuli competing for stakeholder attention and media space if it is to be noticed. Thus, acts of misconduct that capture attention and thus become subject to interpretation are likely to create an initially poor impression (Kiesler & Sproull, 1982). However, follow-up reports can correct the initial story or add context that explains or mitigates that impression. For example, Thevenot (2006) described how gruesome stories of gunfights, murders, and rapes that filled the media in the aftermath of Hurricane Katrina were later recanted. Further, firms are likely to pursue a communications strategy to deny and deflect blame or present contextual factors that lessen the perceived severity of the misconduct (Benoit, 1997).

3.3 Acting

Stakeholders may remain relatively passive while noticing and assessing a firm's actions. Punishing a firm, however, can require significant action. As a result, people may avoid taking on the burden of doing the right thing (Weber & Gillespie, 1998). People vary in their sense of obligation and commitment to taking action to ensure moral outcomes (Eisenberg, 1986; Rest, Narvaez, Bebeau & Thoma, 1999). This variation in what may be termed moral motivation helps explain the loose link between cognition and action when faced with ethical dilemmas (Trevino, Weaver & Reynolds, 2006). Some describe moral motivation as an unconscious urge or need to act to uphold one's moral standards (Blasi, 2005; Oliner & Oliner, 1988), while others describe it as the result of a deliberative process of moral reasoning (Rest, 1979). The stronger one's moral motivation, the more one feels emotional discomfort for failing to act (Blasi, 1999). To avoid this discomfort, those with strong moral motivation are driven to resolve ethical dilemmas despite the personal cost.

Whether realized through unconscious or deliberative processing, moral motivation stems from moral identity, which is "a self-conception organized around a set of moral traits" (Aquino & Reed II, 2002: 1424). People vary in the strength and centrality of morality in their self-conceptualizations (Blasi, 1984), such as how those with strong and central moral identities are more committed "to lines of action that promote or protect the welfare of others" (Hart, Atkins & Ford, 1998: 515). But one's moral identity is not fixed. Through exposure to differing life experiences, one's moral maturity (Rest,

1979) and the content of one's moral identity may change over time (Hart et al., 1998). Further, the centrality of moral identity to one's overall sense of self can vary across contexts (Forehand, Deshpande & Reed II, 2002). Accordingly, a stakeholder's drive to punish an act of misconduct will depend on their moral identity.

At any time, a stakeholder may be aware of a range of acts of misconduct as well as a range of other stimuli that they may be motivated to act upon. However, all stakeholders, even those with the strongest of moral identities, face limits on their abilities to punish misconduct. Though they may not explicitly calculate it, people undertake a sort of cost–reward analysis when deciding what to do. That is, people are motivated to minimize costs and maximize rewards (Piliavin, Dovidio, Gaertner & Clark III, 1981), though these costs and rewards may be subjective. For example, Dovidio et al. (1991) found that situations that decreased the net costs of taking action increased prosocial behavior. In a similar, but less optimistic, vein Vogel (2005) found that the presence of any significant cost could deter action from the vast majority of consumers. After reviewing surveys across multiple countries wherein the majority of respondents reported a willingness to alter purchase behaviors in response to firms' social and environmental actions, yet only a small minority did so (Capron & Qauirel-Lanoizelee, 2004; O'Rourke, 2004), Vogel (2005: 49) concluded that customers are typically unwilling to bear much of a burden to pursue their ethical concerns:

> Consumers will only buy a greener product [if] it doesn't cost more, comes from a brand they know and trust, can be purchased at stores where they already shop, doesn't require a significant change in habits to use, and has at least the same level of quality, performance, and endurance as the less-green alternative.

Because personal convenience trumps ethical concerns in many purchase decisions, some go so far as to describe the ethical consumer as a myth (Carrigan & Attala, 2001; Devinney, Auger & Eckhardt, 2010). Though it is overreaching to dismiss the ethical consumer as fantasy—many certainly exist (for a review, see Newholm & Shaw, 2007)—it is clear that the willingness of consumers and other stakeholders to take action in concert with their moral identity can be dampened by the burden of doing so.

The action-dampening burden of punishing an act of misconduct varies with the stakeholder. For example, a stakeholder wishing to punish BP for its oil spill by boycotting BP gasoline could act relatively easily if a rival supplier is located nearby. However, a stakeholder located in an area where BP is the only supplier may find it too burdensome to drive to another town to purchase gasoline or to stop driving and so may decide not to punish BP. Likewise, an investor searching for a franchise could punish BP relatively easily by purchasing a different franchise, while a current BP franchisee would face a more significant burden to break an existing contract and reorganize to operate a different franchise.

This burden is not an absolute cost but varies with the possible alternative uses of a stakeholder's limited resources. A busy senior executive may willingly punish BP by purchasing gasoline from a rival supplier even if it costs several cents more per gallon. However, they may feel that driving ten minutes out of the way to punish BP is a poor use of limited time. A retired senior citizen, by contrast, may be unwilling to punish a firm by financial expenditure but is willing to punish by time expenditure. This notion of opportunity cost shaping one's actions is validated by many studies that have found that people's tendencies to engage in a variety of prosocial behaviors, such as volunteering in the community (Schneider, 1975; Strober & Weinberg, 1980) and giving blood (Oborne & Bradley, 1975), are moderated by their level of income and available time (Unger, 1991).

Though cost can deter action, reward can motivate it. A stakeholder's reward from undertaking the burden of punishing a firm is that a desired outcome occurs within the target firm. An activist investor may, for example, initiate a proxy fight in hopes of garnering change in a firm's governance practices, or a citizen may attempt to mobilize their community in hopes of closing a polluting plant. But the stakeholder cannot be certain their punishment will have any effect on the target firm. As the uncertainty of creating change rises, the stakeholder's likelihood of action is dampened. Lacking belief that their actions will be noticed, stakeholders may not punish firms for even the most egregious acts of misconduct. This logic is implicit, for example, in the strategic location of polluting industrial plants in those neighborhoods least inclined to act (Brooks & Sethi, 1997).

Faced with uncertainty about which issues to pursue, "people gravitate toward issues more easily when they perceive the issues as having a high probability of resolution" (Dutton & Webster, 1988: 671). Though some are willing to serve as "gadflys" with no realistic hope of success (Ross, 1983), a stakeholder is more likely to expend their limited resources in pursuits that promise success than in those that they believe will fail.

The presence of others influences this. A firm may easily ignore the demands of an individual protestor or a single customer's boycott. But as a protest or boycott grows, the target firm becomes more likely to respond. Recognizing the strength in numbers, a stakeholder is more likely to act alongside others than to stand alone. Simply, the likelihood of successful influence on the target firm—creating reward from action—grows with the size of the active group. Additionally, the cost to the individual decreases once a movement infrastructure is in place.

But when firms team up to fight social control, dispersed stakeholder governance becomes less effective. There are thousands of trade associations within the U.S.A. (Aldrich and Staber, 1988). Almost every industry is represented by at least one, and almost every firm is a member of at least one. Trade associations provide the primary legal means of intentional coordination of industry-wide efforts. Rather than seeking cooperation to better compete within the established rules of the game, trade associations seek to influence the rules themselves.

Through trade associations, firms can legally present a united front and speak with a unified voice. Such collective efforts are critical in changing the rules of the game in the industry's favor (DiMaggio, 1988) and can bring about significant improvements in the performance and survival rates of the members of an industry. For example, the Tobacco Institute protected cigarette manufacturers from a variety of lawsuits and regulations that likely would have resulted in even greater harm to the industry (Miles, 1982), and the coordinated might of the pharmaceutical industry enabled it to co-opt critical resource holders and thereby gain higher average profits and survival rates than the recording industry, despite the similar structural characteristics of these two industries (Hirsch, 1975). Industry-wide cooperation is particularly important in the recovery of entire industries faced with a crisis (King & Lenox, 2000). By presenting a united front, firms can collectively improve the legislative, regulatory, market, and public interest climate for the industry (CMA, 1993), thereby realigning their industry with the demands of its environment (Hoffman, 1997).

But participation in a collaborative group such as a trade association is a mixed motive game involving simultaneous incentives to compete and cooperate (Phillips, Lawrence & Hardy, 2000). Even if firm members share some common interests, they are still rivals. Rivalry is not set aside at the doorstep of a trade association. Those firms with the power to sway trade association agendas actively seek to do so in their favor. Enterprising individuals and organizations have been shown to define, create, and manipulate issues to spur collective action toward some desired end (Davis & Thompson, 1994; McCarthy & Zald, 1977). Dominant firms in an industry are in a particularly opportune position to define, create, and manipulate the problems that their trade association pursues.

The strategic intent behind some agenda-setting efforts may be hidden. For example, a firm may champion a trade association program mandating improvements in the environmental performance of an industry under the premise that the increased standards will improve the industry's standing with regulators, customers, and other stakeholder groups. But if the championing firm can abide by these higher industry standards at a lower cost or in a superior way than can its rivals, it gains competitive advantage. Large firms can have a strong hand in establishing these sorts of self-regulatory programs, shaping these intra-industry policies in ways that play to their scale advantage. For example, Gunningham (1995) discussed the role of Dow Chemical in guiding the development of the chemical industry's self-regulatory program, Responsible Care, and how Dow was able to benefit from this program more easily than smaller firms who could not spread their costs over such a large asset base.

Many issues that trade associations face have subjective goals and largely intangible or distant measures of progress (e.g., choosing an ad campaign to improve public opinion or engaging a lobbyist to enhance the regulatory climate). Moreover, dominant firms hold considerable sway over smaller firms and may use peer pressure or the threat of exclusion from business subcultures to forge cooperation (Galaskiewicz, 1985; Useem, 1984). This makes trade associations a fertile ground for enterprising firms to put forth their favored projects. In fact, a trade association provides a more efficient and effective opportunity to engage in these practices. By engaging a trade association instead of going it alone, a firm can easily spread the costs of its political and regulatory influence efforts.

4 SO, STAKEHOLDERS SORTA' STINK AT SUSTAINING SOCIETY

By consistently rewarding firms for good acts and, conversely, punishing them for their bad acts, stakeholders can push firms away from misconduct and toward greater social and environmental responsibility. But do stakeholders really have the ability to do that? After considering the underlying cognitive processes, the picture that emerges is not one of consistent stakeholder action resulting in widespread social control. Rather, stakeholders' attention is directed in certain ways that bound where they look, limit what they notice, bias their assessment, and constrain their willingness to act. Consequently, firms' bad behaviors may not be consistently extinguished through social control. Thus, firms may continue to "supply" bad behavior because the market does not effectively signal its "demand" for good behaviors (cf. McWilliams & Siegel, 2001). Stated differently, there appears to be a failure in what Vogel (2005) characterized as "the market for virtue" due to stakeholders' limited ability to patrol, perceive, and punish firm misconduct. This is only amplified for corporate sustainability failures, as poor sustainability practices can be less obvious and more difficult to suss out and assess relative to broader forms of firm misconduct.

Cognitive constraints do not simply leave stakeholders unable to see past firms' "smokescreens" or "greenwashing" efforts (Howard, Nash & Ehrenfeld, 2000), as is often the focus of management studies on firm misconduct. Even in the presence of perfect and costless information about all aspects of firm performance, cognitive constraints pose a problem. In fact, more information leads to more problems. As firms increase transparency, stakeholders have no greater prospects for processing this flood of information. Apart from those stakeholders whose livelihood and identities depend upon their relationships or antagonisms with specific firms, more information may not lead to more stakeholder action. Perversely, as more information abounds, the likelihood that any given stakeholder will notice any act of misconduct decreases.

As more and more information about firm practices and consequences surfaces, the uncertainty stakeholders face in deciding what to attend to increases. Williams (2008) describes the stakeholder decision so support "green businesses" as a "green noise" problem, whereby a torrent of information by myriad agencies confuses well-intentioned activists who want to make purchases that further a green agenda. Thus, attentional constraints appear to be increasingly at play in consumer behavior, and stakeholder action in general.

If a stakeholder is not observing a firm's actions or is otherwise occupied and so does not have the desire or ability to respond, then even if powerful and legitimate, the stakeholder has no instrumental relevance to the firm (though ethics may dictate otherwise). Whether primary or secondary, legitimate or illegitimate, powerful or weak, a stakeholder is constrained by limited attention. It is important for firms, themselves with limited resources, to make distinctions regarding the relative importance of stakeholders. Further clarification of the conditions that shape what firm actions stakeholders attend to will help firms in making decisions about where they should focus their attention and how they should behave. That said, business and society scholars should bear in mind that the dark side of developing such insights is increasing firms' abilities to strategically target distribution of negative externalities toward those stakeholders least likely to notice, infer, or act on misconduct. In the pursuit of profits, firms may be prone to, for example, strategic placement of polluting plants (Brooks & Sethi, 1997), so as the business case becomes more explicit, the ethical concerns may become more pronounced.

5 TIME TO (RE)TURN TO THE PROFESSIONALS

Decades of stakeholder management and industry self-regulation have helped to harvest low-hanging fruit, but the wicked problems of sustainability remain beyond our grasp. Stakeholders are dispersed and ineffective. When they do manage to gain ground, firms team up to counter their efforts. Stakeholder pressures must be backed, bolstered, augmented, and given teeth by government. Though stakeholder pressures can bring sustainability issues to the foreground, government intervention is necessary to set the stage for meaningful action and to ensure follow-through. Without government, self-interested stakeholders can pressure firms to move away from the complex, long-term challenges of wicked problems and, without stakeholder pressures, industries may self-regulate in ways that prove little more than "the fox guarding the hen house." Collaboration between business, government, and stakeholders is necessary to resolve the wicked problems of sustainability. Said another way, we must move beyond the established "BS" of just business and stakeholders, to (bear with us) think "BiGS: business interrelating with government and stakeholders."

Government has the power and ability to bring actors to the table and to set the collaborative agenda on wicked problems. Nobel laureate Elinor Ostrom argued that a "polycentric approach" with experimental efforts at multiple levels (governments, business, community) is needed to assess and compare the veracity and efficiency of climate change solution strategies across ecosystems and avoid free-riding (Ostrom, 2014). Figueres et al. (2017: 593), in a *Nature* article regarding climate change, argued that we are running out of time and called on the G20 leaders of the world's largest economies to "highlight the importance of the 2020 climate turning point for greenhouse-gas emissions, and to demonstrate what they and others are doing to meet this challenge." Note that the call is to governments, not stakeholders, because of the urgency and complexity of the matter. More specifically, all levels of government "must help drive the ambition of national governments on climate change, particularly through smart infrastructure and transport policy" (Figueres et al., 2017: 595).

Time is of the essence. Unless we can resolve a myriad of sustainability problems in the very near future, it appears that our choice set will consist of abandoning this planet for another, finding a way to evolve as a species to adapt to the forthcoming drastic changes in this planet's environment, or extinction. As we have seen after decades of stakeholder management, free market approaches are inadequate to bring firms around to addressing anything but the tamest of our sustainability problems. Despite willful and wishful misinterpretation otherwise, the business case has not been made. Firms must traverse a tricky winding path to profit from sustainability, and whether the resulting initiatives achieve social impact is largely ignored.

Voluntary efforts are simply not sufficient to deal with wicked problems. Rather, government intervention is necessary to address the wicked problems that threaten our survival. If we are to live long, long live Leviathan! Of course, governments also have their limitations. Their inefficiency, failure to represent the interests of the people they are elected to serve, and tendency to be captured by special interests or subject to corruption, all provide reasons to be skeptical of governments. However, since the rise and now dominance of stakeholder management, government has been given less and less heed, leaving managerial approaches to organizational sustainability out of balance, unable to guide firms toward it. It is well beyond time to reverse this by bringing business and government back into our research and teaching lexicon. In the next chapter, we trace how government fell out of favor, and in the chapter thereafter, we close by explaining how to bring government back in.

BIBLIOGRAPHY

Aldrich, H., & Staber, U. H. 1988. Organizing business interests: Patterns of trade association foundings, transformations, and deaths. In G. R. Carroll (Ed.) *Eco-logical models of organizations*. Ballinger: Cambridge, MA: 111–126.

Allport, G. 1954. *The nature of prejudice*. Addison-Wesley: Reading, MA.

Aquino, K., & Reed II, A. 2002. The self-importance of moral identity. Journal of Personality and Social Psychology, 83(6): 1423–1440.

Bagdikian, B. 2000. *The media monopoly* (6th edn). Beacon Press.

Barnett, M. 2007a. Stakeholder influence capacity and the variability of financial returns to corporate social responsibility. Academy of Management Review, 32(3): 794–816.

Barnett, M. 2007b. Tarred and untarred by the same brush: Exploring interdependence in the volatility of stock returns. Corporate Reputation Review, 10(1): 3–21.

Barnett, M., Jermier, J. M., & Lafferty, B. 2006. Corporate reputation: The definitional landscape. Corporate Reputation Review, 9(1): 26–38.

Barnett, M., & King, A. 2008. Good fences make good neighbors: A longitudinal analysis of an industry self-regulatory institution. Academy of Management Journal, 51(6): 1150–1170.

Barnett, M., & Salomon, R. 2012. Does it pay to be really good? Addressing the shape of the relationship between social and financial performance. Strategic Management Journal, 33(11): 1304–1320.

Baron, D. 2006. Persistent media bias. Journal of Public Economics, 90: 1–36.

Benediktsson, M. 2010. The deviant organization and the bad apple CEO: Ideology and accountability in media coverage of corporate scandals. Social Forces, 88: 2189–2216.

Benoit, W. 1997. Image repair discourse and crisis communication. Public Relations Review, 23: 177–186.

Bernhardt, D., Krasa, S., & Polborn, M. 2008. Political polarization and the electoral effects of media bias. Journal of Public Economics, 92: 1092–1104.

Berscheid, E., Graziano, W., Monson, T., & Dermer, M. 1976. Outcome dependency: Attention, attribution, and attraction. Journal of Personality and Social Psychology, 34: 978–989.

Blasi, A. 1984. Moral identity: Its role in moral functioning. In W. Kurtines & J. Gewirtz (Eds) *Morality, moral behavior and moral development*. Wiley: New York: York: 128–139.

Blasi, A. 1999. Emotions and moral motivation. Journal for the Theory of Social Behavior, 29(1): 1–19.

Blasi, A. 2005. Moral character: A psychological approach. In D. K. Lapsley & F. C. Power (Eds) *Character psychology and character education*. University of Notre Dame Press: Notre Dame, IN: 67–100.

Brooks, N., & Sethi, R. 1997. The distribution of pollution: Community characteristics and exposure to air toxics. Journal of Environmental Economics and Management, 32(2): 233.

Bruner, J. 1957. On perceptual readiness. Psychological Review, 64: 123–152.
Burke, L., & Logsdon, J. M. 1996. How corporate social responsibility pays off. Long Range Planning, 29: 495–502.
Capron, M., & Qauirel-Lanoizelee, F. 2004. *Mythes et realities de l'entreprise responsible*. La Decouverte: Paris.
Carrigan, M., & Attala, A. 2001. The myth of the ethical consumer—do ethics matter in purchase behaviour? Journal of Consumer Marketing, 18: 560–577.
Chemical Manufacturers Association Report. 1993. On the road to success (Responsible Care progress report). Author: Washington, D.C.
Cyert, R. M., & March, J. G. 1963. *A behavioral theory of the firm*. Prentice-Hall: Englewood Cliffs, NJ.
Davis, G., & Thompson, T. 1994. A social movement perspective on corporate control. Administrative Science Quarterly, 39: 141–173.
Deephouse, D. 2000. Media reputation as a strategic resource: An integration of mass communication and resource-based theories. Journal of Management, 26: 1091–1112.
Delli Carpini, M., & Williams, B. 1987. Television and terrorism: Patterns of presentation and occurrence, 1969 to 1980. Western Political Quarterly, 40: 45–64.
Devinney, T., Auger, P. & Eckhardt, G. 2010. *The myth of the ethical consumer*. Cambridge University Press: Cambridge, U.K.
DiMaggio, P. 1988. Interest and agency in institutional theory. In L. Zucker (Ed.) *Institutional patterns and organizations*. Ballinger: Cambridge, MA: 3–22.
Dutton, J., & Webster, J. 1988. Patterns of interest around issues: The role of uncertainty and feasibility. Academy of Management Journal, 31(3): 663–675.
Einhorn, H., & Hogarth, R. 1986. Judging probable cause. Psychological Bulletin, 99: 3–19.
Eisenberg, N. 1986. *Altruistic emotion, cognition and behavior*. Erlbaum: Hillsdale, NJ.
Eisensee, T., &. Stromberg, D. 2007. News droughts, news floods, and US disaster relief. The Quarterly Journal of Economics, May: 693–728.
Fama, E. F. 1980. Agency problems and the theory of the firm. Journal of Political Economy, 88(2): 288–307.
Fazio, R., & Williams, C. 1986. Attitude accessibility as a moderator of the attitude–perception and attitude–behavior relations: An investigation of the 1984 Presidential election. Journal of Personality and Social Psychology, 51: 505–514.
Figueres, C., Schellnhuber, H. J., Whiteman, G., Rockström, J., Hobley, A., and Rahmstorf, S., 2017. Three years to safeguard our climate. Nature News, 546(7660): 593–595.
Fiske, A. P. 1991. *Structures of social life: The four elementary forms of human relations*. Free Press: New York.
Fiske, S., & Taylor, S. 1991. *Social cognition* (2nd edn). Random House: New York.
Fombrun, C., Gardberg, N., & Barnett, M. 2000. Opportunity platforms and safety nets: Corporate citizenship and reputational risk. Business and Society Review, 105(1): 85–106.
Forehand, M., Deshpande, R., & Reed II, A. 2002. Identity salience and the influence of differential activation of the social self-schema on advertising response. Journal of Applied Psychology, 87(6): 1086–1099.
Freeman, R. 1984. *Strategic management: A stakeholder approach*. Pitman: Marshfield, MA.

Galaskiewicz, J. 1985. Interorganizational relations. Annual Review of Sociology, 11: 281–304.
Gardberg, N., & Fombrun, C. 2006. Corporate citizenship: Creating intangible organizational assets across institutional environments. Academy of Management Review, 31(2): 329.
Godfrey, P. 2005. The relationship between corporate philanthropy and shareholder wealth: A risk management perspective. Academy of Management Review, 30(4): 777–798.
Godfrey, P., Merrill, C., & Hansen, J. 2009. The relationship between corporate social responsibility and shareholder value: An empirical test of the risk management hypothesis. Strategic Management Journal, 30: 425–445.
Groseclose, T., & Milyo, J. 2005. A measure of media bias. The Quarterly Journal of Economics, 120: 1191–1237.
Gunningham, N. 1995. Environment, self-regulation, and the chemical industry: Assessing responsible care. Law & Policy, 17: 57–108.
Hambrick, D., & Mason, P. 1984. Upper echelons: The organization as a reflection of its top managers. Academy of Management Review, 9(2): 193–206.
Hart, D., Atkins, R., & Ford, D. 1998. Urban America as a context for development of moral identity in adolescence. Journal of Social Issues, 54: 513–530.
Hirsch, P. 1975. Organizational effectiveness and the institutional environment. Administrative Science Quarterly, 20: 327–344.
Hockerts, K. 2007. Managerial perceptions of the business case for corporate social responsibility. Copenhagen Business School Working Paper No. 03-2007.
Hoffman, A. 1997. *From heresy to dogma: An institutional history of corporate environmentalism*. The New Lexington Press: San Francisco, CA.
Howard, J., Nash, J., & Ehrenfeld, J. 2000. Standard or smokescreen? Implementation of a voluntary environmental code. California Management Review, 42(2): 63–82.
James, W. 1890/1983. The principles of psychology. Harvard University Press: Cambridge, MA.
Jensen, M. C., & Meckling, W. H. 1976. Theory of the firm: Managerial behavior, agency costs and ownership structure. Journal of Financial Economics, 3(4): 305–360.
Jones, T. 1982. An integrating framework for research in business and society: A step toward the elusive paradigm? Academy of Management Review, 8: 559–564.
Jones, T. 1995. Instrumental stakeholder theory: A synthesis of ethics and economics. Academy of Management Review, 20(2): 404–437.
Kahneman, D. 1973. *Attention and effort*. Prentice-Hall: Englewood Cliffs, NJ.
Kahneman, D., Knetsch, J. L., & Thaler, R. H. 1986. Fairness and the assumptions of economics. Journal of Business, 59: 285–300.
Kiesler, S., & Sproull, L. 1982. Managerial response to changing environments: Perspectives on problem sensing from social cognition. Administrative Science Quarterly, 27: 548–570.
King, A. A., & Lenox, M. J. 2000. Industry self-regulation without sanctions: The chemical industry's responsible care program. Academy of Management Journal, 43(4): 698–716.
King, A. A., Lenox, M., & Barnett, M. 2002. Strategic responses to the reputation commons problem. In A. Hoffman & M. Ventresca (Eds) *Organizations, policy and the natural environment: Institutional and strategic perspectives*. Stanford University Press: Stanford, CA: 393–406.

Lee, S., Oh, K., & Eden, L. 2010. Why do firms bribe? Insights from residual control theory into firms' exposure and vulnerability to corruption. Management International Review, 50: 775–796.
March, J. G., & Simon, H. A. 1958. *Organizations*. Wiley: New York.
Margolis, J., & Walsh, J. 2003. Misery loves company: Rethinking social initiatives by business. Administrative Science Quarterly, 48: 268–305.
Mauro, P. 1998. Corruption causes, consequences, and agenda for further research. Finance Development, 35: 11–14.
McCarthy, J., & Zald, M. 1977. Resource mobilization and social movements: A partial theory. American Journal of Sociology, 82: 1212–1241.
McWilliams, A., & Siegel, D. 2001. Corporate social responsibility: A theory of the firm perspective. Academy of Management Review, 26: 117–127.
Miles, R. H. 1982. *Coffin nails and corporate strategies*. Prentice-Hall: Englewood Cliffs, NJ.
Mullainathan, S., & Shleifer, A. 2005. The market for news. The American Economic Review, 95: 1031–1053.
Newholm, T., & Shaw, D. 2007. Studying the ethical consumer: A review of research. Journal of Consumer Behaviour, 6: 253–270.
Nossiter, A. 2010, June 16. Far from Gulf, a spill scourge five decades old. *New York Times*. Available at: www.nytimes.com/2010/06/17/world/africa/17nigeria.html. Accessed January 27, 2022.
Oborne, D., & Bradley, S. 1975. Blood donor and nondonor motivation: A transnational replication. Journal of Applied Psychology, 60: 409–410.
Ocasio, W. 1997. Towards an attention-based view of the firm. Strategic Management Journal, 18: 187–206.
Oliner, S. P., & Oliner, P. M. 1988. *The altruistic personality*. The Free Press: New York.
O'Rourke, D. 2004. Opportunities and obstacles for corporate social reporting in developing countries. World Bank/International Finance Corporation, March: 22.
Ostrom, E. 2014. Do institutions for collective action evolve? Journal of Bioeconomics, 16(1): 3–30
Patterson, T., & Donsbach, W. 1996. News decisions: Journalists as partisan actors. Political Communication, 13: 453–468.
Pettigrew, T. 1979. The ultimate attribution error: Extending Allport's cognitive analysis of prejudice. Personality and Social Psychology Bulletin, 5: 461–476.
Phillips, N., Lawrence, T., & Hardy, C. 2000. Inter-organizational collaboration and the dynamics of institutional fields. Journal of Management Studies, 37: 23–43.
Piliavin, J., Dovidio, J., Gaertner, F., & Clark III, R. 1981. *Emergency intervention*. Academic Press: New York.
Porter, L., & Roberts, K. 1976. Organizational communication. In M. Dunnette (Ed.) *Handbook of industrial and organizational psychology*. Rand McNally: Chicago: 1553–1589.
Rest, J. 1979. *Revised manual for the defined issues test: An objective test of moral judgment development*. Minnesota Moral Research Projects: Minneapolis.
Rest, J., Narvaez, M., Bebeau, J., & Thoma, S. 1999. *Postconventional moral thinking: A neo-Kohlbergian approach*. Lawrence Erlbaum Press: Mahway, NJ.
Ross, N. 1983, April 17. Gadflies set to buzz shareholders' meetings. *The Washington Post*: G1.

Rowley, T., & Moldoveanu, M. 2003. When will stakeholder groups act? An interest- and identity-based model of stakeholder group mobilization. Academy of Management Review, 28(2): 204–219.
Ruscher, J., & Fiske, S. 1990. Interpersonal competition can cause individuating impression formation. Journal of Personality and Social Psychology, 58: 832–842.
Schneider, K. 1975. Altruistic behavior: The effects of two experimental conditions on helping behavior and personality correlates of this behaviour. Unpublished doctoral dissertation, Purdue University.
Simon, H. 1947. *Administrative behavior*. The Free Press: New York.
Starbucks full-page ad. 2005, July 24. *The New York Times*: 13.
Strober, M., & Weinberg, C. 1980. Strategies used by working and nonworking wives to reduce time pressures. Journal of Consumer Research, 6: 338–348.
Sunstein, C. 2001. *Republic.com*. Princeton University Press: Princeton, NJ.
Taylor, S. 1981. A categorization approach to stereotyping. In D. Hamilton (Ed.) *Cognitive processes in stereotyping and intergroup behavior*. Erlbaum: Hillsdale, NJ: 88–114.
Taylor, S., & Fiske, S. 1975. Point-of-view and perceptions of causality. Journal of Personality and Social Psychology, 32: 439–445.
Thevenot, B. 2006. Myth-making in New Orleans. American Journalism Review, Dec/Jan.
Trevino, L., Weaver, G., & Reynolds, S. 2006. Behavioral ethics in organizations: A review. Journal of Management, 32(6): 951–990.
Turban, D., & Greening, D. 1997. Corporate social performance and organizational attractiveness to prospective employees. Academy of Management Journal, 40(3): 658–672.
Turillo, C. J., Folger, R., Lavelle, J. J., Emphress, E., & Gee, J. 2002. Is virtue its own reward? Self-sacrificial decisions for the sake of fairness. Organizational Behavior and Human Decision Processes, 89: 839–865.
Tversky, A., & Kahneman, D. 1974. Judgment under uncertainty: Heuristics and biases. Science, 185: 1124–1131.
Unger, L. 1991. Altruism as a motivation to volunteer. Journal of Economic Psychology, 12(1): 71–100.
Useem, M. 1984. *The inner circle: Large corporations and the rise of business political activity in the U.S. and U.K.* Oxford University Press: New York.
Virag, G. 2008. Playing for your own audience: Extremism in two-party elections. Journal of Public Economic Theory, 10: 891–922.
Vogel, D. 2005. *The market for virtue: The potential and limits of corporate social responsibility*. Brookings Institution Press: Washington, D.C.
Wallace, A. R. 1903. *Man's place in the universe*. McClure, Phillips & Co: New York. Available at: https://people.wku.edu/charles.smith/wallace/S728-1.htm. Accessed January 27, 2022.
Walmart. 2006, March 2. Wal-Mart is taking the lead on environmental sustainability. Available at: https://corporate.walmart.com/newsroom/2006/03/02/wal-mart-is-taking-the-lead-on-environmental-sustainability. Accessed January 27, 2022.
Wason, P. C. 1960. On the failure to eliminate hypotheses in a conceptual task. Quarterly Journal of Experimental Psychology, 12: 129–140.
Weber, J., & Gillespie, J. 1998. Differences in ethical beliefs, intentions, and behaviors. Business & Society, 37(4): 447–467.
Weick, K. 1995. *Sensemaking in organizations*. Sage: Thousand Oaks, CA.

Weick, K., Sutcliffe, K., & Obstfeld, D. 2005. Organizing and the process of sensemaking. Organization Science, 16: 409–421.
Williams, A. 2008, June 15. That buzz in your ear may be green noise. *New York Times*.
Wood, D. 1991. Corporate social performance revisited. Academy of Management Review, 16: 691–718.
Yu, T., Sengul, M., & Lester, R. 2008. Misery loves company: The spread of negative impacts resulting from an organizational crisis. Academy of Management Review, 33(2): 452–472.

8. Gripes against government

In *The Great Transformation: The Political and Economic Origins of our Time*, Karl Polanyi (1944) argued the state's critical role in shaping and creating markets for the good of all. Governments have long been "able to take risks and create a highly networked system of actors that harness the best of the private sector for the national good over a medium- to long-term horizon" (Mazzucato, 2015: 27). In the U.S., for example, there is a rich history of the federal government catalyzing innovation and laying the groundwork for success (Erickson, 2012), including investment in the Panama Canal (1904–1914), the Hoover Dam (1931–1936), the Apollo Space Program (1961–1969), the Defense Advanced Research Projects Agency (DARPA, 1958), and the Elementary and Secondary Education Act (1965). Governments across the globe have gone beyond addressing market failures to undertaking risky investments in people and infrastructure. These governmental undertakings have ameliorated social problems while providing enormous positive spillovers to the private sector, such as funding technological research and creating a highly educated workforce.

Despite this history, Ronald Regan famously declared in his 1981 inaugural address that "government is not the solution to our problem; government is the problem" (Ronald Reagan Presidential Foundation & Institute, 1981). This ushered in a broad and deep shift toward deregulation in the U.S. and beyond, under the assumption that markets achieve the best outcomes when left largely unburdened by government intervention. It was in this period that the stakeholder view of the firm arose (Freeman, 1984).

In this chapter we describe how, consonant with stakeholder theory's libertarian underpinnings (Freeman & Phillips, 2002), the business and society literature has downplayed government's role in tackling sustainability issues. The stakeholder view suggests that government intervention is unnecessary in inducing firms to serve the greater good, arguing that firms serve their own interests by fulfilling stakeholder interest. Glad to avoid the heavy hand of government regulation, firms were quick to adopt this view, thereby helping to legitimize and promulgate it across both scholarship and practice (Rowley & Berman, 2000). Today, the notion that firms produce widespread "win–win" outcomes through stakeholder management dominates the business and society literature (Harrison et al., 2010). Along the way, the role of government in regulating firm behavior has fallen to the wayside, and this has limited the substantiveness of sustainability solutions.

1 LEARNING TO LOATHE LEVIATHAN

Unlike the long-established dictum of shareholder management, stakeholder management drives firms to consider the interests of a broader set of stakeholders. However, by selectively responding to the most powerful, legitimate, and urgent demands of their stakeholders to seek profit (Mitchell, Agle & Wood, 1997), firms are unlikely to traverse a path to sustainability. Instead, firms tend to harvest low-hanging fruit that heavily depends on independent advances in technology and rising consumerism. Yet sustainability issues require cooperation across parties and a significant amount of time to resolve, or even just to define (Rittel & Webber, 1973). Managing by prioritizing the demands of some stakeholders over others retards the cross-stakeholder cooperation that is needed to discover, design, and implement effective solutions to our sustainability challenges.

This is where government should step in. Cooperation is sorely needed, and government has the power to incentivize and direct cooperation even in competitive markets. Why has this major actor been sidelined in the battle to bring about a sustainable society?

The stakeholder framework that underpins the business and society literature has not been theorized in a way that carves out a clear space for government. Freeman's (1984) original "broad" stakeholder view implicitly categorized government as a stakeholder since government can affect and is affected by the firm. But almost anyone and anything can fit into this broad definition of a stakeholder. Orts and Strudler (2002) outlined a "narrower" view that excluded government from stakeholder status, since government has no economic stake at risk in the firm. Moreover, stakeholder theory's broad prescription of sorting out how to balance competing stakeholder interests makes no sense in terms of the government, since firms lack the discretion to trade off their duties to obey the law with other stakeholder interests. Thus, there has been no clear conceptual role for government in the dominant stakeholder framework that guides the business and society literature—apart from enforcing the law, of course.

A minimal role for government is consonant with stakeholder theory's foundational libertarian leanings (Buchholz & Rosenthal, 2004). The concept of voluntarism, at least in the U.S. context, was highlighted in Freeman's (1984: 74) initial work: "Voluntarism means that an organization on its own will undertake to satisfy its key stakeholders. A situation where a solution to a stakeholder problem is imposed by a government agency or the courts must be seen as a managerial failure." Freeman and Phillips (2002) later defend stakeholder theory from a libertarian perspective. In their essay, they lay the groundwork for understanding how stakeholder theory is compatible with libertarian principles, especially concepts such as consent, voluntariness, and negotiation. They explain: "Business is founded (and businesses are created) on this idea of making agreements with each other. And we are free to make these agreements because others are not permitted to interfere (so long as they are not substantially affected)" (Freeman & Phillips, 2002: 341). Hence stakeholder theory fits well with the minimal "night watchman" state (Nozick, 2013).

Whether government is classified as a stakeholder—one of many—or as a night watchman that protects citizens from fraud, theft, and violence, stakeholder theory has had minimal use for the apparatus of government regulation in driving firms toward more responsible behavior. Despite ongoing and worsening challenges to sustainability after decades of stakeholder theory, governmental minimalism remains a central feature, still not widely viewed as a major part of the solution. As we next outline, beliefs that government regulation is inefficient and costly and subject to capture and corruption continue to drive out consideration of government, enabling ongoing beliefs that voluntary efforts by companies are sufficient to address all externalities, and stakeholder pressures are sufficient to get companies to change.

1.1 Government Regulation is Costly and Inefficient

The primary knock against government is that it is a blunt instrument which does more harm than good in competitive markets. Its byzantine rules and broad mandates, backed by the force of the state, can cripple industry. Long lines, blustery employees, and outdated and insufficient stocks instantly come to mind when picturing government-run organizations.

Welfare economics argues that a competitive market leads to an efficient allocation of resources (Arrow & Hahn, 1970) if there are no externalities, information is perfect, and markets are complete (Debreu, 1959). In such a world, the intervention of government, with the costs and inefficiency this can bring, is unnecessary because the market efficiently allocates resources.

Unfortunately, we do not live in such a world. Instead, there are spillovers and externalities in production and consumption, imperfect and asymmetric information, incomplete and/or monopolistic markets, poorly or undefined property rights, positive transactions costs, and economies of scope and scale (Mahoney & Qian, 2013). Thus, government has an important role to play.

Rather than exclude government, the aim must be to organize it so that it can fulfill its essential function in less burdensome ways. North (1984: 255) suggests that "transaction costs are the basic determinants of institutions and provide the framework within which economic activity occurs." He examined four major costs of exchange; the first is the cost of measuring to determine what participants are receiving from the exchange. The second is the nature of the exchange process which impacts enforcement costs. The third is the enforcement mechanism to determine the costs to parties when the terms of the agreement are violated. The fourth is the strength of ideology defined as the cost of one's convictions which can "vary according to one's beliefs about the justice of the rules and the contractual arrangements of society, and … influenced by education, propaganda and symbols" (North, 1984: 258). He concludes that there are "no cases of complex urban societies that do not have an elaborate structure of government" and that "one cannot have the productivity of an industrial society with political anarchy" (North, 1984: 259). Thus, the government, as an institution, is here to stay and is a significant entity influencing industry and civil society.

Kourula et al. (2019) provide a succinct historical trajectory of government roles from the 1970s to today. In the 1970s, governments were primarily regulators of business conduct, with firms lobbying governments to enact favorable regulation. In the 1980s and 1990s, with the neoliberal drives to privatize, liberalize, and deregulate markets, government responsibility decreased under the guise that companies were better problem solvers. It is during this period that companies began developing and participating in self-regulatory mechanisms such as voluntary environmental management systems (e.g., ISO 14001 and the EU Eco-Management and Audit Scheme (EMAS)). The 2000s saw a "shift towards a partnership society, where all sectors increasingly work together to address local and global societal challenges" (Kourula et al., 2019: 1109). Here, multi-stakeholder initiatives and public–private partnerships enable governments to take on both a traditional role of regulator as well as an active role as convener (Koontz et al., 2004; Pedersen, Lüdeke-Freund, Henriques & Seitanidi, 2021).

Conventional economic logic stipulates that the opportunity costs of environmental regulation increases costs and reduces profits, which then negatively affects growth and the level of per capita gross domestic product (Altman, 2001). Economists do not deny that such regulations may give rise to social benefits; however, such benefits cannot be obtained without significant private costs (Cropper & Oates, 1992; Jaffe, Peterson & Portney, 1995). On the other hand, Porter (1991) argued that properly constructed regulatory standards that target outcomes would encourage innovation and upgrading, which would not only reduce emissions but lower costs and improve quality. The reality is that command-and-control environmental measures tell people what they cannot do—not what they *should* do—to protect the environment. With the growth in grassroots concern about the environment in the early 1990s, government agencies faced increasing pressure to examine alternative means to solve environmental problems such as corporate and industry voluntary environmental management programs, which demanded greater involvement of a more diverse group of stakeholders in the decision-making process (Koontz et al., 2004).

This tug-of-war between regulatory costs and societal benefits forced regulatory agencies to assess the viability of their policies using cost–benefit analyses. Regulators' costs (e.g., cost of technology upgrades, investments) are, predictably, much easier to calculate because they are market-based, incurred in the short term, and internal to the company. Societal benefits (e.g., the impact of cleaner air or waterways), on the other hand, are more difficult to ascertain because they tend to be non-market based (e.g., quality of life improvements, health impacts and biodiversity improvements), occur in the long run and are external to the firm. So, while governments sought alternatives to regulation, firms made a habit of disregarding regulatory societal benefits, leading to the current favoring of free market solutions.

1.2 Government can be Corrupted

Even if it were cheap and efficient, government still faces the problem of being captured and corrupted, used to serve private interests at public expense. The media's portrayal of government corruption, both at home and abroad, has done little to improve the image of governments. Stories include journalists being arrested for uncovering government corruption (Roth, 2021), the Estonian government collapsing over a corruption investigation (Henley, 2021) and the Mexican government using billions in government cash to control the news media (Ahmed, 2017).

Government corruption can take two forms, with differing effects on firms' decision making: policy-specific corruption and general corruption (Montiel, Husted & Christmann, 2012). Policy-specific corruption is typically based on a firm's experiences with the enforcement of regulations and policies by specific government agencies, whereas general corruption is based on experiences with a variety of transactions with different government agencies, levels of government, and private sector entities. General corruption is conceptually similar to the aggregate measures of corruption in common use, while policy-specific corruption is a narrower theoretical construct that captures one specific dimension of corruption.

In jurisdictions with high levels of policy-specific corruption, firms' apparent compliance with regulations does not reveal credible information about their actual conduct relative to the regulated issue. For example, firms can fail to comply with environmental regulations, but give the appearance of compliance by bribing government officials to obtain environmental permits such as hazardous waste or wastewater discharge permits, or to avoid penalties for regulatory violations. Conversely, in jurisdictions with low policy-specific corruption, external stakeholders can presume that most firms that are not fined for violations and possess appropriate permits generally do comply with regulations (Ivanova, 2007). Thus, information asymmetries about policy-specific conduct between firms and their external stakeholders are larger in jurisdictions with high policy-specific corruption.

In the case of firms with good conduct, the firm would use certification as a signal to reveal this information but only if the value derived from certification exceeds the cost (Delmas & Montiel, 2009; King et al., 2005). While the costs of obtaining, say, environmental certification do not differ across jurisdictions with different levels of policy-specific corruption, its signaling value is expected to be larger in jurisdictions with high levels of policy-specific corruption, since apparent regulatory compliance conveys little information regarding true policy-specific conduct. In such jurisdictions, policy-relevant certification—i.e., certification that addresses the regulated issue—reveals additional information by separating firms with good conduct from those with poor conduct. Thus, high levels of policy-specific corruption increase the value of private certification.

Previous research has found that people's perceptions of widespread governmental corruption, which involves many agencies and a wide range of transactions with the government, affect their assessments of other societal institutions as well as their perceptions of general corruption. This general perception of corruption is defined as the public's belief that corruption cuts a wide swath across both the public and private sectors. Perceptions of or experience with widespread corruption appear to correlate with reduced trust in individuals and institutions (Bailey & Paras, 2006; Canache & Allison, 2005). In addition, perceptions of widespread public corruption seem to be highly correlated with perceptions of private sector corruption (Melgan, Piani & Rossi, 2009). While private corruption frequently coexists with public corruption, the press, politicians, and civil society tend to focus their attention on the government, such that only limited information is available on private sector corruption in many places like Central America, Mexico, and the Caribbean (Transparency International, 2003).

General corruption is inextricably tied to private sector corruption, so private auditors, who issue the certification in countries with high levels of general corruption, will almost certainly be viewed as more corrupt. In environments with high levels of general corruption, it may be possible for firms to obtain certification by bribing the private auditors assessing firms' conformance with standard requirements, rather than by substantively implementing the standard and using it in their daily operations. The possibility that undeserving firms may obtain certification by bribing private auditors affects the costs of obtaining certification for these firms as well as the signaling benefits that they derive from achieving the certification.

In jurisdictions with high levels of general corruption, firms can avoid the high costs of standard implementation by paying a bribe to a private auditor while implementing the standard symbolically and not using it in their daily operations (Boiral, 2007; Christmann & Taylor, 2006). Firms will only bribe auditors if the total cost of obtaining certification (i.e., implementation and certification costs plus the cost of the bribe) is less than the cost of obtaining certification via substantive standard implementation. Given that firms with poor performance incur higher implementation costs, they will be more likely to bribe the auditors to lower their total costs of obtaining certification. Thus, general corruption lowers the costs of certification for poor performers, which suggests that a separating equilibrium—that is, a situation in which high-performing firms incur lower signaling costs than low-performing firms—does not exist for certification in jurisdictions with high levels of general corruption. As a result, the signaling value of certification is compromised in these jurisdictions and neither type of firm (high or low performers) will want to incur the costs of a valueless certification. It is important to point out that public *perception* of high levels of general corruption (rather than *actual* high levels of general corruption) are sufficient to generate this effect. If external stakeholders perceive general corruption to be high, they will infer that a separating equilibrium does not exist. Hence, the signaling value of certification is reduced, which reduces firms' likelihood of certification. Interestingly, Montiel et al. (2012), using a sample of automotive supplier facilities in Mexico, found that policy-specific corruption increased firms' certification likelihood, while general corruption lowered certification likelihood.

Corruption continues to be a serious problem around the world. Husted (2002) suggests that the battle against corruption in Latin America, for example, must work at the level of group norms, with strong executive leadership and unambiguous rules that seek to harness individual and group interests in ways that promote the fight against corruption. In addition, sanctions must be sensitive to national differences in the individualism–collectivism and masculinity–femininity dimensions. As a collectivistic society, the Latin American experience of shame is a particularly important means of social control. It is thus necessary that programs be developed to emphasize corruption as a violation of community ideals for behavior. Such shame-based forms of control should prove more effective than the guilt-based approach of the Inter-American Corruption Convention (which was approved by the Organization of American States (OAS) in 1996), and the OECD Convention signed in 1997. In the masculine countries of Latin America such as Mexico, Venezuela, and Colombia, fines are likely to be more effective than in the feminine countries such as Uruguay and Costa Rica. Conversely, jail terms are more likely to be effective in feminine cultures.

The OAS and OECD conventions certainly acknowledge the Latin American governments' seriousness over the corruption issue that these countries face. However, unless efforts are made to develop culturally consonant modes of corruption control, the implementation and enforcement of these agreements should prove to be elusive and, in turn, make it difficult for governments to guide their citizens on a more sustainable path. The reality is that most countries that are recognized today for their integrity were, at some point in their history, afflicted with pervasive corruption. In fact, Cuellar and Stephenson (2020: 2) found that the "U.S. anticorruption experience involved a combination of 'direct strategies', such as aggressive law enforcement and 'indirect strategies'" (like civil service reform and other institutional changes), which "coincided with a substantial expansion of government size and power."

1.3 Voluntary Efforts by Companies are Sufficient to Address Environmental Problems

Despite the risks inherent in "the fox guarding the henhouse," concerns about the costs and corruption of government have led to a rise in the self-regulation of firms and industries. Many governments now encourage—which industry groups and individual firms now use—voluntary environmental programs (VEPs) to address sustainability problems in more flexible and cheaper ways (Morgenstern & Pizer, 2007; Paton, 2000).

VEPs are commitments not required by law, are meant to influence or regulate behavior, and are implemented to achieve a consistent outcome (Webb, 2004). VEPs can be classified as public voluntary programs, i.e., negotiated agreements between business and government, or unilateral agreements by industrial firms (Morgenstern & Pizer, 2007). Public VEPs involve environmental agencies inviting firms to voluntarily meet specified standards or adopt clean technologies (Khanna, 2001). Participants in these programs sign non-binding letters of intent and their progress is tracked by self-reporting. Governmental bodies then develop the programs which firms can join. Specific terms of the program are, in general, not negotiated. Examples of public VEPs in the United States include the 33/50 Program, Green Lights, and the Climate Wise Program (Morgenstern & Pizer, 2007). Examples of Canadian public voluntary programs include the Voluntary Challenge and Registry (VCR) Program and the Accelerated Reduction and Elimination of Toxics Initiative (ARET).

Negotiated VEPs involve the government's environmental agencies negotiating with a firm or trade association on abatement targets, timelines, and plans (Khanna, 2001; Morgenstern & Pizer, 2007). Such negotiations usually provide regulatory relief in exchange for pollution reductions more than status quo standards (Khanna, 2001). These agreements, whose implementations vary across countries like Canada, the European Union, Japan, and the United States, are usually legally non-binding. Examples of negotiated VEPs include the U.S. Environmental Protection Agency's (USEPA) Common Sense Initiative and Project XL, Denmark's program on industrial energy efficiency, the United Kingdom's Voluntary Climate Agreements, and Japan's Keidanren Voluntary Action Plan on the Environment (Morgenstern & Pizer, 2007). Examples of negotiated national voluntary agreements in Canada include industry-specific environmental performance agreements, the Canadian Pesticide Container Management Program, the Recycling Program for Rechargeable Batteries, and the Refrigerant Management Canada Program. Consequently, both public and negotiated VEPs entail some level of government engagement (Henriques & Sadorsky, 2008).

Unilateral agreements, on the other hand, occur without direct government involvement and include unilateral corporate programs aimed at environmental stewardship. The interest in promoting voluntary environmental action and pollution prevention has been accompanied by a growing number of business-initiated unilateral actions to change corporate culture and management practices via the introduction of environmental management systems (EMS), industry-level codes of environmental management (such as the Responsible Care Program developed by the Canadian Chemical Producers' Association (CPPA)), and international EMS certification programs (e.g., the International Standards Organization's (ISO) 14001). EMSs represent corporations' efforts for self-regulation by defining a set of formal environmental policies, goals, strategies, and administrative procedures for improving environmental performance (Coglianese & Nash, 2001).

Voluntary self-regulation relies on the discipline of markets rather than formal command and control to regulate corporate behavior, making it cheaper and easier to implement and enforce. This provides a relatively easy sell to many governments eager to offload the burden of regulation. Voluntary corporate sustainability programs have thrived, as self-regulation has partially supplanted formal regulation (Cashore, 2002). Under a free market ethos, corporations have come to view sustainability initiatives as any other business investment, seeking to establish business cases to profit from addressing environmental problems. Following the discovery of numerous instances in which the market promotes such efforts and penalizes their absence, the majority of the world's leading firms are now devoting considerable resources to sustainability projects (Eccles, Ioannou & Serafeim, 2014).

Unfortunately, as noted in Chapter 5, voluntary self-regulation is not sufficient to deal with the enormity and urgency of the sustainable challenges we currently face. Despite the many voluntary initiatives, the planet has suffered significant ecological damage and is nearing the point of no return for sustaining life (IPCC, 2018). This fact is not lost on King and Pucker (2021: 37), who argued:

> When US citizens were faced with dirty rivers in the 1970s, they didn't encourage firms to consider that it might pay to be green; they demanded that pollutants be regulated. When smog overcame many US cities, activists didn't ask firms to create shared value; they called for emission standards. When the world faced its first global threat to our shared atmosphere, growing damage to our ozone layer, citizens did not ask for companies to create new "social purpose" charters; they forced global leaders to negotiate a worldwide ban on chlorofluorocarbons. As a result, our rivers are healthier, our air is safer, and the hole in the ozone layer is closing.

1.4 Stakeholder Pressures are Sufficient to Affect Change

Stakeholders can influence firms through control over resources, social movements, and private politics (Barnett, Henriques & Husted, 2020). Typologies of stakeholder influence strategies have been developed based on essentially two dimensions: firm power and stakeholder power (Frooman, 1999). When there is low interdependence between the firm and its stakeholders, the firm will avoid the indirect pressure generally exerted from its stakeholders through allied parties. However, when there is high interdependence because the firm is centrally located in a dense stakeholder network, the firm will negotiate with those stakeholders who deal directly with the firm by attaching strings to resource usages. Stakeholder power arises from dense networks where stakeholder interests converge and thus allow stakeholders to "speak with a clear voice" (Mintzberg, 1983: 98, cited by Rowley, 1997: 903). In short: power matters.

Frooman (1999) argues that firms not resource dependent on stakeholders may exercise indirect influences via other stakeholders on whom the firm is resource dependent. Such stakeholders usually have social and ecological stakes and include non-governmental organizations (NGOs), wildlife protection groups, aboriginal groups, and the media (Feddersen & Gilligan, 2001). To achieve their social and/or ecological objectives, these stakeholders will enhance their power (Mitchell et al., 1997) by influencing other stakeholders who control resources critical for the firm. For example, Greenpeace pressured British investment firm Friends Ivory & Sime Plc to divest its equity holdings in the Canadian forestry company Interfor as part of its ongoing campaign to pressure British financial firms into divesting Canadian forestry companies with poor sustainability practices (Stueck, 2001). The methods used by social movements in this case become much more relevant by inciting a larger group of individuals to exercise their influence (King, 2008a). Sharma and Henriques (2005) found substantial evidence in the effectiveness of both withholding and using strategies to foster sustainability practices among Canadian forest products firms. Zietsma and Winn (2008) focus specifically on secondary stakeholders and discover how their influence tactics change over time through issue raising, issue suppression, positioning, and solution-seeking.

Protests are influential when they target issues dealing with critical stakeholder groups (i.e., groups that are highly interdependent with the firm such as labor and consumers) (King & Soule, 2007) or highly legitimate groups with compelling claims (King & McDonnell, 2011). The influence of stakeholders depends on three elements: (1) mobilizing structures like formal organizations and interpersonal networks, (2) political opportunities such as changes in corporate leadership or industry competition, and (3) framing processes (King, 2008b). Framing processes are especially relevant because stakeholder influence can often be conceived of as a kind of framing contest with the firm (Benford & Snow, 2000). Frames refer to "schemata of interpretation," which convert "what would otherwise be a meaningless aspect of the scene [or event] into something that is meaningful" (Goffman, 1974: 21). The ability of these stakeholders to influence the firm thus resides largely in their ability to frame issues; that is, to construct meaning around an issue and thereby facilitate mobilization (King, 2008b). The digital age has increased the ability of individual stakeholders to influence firms by decreasing the cost of mobilization to virtually nil. As addressed in Chapter 6, however, the resulting cacophony from everyone using a virtual megaphone has not led to widespread social control of firms.

2 CONCLUSION

Governments have problems. Regulation can be costly and inefficient; governments can be corrupted; alternative forms of governance can drive firms to voluntarily do the right thing without government intervention. Over the last several decades, political emphasis on the problems of government promoted the ideology that only markets offer efficient and effective solutions. Kourula et al. (2019) argue that regulatory authority has shifted to private-led business initiatives in sectors that were once under the purview of government, such as healthcare, education, accounting, and human rights.

But government must become a critical part of the solution for sustainability. As depicted in Figure 8.1, perspectives must change so that governments take the lead. There is still hope. Governments have begun to make mandatory what was previously voluntary and have taken on influential partnership roles with the private sector, including large clean-energy infrastructure projects (Kourula et al., 2019). As governments start to take the lead and address our planet's sustainability challenges with the private sector and other stakeholders, they must be careful to avoid what Mazzucato calls the "socialization of risk and the privatization of rewards" (Mazzucato, 2015: 9). In the next chapter, we argue that governments need to take the lead in setting overall sustainability goals based on societal net benefits and scientific evidence, with stakeholders continuing to pressure government and companies on their societal concerns, and companies employing their ingenuity to meet these goals.

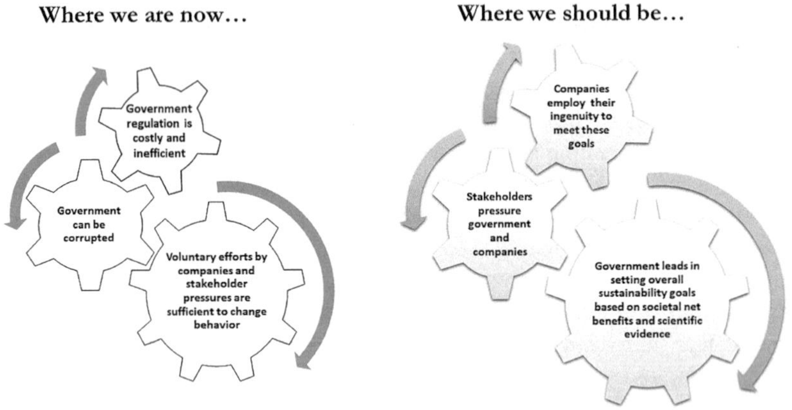

Figure 8.1 *Process change to achieve sustainability goals*

BIBLIOGRAPHY

Ahmed, A. 2017, December 25. Using billions in government cash, Mexico controls news media. *New York Times*. Available at: www.nytimes.com/2017/12/25/world/americas/mexico-press-government-advertising.html. Accessed January 27, 2022.

Altman, J. 2001. When green isn't mean: economic theory and the heuristics of the impact of environmental regulations on competitiveness and opportunity cost. Ecological Economics, 36(1): 31–44.

Arrow, K. J., & Hahn, F. 1970. *General competitive analysis*. Holden Day: San Francisco, CA.

Bailey, J., & Paras, P. 2006. Perceptions and attitudes about corruption and democracy in Mexico. Mexican Studies, 22(1): 57–81.

Barnett, M. L., Henriques, I., & Husted, B. W. 2020. The rise and stall of stakeholder influence: How the digital age limits social control. Academy of Management Perspectives, 34(1): 48–64.

Benford, R. D., & Snow, D. A. 2000. Framing processes and social movements: An overview and assessment. Annual Review of Sociology, 26(1): 611–639.

Boiral, O. 2007. Corporate greening through ISO 14001: A rational myth? Organization Science 18(1): 127–146.

Buchholz, R. A., & Rosenthal, S. B. 2004. Stakeholder theory and public policy: How governments matter. Journal of Business Ethics, 51(2): 143–153.

Canache, D., & Allison, M. 2005. Perceptions of political corruption in Latin American democracies. Latin American Politics & Society, 47(3): 91–111.

Cashore, B. 2002. Legitimacy and the privatization of environmental governance: How non-state market-driven (NSMD) governance systems gain rule-making authority. Governance, 15(4): 503–529.
Christmann, P., & Taylor, G. 2006. Firm self-regulation through international certifiable standards: Determinants of symbolic versus substantive implementation. Journal of International Business Studies, 37(6): 863–878.
Coglianese, G., & Nash, J. 2001. *Regulating from the inside: Can environmental management systems achieve policy goals*. Resources for the Future: Washington, D.C.
Cropper, M. L., & Oates, W. E. 1992. Environmental economics: A survey. Journal of Economic Literature, 30: 675–740.
Cuellar, M.-F., & Stephenson, M. C. 2020. Taming systemic corruption: The American experience and its implications for contemporary debates. The Quality of Government Institute (QOG), Department of Political Science, University of Gothenburg, Working Paper Series 2020-6 September. Available at: Taming Systemic Corruption: The American Experience and its Implications for Contemporary Debates by Mariano-Florentino Cuéllar, Matthew Stephenson: SSRN
Debreu, G. 1959. *The theory of value*. Wiley: New York.
Delmas, M., & Montiel, I. 2009. Greening the supply chain: When is customer pressure effective? Journal of Economics and Management Strategy, 18(1): 171–201.
Dovidio, J., Piliavin, J., Gaertner, S., Schroeder, D., & Clark, R. III. 1991. The arousal: cost–reward model and the process of intervention: a review of the evidence. In Clark, M. S. (Ed.) *Review of personality and social psychology, Vol. 12, Prosocial behavior*, Sage: Newbury Park, CA: 86–118.
Eccles, R. G., Ioannou, I., & Serafeim, G. 2014. The impact of corporate sustainability on organizational processes and performance. Management Science, 60(11): 2835–2857.
Erickson, J. 2012, January 6. Top 10 U.S. government investments in 20th century American competitiveness. *Center for American Progress*. Available at: www.americanprogress.org/issues/economy/reports/2012/01/06/10930/top-10-u-s-government-investments-in-20th-century-american-competitiveness/. Accessed January 27, 2022.
Feddersen, T. J., & Gilligan, T. W. 2001. Saints and markets: Activists and the supply of credence goods. Journal of Economics & Management Strategy, 10(1): 149–171.
Freeman, R. E. 1984. *Strategic management: A stakeholder approach*. Pitman: Boston, MA.
Freeman, R. E., & Phillips, R. A. 2002. Stakeholder theory: A libertarian defense. Business Ethics Quarterly, 12(3): 331–349.
Frooman, J. 1999. Stakeholder influence strategies. Academy of Management Review, 24(2): 191–205.
Goffman, E. 1974. *Frame analysis: An essay on the organization of experience*. Northeastern University Press: Boston, MA.
Harrison, J. S., Bosse, D. A., & Phillips, R. A. 2010. Managing for stakeholders, stakeholder utility functions, and competitive advantage. Strategic Management Journal, 31(1): 58–74.
Henley, J. 2021, January 13. Estonian government collapses over corruption investigation. *The Guardian*. Available at: www.theguardian.com/world/2021/jan/13/estonian-government-collapses-over-corruption-investigation. Accessed January 27, 2022.
Henriques, I., & Sadorsky, P. 2008. Voluntary environmental programs: A Canadian perspective. The Policy Studies Journal, 36(1): 143–166.

Hobbes, T. 1968. *Leviathan*. Penguin Books: Baltimore, MD.

Husted, B. W. 2002. Culture and international anti-corruption agreements in Latin America. Journal of Business Ethics, 37(4): 413–422.

IPCC 2018. Special Report: Global warming of 1.5°C. World Meteorological Organization, United Nations: Geneva, Switzerland.

Ivanova, K. 2007. Corruption, illegal trade, and compliance with the Montreal protocol. Environmental Resource Economics, 38(4): 475–496.

Jaffe, A. B., Peterson, S. R., & Portney, P. R. 1995. Environmental regulation and the competitiveness of US manufacturing: What does the evidence tell us? Journal of Economic Literature, 33: 132–163.

Khanna, M. 2001. Non-mandatory approaches to environmental protection. Journal of Economic Surveys, 15(3): 291–324.

King, A., Lenox, M. J., & Terlaak, A. K. 2005. The strategic use of decentralized institutions: exploring certification with the ISO 14001 management standard. Academy of Management Journal, 48(6): 1091–1106.

King, A. & Pucker, K. P. 2021. The dangerous allure of win–win strategies. Stanford Social Innovation Review, Winter 2021: 35–39.

King, B. G. 2008a. A political mediation model of corporate response to social movement activism. Administrative Science Quarterly, 53(3): 395–421.

King, B. G. 2008b. A social movement perspective of stakeholder collective action and influence. Business & Society, 47(1): 21–49.

King, B. G., & McDonnell, M. H. 2011, November 21. Case study–Delta Airlines boycott. *Financial Times*.

King, B. G., & Soule, S. 2007. Social movements as extra-institutional entrepreneurs: The effect of protests on stock price returns. Administrative Science Quarterly, 52(3): 413–442.

Koontz, T. M., Steelman, T. A., Carmin, J., Korfmacher, K. S., Moseley, C., & Thomas, C. W. 2004. Collaborative environmental management: What roles for government? Resources for the Future: Washington, D.C.

Kourula, A., Moon, J., Salles-Djelic, M.-L., & Wickert, C. 2019. New roles of government in the governance of business conduct: Implications for management and organizational research. Organization Studies, 40(8): 1101–1123.

Mahoney, J. T., & Qian, L. 2013. Market frictions as building blocks of an organizational economics approach to strategic management. Strategic Management Journal, 34(9): 1019–1041.

Mazzucato, M. 2015. The entrepreneurial state: Debunking public vs private sector myths. Public Affairs: New York.

Melgan, N., Piani, G., & Rossi, M. 2009. Are there differences between perception of corruption at public and private sector? A multi-country analysis. Working Paper 01/09, Department of Economics, University of the Republic, Uruguay.

Mintzberg, H. 1983. *Power in and around organizations*. Prentice-Hall: Englewood Cliffs, N.J.

Mitchell, R. K., Agle, B. R., & Wood, D. J. 1997. Toward a theory of stakeholder identification and salience: Defining the principle of who and what really counts. Academy of Management Review, 22(4): 853–886.

Montiel, I., Husted, B. W., & Christmann, P. 2012. Using private management standard certification to reduce information asymmetries in corrupt environments. Strategic Management Journal, 33(9): 1103–1113.

Morgenstern, R. D., & Pizer, W. A. 2007. Reality check: The nature and performance of voluntary environmental programs in the United States, Europe, and Japan. Resources for the Future: Washington, D.C.

North, D. C. 1984. Government and the cost of exchange in history. The Journal of Economic History, 44(2): 255–264.

Nozick, R. 2013. *Anarchy, state, and utopia*. Basic Books: New York.

Organization of American States (OAS) 1996. Inter- American Convention against Corruption. Available at: www.oas.org/en/sla/dil/inter_american_treaties_b-58_against_corruption.asp. Accessed January 27, 2022.

Organization of Economic Cooperation and Development (OECD) 1997, December 17. Convention on Combating Bribery of Foreign Public Officials in International Business Transactions. Available at: www.oecd.org/corruption/oecdantibriberyconvention.htm. Accessed January 27, 2022.

Orts, E. W., & Strudler, A. 2002. The ethical and environmental limits of stakeholder theory. Business Ethics Quarterly, 12(2): 215–233.

Paton, B. 2000. Voluntary environmental initiatives and sustainable industry. Business Strategy & the Environment, 9: 328–38.

Pedersen, E., Lüdeke-Freund, F., Henriques, I., & Seitanidi, M. M. 2021. Toward collaborative cross-sector business models for sustainability. Business & Society, 60(5): 1039–1058.

Polanyi, K. 1944. *The great transformation: The political and economic origins of our time*. Beacon: Boston, MA.

Porter, M.E. 1991. America's green strategy. Scientific American, 264: 168.

Rittel, H. W. J., & Webber, M. M. 1973. Dilemmas in a general theory of planning. Policy Sciences, 4(2): 155–169.

Ronald Reagan Presidential Foundation & Institute. 1981. 1981 Inaugural Address. Available at: https://www.reaganfoundation.org/programs-events/webcasts-and-podcasts/podcasts/words-to-live-by/1981-inaugural-address/. Accessed January 27, 2022.

Roth, A. 2021, June 29. Russian police raid journalists probing government corruption. *The Guardian*. Available at: www.theguardian.com/world/2021/jun/29/russian-police-raid-proekt-journalists-probing-government-corruption. Accessed January 27, 2022.

Rowley, T. J. 1997. Moving beyond dyadic ties: A network theory of stakeholder influences. Academy of Management Review, 22(4): 887–910.

Rowley, T., & Berman, S. 2000. A brand-new brand of corporate social performance. Business & Society, 39(4): 397–418.

Sharma, S., & Henriques, I. 2005. Stakeholder influences on sustainability practices in the Canadian forest products industry. Strategic Management Journal, 26(2): 159–180.

Stueck, W. 2001, January 25. British investor pulls Interfor stake. *The Globe and Mail*. B5.

Transparency International 2003. Global Corruption Report. Available at: www.transparency.org/en/publications/global-corruption-report-2003-access-to-information. Accessed January 27, 2022.

Webb, K. 2004. *Voluntary codes: private governance, the public interest and innovation*. Carleton Research Unit for Innovation, Science and Environment: Ottawa, Canada.

Zietsma, C., & Winn, M. I. 2008. Building chains and directing flows: Strategies and tactics of mutual influence in stakeholder conflicts. Business & Society, 47(1): 68–101.

9. Learning to lean on Leviathan

After decades of extensive implementation and expansion of corporate sustainability programs, sustainability remains the central challenge facing society. Given the shortcomings now apparent in free-market sustainability solutions, we must look beyond the business case if we hope to overcome the wicked problems we still face. We must better incorporate formal government regulation warts and all.

In the previous chapter, we discussed the widespread beliefs framing government as the problem for sustainability challenges rather than as the solution. These beliefs include government's cost and inefficiency, corruption, the notion that a firm's voluntary efforts are sufficient, and that stakeholder pressures consistently change firm behaviors. In this closing chapter, we challenge these beliefs and argue that the solution to our sustainability challenges is not to minimize government but to improve its function. As Lazarus (2020) put it: "We can disagree on where the lines may fall at any particular moment, and that's fine. But we'll be better off, and safer, and healthier, if we get past this childish idea that government authority is by definition a bad thing." To that end, we outline a research agenda that can enable the corporate sustainability literature to better draw the line between over- and under-regulation.

1 WHY GOVERNMENT IS NOT THE PROBLEM FOR SUSTAINABILITY

The centralized power of government can be frightening, especially in a country like the United States that has a penchant for rugged individualism. But the costs of government intervention have been overstated relative to sustainability, as have the relative benefits of self-regulation. We next counter the arguments against substantive government involvement in corporate sustainability that were proffered in the prior chapter.

1.1 Government Regulation can be Efficient and Effective

Sure, governments can screw things up. But regulation can also be designed effectively; the key is in aligning incentives for public good production. North (1990) argued that the institutional environment determines the formal and informal rules of the game by placing constraints on human action and reducing uncertainty. In this environment, government is a critical actor and its regulatory toolkit—which includes taxation and the ability to create tradable markets—is particularly effective in aligning private action with public goals.

Government regulation has been effectively used to address environmental problems and could be applied to many other issues. Take the case of income inequality. Goal 10 of the UN Sustainable Development Goals (SDGs) established targets to reduce inequality within and among countries. Income inequality is of vital importance to both economic prosperity and social sustainability (Stymne & Jackson, 2000). Shiller (2003) even argues that increasing income inequality is one of the greatest sources of financial risk for the twenty-first century. Risks include impacts on health (Lynch et al., 2001; Pham-Kanter, 2009; Wilkinson, 2006; Wilkinson & Pickett, 2008), social unrest (Sen, 1995), crime (Bourguignon, 2000; Fajnzylber, Lederman & Loayza, 2002; Kelly, 2000), and environmental degradation (Islam, 2015; Kasuga & Takaya, 2017; Mahedi, Binti, Banna & Saifullah, 2018; Ridzuan, 2019; Torras & Boyce, 1998; Uzar & Eyuboglu, 2019).

Despite increasing academic and popular interest, issues of income inequality are largely analyzed at a societal level, rather than at firm level. Analogous to efforts in controlling environmental pollution, the failure to recognize the contribution of specific firms and organizations to the generation of income inequality has led to "end-of-pipe" solutions, where an unequal distribution created by firm-level decisions must be resolved by government authorities through the redistribution of income and wealth. Government policy usually involves fiscal policy (e.g., progressive personal income taxation) as well as subsidies to improve access to health and education opportunities for the very poor. Unfortunately, these approaches fail to isolate the responsibility of individual firms. Instead, firms operate in a kind of tragedy of the common environment by exploiting levels of labor income inequality—the most important component of income inequality—without regard to its impact on the overall system. The key is to price income inequality, because without it, firms lack any incentive to set compensation to achieve socially desirable levels of income inequality.

Aligning incentives through a market for "social bads" (negative externalities like income inequality) entails setting an overall income inequality reduction target for a relevant population of firms. This population could be at the national, state, county, or other levels. The population target is set by the governmental authority and should be determined through scientific research to establish the desirable level of income inequality, given its impact on economic growth, health, violence, and the environment, among other factors (Kasuga & Takaya, 2017; Ridzuan, 2019; Shiller, 2003; Torras & Boyce, 1998; Uzar & Eyuboglu, 2019; Wilkinson, 2006; Wilkinson & Pickett, 2008).

The government could require each firm to comply with its income inequality reduction target. However, given firm heterogeneity, it may be cheaper for some firms to buy income inequality allowances from other firms that have a comparative advantage in reducing income inequality. Moreover, firm income inequality is more likely to enhance firm profitability in owner-controlled or owner-managed firms than in manager-controlled firms (Fong, Misangyi & Tosi, 2010), which means that firms with comparable decreases in inequality may find it more costly, given the reduced profits and increased turnover. Therefore, each firm must estimate its own marginal income reduction cost curve to determine an appropriate target.

Should a firm not meet their income inequality target, they will be obligated to buy income inequality certificates from firms contributing less income inequality to the population (national or local) than their target requires. This market for income inequality certificates will ultimately generate incentives for firms to reduce their own levels of income inequality to the extent that they can generate revenue streams through the sale of income inequality certificates.

Overall, markets for social bads (negative externalities) provide a way for societies to put a price on the social costs that firms are generating and to value intangible public goods like biodiversity. As Haque writes (2008): "And so when we capitalize rainforests, endangered species, community, the foregone opportunities of the poor, our own well-being – then they will finally have value: they can finally be priced, and so the fat-cats of the world won't be free to destroy them with impunity." In a capitalist society, value is determined in markets, and what we value is what we will preserve. Whether equitable income distributions or linguistic diversity, markets can attach value to these public goods.

In the same way that it creates efficient and effective markets to overcome income inequality, regulation can also create markets designed to achieve other sustainability outcomes. The advantage of this kind of approach is that it does not require firms to make structural changes to comply with public targets if it is not in their best interest. The markets may simply choose to reward those firms that do make necessary changes to foster and support a more equitable and sustainable world. In other words, government intervention can be efficient and effective—but we must let it act.

1.2 Government Corruption can be Controlled

The issue of government corruption is a weak link in our argument for a stronger role for government. Corruption can undermine the ability of governments to effectively regulate markets in favor of social equity and environmental quality. If corrupt, government intervention only amplifies these problems. Achieving a sustainable planet thus requires attention to institutional weakness. As Rodriguez, Uhlenbruck, and Eden (2005: 383) note, "corruption is everywhere, to be sure, but it is not the same everywhere … corruption varies across countries as much as labor costs or corporate tax rates." The answer, therefore, is not less governance, but *better* governance. Stronger institutions are needed. Business must play its role in strengthening institutions by paying taxes, staying out of self-serving politics, and letting government set standards.

Paying taxes is how organizations can distribute value to society and government (Lepak, Smith & Taylor, 2007). Ideally, taxation revenues allow the state to promote the development of human capital through education and health as well as enabling social safety nets designed to protect citizens against adverse shifts in their material well-being. Such actions allow for upward mobility by preventing long-term disadvantages stemming from poverty and income shortfalls (DiPrete & McManus, 2000; Kenworthy, 1999). That is, tax revenue allows the state to develop human capital and determine the conditions necessary for firms to create and appropriate value.

Although governments seek a share of the retained earnings through various forms of taxation, firms often resist these attempts to achieve a favorable tax regime. For example, research has found that firms devoting resources to tax lobbying accrue considerable benefits in terms of their effective tax rates (Richter, Samphantharek & Timmons, 2009). When tax systems are biased by exemptions targeted at the rich, the tax base and progressivity may shrink, increasing income inequality (Gupta, Davoodi & Alonso-Terme, 2002).

Clearly, firms need to resist the impulse to lobby tax policy. As Reich (1998: 16) argued, corporations have "a social responsibility to refrain from politics." Corporate sustainability must therefore involve efforts to strengthen institutions by respecting government decisions and staying out of politics since, to some extent, we make institutions strong by respecting them.

Government can also play an essential role in helping corporations prioritize environmental problems. By setting reporting standards, government can establish a common lens through which stakeholders can evaluate corporations. This can help fix broken links within virtuous markets, enabling stakeholders to be more consistent in rewarding good and punishing bad corporate behaviors. At present, the International Financial Reporting Standards have enhanced market exchange by ensuring that financial statements are consistent, transparent, and comparable around the world (Cuadrado-Ballesteros, Martínez-Ferrero & García-Sánchez, 2017), suggesting that the implementation of an International Environmental Reporting Standard attributed to science-based targets can do the same.

1.3 Voluntary Corporate Initiatives are Insufficient

The environmental management literature suggests that participation in voluntary environmental programs (VEPs) provides a variety of benefits to firms, such as relief from existing environmental regulation (like a burdensome tax), the preemption of regulatory threats, influencing future regulations (Alberini & Segerson, 2002; Henriques & Sadorsky, 1996; Khanna & Anton, 2002; Lyon & Maxwell, 2002), cost-efficiency (Hart & Ahuja, 1996), improved stakeholder relations (Arora & Cason, 1999; Henriques & Sadorsky, 1996, 1999), and the possibility of receiving technical assistance. Hence, firms are motivated to undertake these programs to increase their internal efficiency and external legitimacy, which can lead to competitive advantage and shareholder value creation (Hart, 1995; Hart & Milstein, 2003).

Many sustainability problems, however, involve uncertain and disagreeable time frames. Although a manager may be able to define, say, corporate carbon emission targets for the firm, the outcome of such efforts may not be apparent or visible to stakeholders. Given the complex nature of climate change, the participation of all emitters is required for there to be any improvements in the damaged ecosystem (Pogutz, Micale & Winn, 2011). But a manager's tendency toward risk avoidance (Cyert & March, 1963) means that such problems are not prioritized, since it is difficult to demonstrate certain, direct, and timely returns to the firm.

Others may see the strategic benefit in circumventing future environmental regulation (Henriques & Sadorsky, 1996) and choose to adopt a VEP (such as ISO 14001) or join forces with their trade association's environmental management program (e.g., Chemical Industry's Responsible Care Program). But these approaches may fail to protect the environment. Henriques, Husted and Montiel (2013) argue that the provision of environmental protection has two salient properties. The first arises once an investment is made and ensures that the benefits of said investment are non-excludable for all stakeholders. For example, if firm A were to change its processes to improve air quality, everyone benefits, including competitors. Second, the consumption of the benefits (e.g., improved air quality) by a firm does not affect the consumption of other firms—that is, it is non-rival. Given the existence of these two characteristics, one would predict that the private provision of environmental protection would be undersupplied (McNutt, 2002). Because firm B cannot be excluded from securing the environmental benefits supplied by firm A, there is no incentive for firm B to pay the costs of undertaking such an investment. Environmental protection is, therefore, a public good whose benefits are both non-excludable and non-rival. Consequently, private provision (i.e., the market) will not be sufficient to meet demand—a market failure.

A well-designed and certifiable VEP can overcome the problem of asymmetric information by creating a brand that credibly signals the environmental stewardship of participating firms, which stakeholders are otherwise unable to assess, and thereby confers on participants a valuable intangible asset (Conroy, 2007; Klein & Leffler, 1981). Certified firms capture benefits from the program's certification (e.g., its reputation, the development of environmental management resources and capabilities, and improved environmental conduct), and they also become distinguishable from non-certifiers. Unfortunately, poorly designed programs can create problems of adverse selection and attract firms that engage in greenwashing and free-riding (Delmas & Montes-Sancho, 2010).

VEPs have significantly different impacts in reducing targeted and untargeted emissions. Managers, VEP sponsors, and policymakers should be aware of what leads to these differences—specifically, differences in environmental performance and design attributes—when developing or adopting such programs. Due to these issues, VEPs cannot be counted on to solve environmental problems. Governments are slowly realizing this and taking on leadership roles when partnering with the private sector to address societal issues (Kourula et al., 2019).

1.4 Stakeholder Pressures are Insufficient to Change Firm Behavior

Though stakeholders now voice greater concern for social and environmental performance (Dawkins and Lewis, 2003), their bark often proves worse than their bite. Consider consumers: they widely prefer firms that engage in sustainable business practices, but the vast majority will not follow through on their preferences if it requires any significant cost for them to do so (Vogel, 2007). Whelan and Fink (2016) estimate that consumers are only willing to pay up to a 20 percent price premium for sustainable products.

The void between consumer claims and actions is so large that some scholars believe consumer actions to promote corporate social and environmental responsibility are a myth (Devinney, Auger & Eckhardt, 2010). Harrison and Wicks (2013: 111) argue: "While stakeholders through their cooperation in firms will want to improve society and not harm the environment, it isn't clear the extent to which they will do so in their capacity as stakeholders." For example, new recruits may be more attracted to and accept lower pay from a company with a good reputation for CSR (Turban & Greening, 1997), but there is no hard evidence as to the percentage of the labor pool that willingly does this. Employees may indicate a preference to work for clean firms, but their employers are more likely to keep them satisfied by increasing employee pay and benefits than by reducing emissions. Thus, sustainability issues "are not clearly or directly tied to value creation for stakeholders and the utility they seek in the firm" (Harrison & Wicks, 2013: 111).

Stakeholders may also fail to promote sustainable options or make strong sustainability demands. Further, industries that produce products higher up the value chain can avoid stakeholder pressures altogether if their detrimental activities are not visible to the end consumer. Doonan, Lanoie, and Laplante (2005: 82) found in their study of the Canadian pulp and paper industry that "capital markets and consumer markets did not appear as statistically significant sources of pressure" insofar as environmental performance was concerned and that the most important source of pressure was government. Moreover, industry resistance to improving environmental practices can be bolstered by union and employee fears that environmental efforts may negatively impact competitiveness and thereby threaten their jobs (Räthzel & Uzzell, 2011).

Nonetheless, sustainability is an actionable concern to at least some stakeholders, including those whose demands may be powerful, legitimate, and urgent. But cognitive constraints forge a gap between the occurrence of sustainability problems and their demands for firms to act, even for the most actionable stakeholders. As Barnett (2014: 695) notes, "Whether primary or secondary, legitimate or illegitimate, powerful or weak, a stakeholder is constrained by limited attention." This binding constraint means that stakeholders, no matter how concerned with sustainability issues, will overlook a significant portion of the socially and environmentally destructive behaviors of firms. Gao and Bansal's (2013: 251) claim that "in most issue domains, stakeholders are unaware of relatively small improvements in a firm's social and environmental management, partly because the firm's operations are not completely transparent and partly because such small improvements are difficult to measure" further widens this gap. Firms' sustainability programs can be slow to produce substantial change. If the small changes along the way are unlikely to be noticed and rewarded by stakeholders, firms may be even less likely to undertake the costly and lengthy burden. As are many managers and their firms (Laverty, 1996), stakeholders are myopic, favoring near-term gains over distant potential (March, 1991).

The actions firms undertake to appease stakeholder demands for sustainability may prove inadequate to abate such wicked problems. Again, consider climate change. There is no direct link between stakeholder demands and the total amount of climate change mitigation that individual firms must provide. Moreover, stakeholder management does not provide a mechanism for coordinating action across unrelated firms. For example, there may be no relationship between Mexican beverage company FEMSA and Oneida Silver, a manufacturing company in the U.S., yet if both firms need to reduce greenhouse gas emissions, how do they coordinate their reductions? When has each one done enough? The bargaining problem across firms can be unmanageable.

Firms develop an incentive to reduce efforts in abating climate change whenever competition is involved, enabling them to instead focus on gaining a competitive advantage with respect to firms that do more. Heterogeneous stakeholders have little interest in or ability to punish unrelated and distant climate change laggards. The firm's ability to reason when faced with self-interested, myopic, and heterogeneous demands is further distorted by media where "the economic and ideological interests of those who stand to lose in the face of climate change solutions have tremendous power to sway public debate that is marked by low scientific literacy, expanding sources of information, and a fractured and conflicted world of 24-hour news cycles" (Hoffman, 2015: 47).

Sustainability is also an intergenerational dilemma, meaning that time is not on our side. These kinds of dilemmas are defined as "decisions that entail a tradeoff between one's own self-interest in the present and the interests of other people in the future" (Wade-Benzoni & Tost, 2009: 165). Decisions to ignore climate change, for example, affect other people in the future. An intergenerational perspective broadens the definition of economic interests to include multiple parties across time (Wade-Benzoni, 1999). Wade-Benzoni and Tost (2009) argue that intergenerational reciprocity, uncertainty, and legacy creation can help reduce both the intertemporal and interpersonal distances that tend to increase intertemporal and social discounting of the future. More specifically, where prior generations pass on benefits to future ones based on how well they were treated previously, where the uncertain outcome suggests that future generations may receive nothing, and where the generation's legacy becomes a great burden for future generations, there will be a greater intergenerational beneficence or generosity (Wade-Benzoni, Sondak & Galinsky, 2010). However, the question remains: Who has the hindsight and foresight to take on this intergenerational analysis? Given that stakeholders tend to be self-interested, myopic, and heterogeneous, it is unlikely that an intergenerational dilemma such as climate change can be addressed by firms, customers, employees, investors, communities, or suppliers; however, the government certainly can.

2 GOVERNMENT AS THE SOLUTION: A RESEARCH AGENDA

Government need not be the problem. As we have just explained, government can efficiently and effectively facilitate corporate sustainability, goading and guiding firms toward substantive solutions that will not arise in the absence of meaningful government intervention. Given the systemic nature of the wicked problems that sustainability presents, government is needed to facilitate cooperation across actors. Government reduces the bargaining costs between individual firms and is the most cost-effective way of enabling an entire economy to become sustainable. Governments can establish clear standards for sustainability so that firms meet acceptable minimum standards. If they want to go beyond those minimums, then firms have an opportunity to develop a competitive strategy based on sustainability. Finally, governments can act for the long term, unhindered by the usual pressure on public firms for quarterly profits. Profits may sometimes coincide with the needs of future generations, but when they collide, governments can align them.

However, government can also be a burden that misdirects incentives and harms corporate sustainability. In this section, we outline a research agenda to help find the most effective means of government intervention to maximize the benefits of corporate sustainability. Recent studies have begun to model the natural environment as a constrained resource. That's a start. But developing strategies to buffer firms from the risks associated with ecological constraints is not enough. Even developing plans to reduce or eliminate the damage that firms cause to the natural environment is not enough to achieve sustainability (Barnett et al., 2018). To address our planet's urgent sustainability issues, firms must treat all their environments not as exogenous, but as key parts of an essential and vulnerable system that they are responsible for sustaining.

Because sustainability is achieved at the level of the system while firms are only part of the subsystem of users (Ostrom, 2009; Young et al., 2006), firms too easily ignore their role in resolving this larger problem. Rather than perfecting constrained optimization, firms must instead seek to understand and manage their interdependencies within the social-ecological system in which they are embedded (Williams et al., 2017). For example, climate change, caused in large part by economic activity, has led to devastating forest fires in California, Australia, and elsewhere. Firms must do more than develop plans to safeguard and insure against the risks they now face from such events. They must understand how their activities contribute to these events and develop plans to counter the climate change that drives them.

Profitable firms and a roaring economy are not sustainable if they lead to global pandemics, irreversible climate change (Lenton et al., 2019), or worse. Of course, not every short-sighted firm action leads to global devastation. Applying Rittel and Webber's (1973) distinction between "tame" and "wicked" problems, we define tame sustainability problems as those possessing scientific protocols that are associated with a system of components and outcomes possessing a low uncertainty, can guide solutions, are confined to one area, and remain unchanged across time. In contrast, wicked sustainability problems (such as climate change and biodiversity loss) possess none of those agreed-upon scientific protocols (Barnett, et al., 2018; Batie, 2008).

Firms may pursue strategies in which they respond to either type of sustainability problem with a solution that addresses the firm or the system level. For example, a firm could address the problem of income inequality—a wicked problem—by increasing its employee pay scale—a firm-level solution—or it could act on a system-level solution, such as lobbying state or federal governments to increase the minimum wage (Grant, 2013). To the extent that problems reach across generations and are systemic in nature, the role of government in coordinating solutions becomes key.

In Barnett, Henriques, and Husted's (2021) framework, we set the type of problem and solution level as determinants to identify four sustainability strategies and corresponding research agendas that populate the quadrants of Figure 9.1. We next examine each quadrant and discuss how researchers might find an equilibrium between over- and under-regulation. The evidence for both market failure and regulatory failure is clear. Hence, we need a point of balance between over- and under-regulation so that both the private sector and the public sector may effectively work together.

Type of Problem	Level of Solution	
	Firm	**Social-ecological System**
Tame	*Calculative* → Firm-level calculation (e.g., local cost–benefit analysis) **1**	*Cooperative* Compromise – government and firm **2**
Wicked	**3** *Concerned* → Within-firm learning; create shared value to benefit firm but unable to find solutions	**4** *Co-creative* Co-creation/collaboration/co-learning with multiple actors such as government, universities, health facilities, NGOs, Indigenous communities

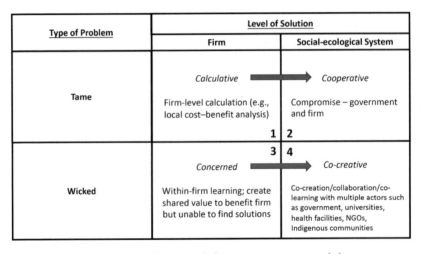

Figure 9.1 *A research framework for corporate sustainability*

The Calculative strategy (Quadrant 1) is common in practice and represents the business case for sustainability, seeking ways to profit from the implementation of sustainable business practices. For example, a firm may implement a "paperless office" practice that reduces its consumption of paper products, thereby helping to lessen the deforestation needed to supply paper while also saving the firm the costs of buying paper. Firms using this strategy recognize that their activities cause harm and that they can create post-hoc solutions when the associated problems are tame. However, firms only act when it pays to do so. Since it is not feasible for firms to capture benefits that accrue to the system, calculations are confined to the firm level.

In this quadrant, government does not need to facilitate coordination, but regulation helps to ensure that each firm meets the required minimum. Local governments may play a particularly important role in making sure that tame problems do not become wicked. For example, suppose there is a lake that has five polluters. These polluters may face a threshold over which they cannot pollute. However, as the number of polluters increase or the lake conditions change, it is imperative that government and its scientists evaluate the sustainability of the watershed so that the problem remains tame. Here, the government acts as a steward as well as a regulator. In the latter case, command-and-control regulation can be useful to assure compliance with minimum environmental emissions standards. Potential fines can help firms recalculate the costs and benefits of compliance.

In the Cooperative strategy shown in Quadrant 2, the problems remain tame, but the firm develops solutions that account for the affected system and stakeholders, thereby increasing the solution's ability to mitigate the damage or restore the system to its original state. These solutions may require the firm to organize agreements with other firms, NGOs, or governmental agencies. Examples include global, sectoral, and regional voluntary environmental programs to address environmental issues (Prakash & Potoski, 2012), such as the Responsible Care program developed by the chemical industry (Li, Khanna & Vidovic, 2018), and certification standards such as ISO 14001 (Arimura, Darnall & Katayama, 2011) and energy efficiency certifications (Delmas & Pekovic, 2015).

When these voluntary programs are enhanced with government sanctions for failure to comply with the program, their effectiveness increases (Henriques et al., 2013). However, the literature currently lacks clear guidance on how to achieve the right balance between self-determined industry standards and government-supported sanctions. Furthermore, the institutional context in which such cooperative strategy programs operate vary considerably. Corruption, for example, can differ significantly at the local level within the same country (Montiel, Husted & Christmann, 2012), thus impacting the effectiveness of some VEPs. Thus, researchers must pay attention to the contours of the institutional context and recognize the link between government effectiveness and VEPs.

Firms attempting to address wicked problems at the firm level use what we call a Concerned strategy (Quadrant 3). Though corporate concern for wicked problems represents a sustainability advancement in the Calculative strategy, decisions about which problems to pursue remain in the firm's favor. Firms seldom have both the desire and ability to assess the impact of their social interventions on their targets. Thus, the Concerned strategy often collapses into concern for the firm, which, as revealed in practice and academic research, fails to achieve environmental and societal impact (Barnett et al. 2020). For example, Royal Dutch Shell sought to invest in more renewable energy sources and move its core businesses from hydrocarbons to electrons. However, just weeks prior to announcing its strategy to become a net zero emissions business, a number of Shell executives responsible for leading the clean energy transition quit due to deep divisions over the time frame for reducing the company's dependence on oil and gas revenues (Raval & Hook, 2020).

Research must go beyond analyzing firm-level impacts of corporate sustainability programs to determine what difference such programs make in resolving social and environmental problems. Even with good intentions, the intractability of wicked problems suggests that firm-level solutions are symbolic at best or greenwashing at worst. Firms tend to deflect, deny, and blame others for wicked sustainability problems while lobbying the government to not impose or to reduce regulation (Duchon & Drake, 2009). Governments, particularly local governments, may therefore play an important role in coordinating local firm initiatives, avoiding spillovers from one jurisdiction to another (Sigman, 2005), and providing a propitious local environment for corporate action through programs such as local education and green municipal purchasing (Kern & Alber, 2009; Leal, Perez-Castillo, Amorós & Husted, 2020). Identifying and appreciating the role of local governments as they relate to private firms is particularly important for business scholars, who tend to collapse governments into a single black box.

Finally, in the Co-creative strategy (Quadrant 4), firms may spearhead system-level solutions to wicked sustainability problems. Using this strategy, firms acknowledge that problems involve many stakeholders with differing values and priorities who possess complex and tangled roots dispersed amongst a host of actors and across borders, meaning these problems cannot be resolved by a singular actor with a singular solution. Thus, solutions must entail complex interactions among different sectors with a focus on "understanding connections, synergies and trade-offs" among different sustainability goals (Liu, et al., 2018: 466). Unfortunately, the sort of nexus-thinking required to implement such a strategy has been found to be embryonic at best among firms (Dahlmann & Bullock, 2020).

Ultimately, governments must play a leadership role in working with all relevant actors to develop and coordinate solutions to wicked problems in this quadrant. As Blackrock's former chief investment officer for sustainability, Tariq Fancy (2021), wrote: "... one lesson COVID-19 has hammered home is that systemic problems – such as a global pandemic or climate change – require systemic solutions. Only governments have the wide-ranging powers, resources and responsibilities that need to be brought to bear on the problem … The vast majority of our work at BlackRock helped the bottom line, but showed no demonstrable positive impact on society." There is a significant need for work focused on the creation of effective models of stakeholder collaboration toward system solutions. What role should governments play in helping firms spearhead system-level solutions? Who should be at the table? What type of relationship is best for co-creating the knowledge necessary to bridge the social, environmental, and economic tensions that such collaborations entail? These are the issues that need to be studied in the co-creative strategy quadrant.

This simple two-by-two typology opens a myriad of directions for future research. We have mentioned some of the possibilities relevant to each quadrant. As indicated by the thick arrows between quadrants, there are also important opportunities for scholars as they determine the conditions under which firms begin to recognize the systemic nature of problems and solutions and seek to transition between these positions. As we have noted throughout this book, we are bumping into physical limits that will constrain the ability of firms to pursue limitless economic growth. Even putatively "green products" such as windmills and electric cars have serious negative impacts on the environment. Thus, the concept of the limits to growth and the importance of what is sufficient will become key to operating within material limits. As Dhara and Singh (2021) ask: "The real question is this: how do we transition to alternative economic paradigms founded on the reconciliation of equitable human well-being with ecological integrity?" Thus, more research on business models is needed if we hope to successfully implement this transition—a transition where government sets the rules of the game for all actors. Scholars will need to study business models that generate profits by using fewer material resources at the environmental level. They will need to construct a business case for non-consumption and zero, if not negative, growth!

Firms are naturally inclined toward firm-level solutions. The reluctance to move from the firm to the system is evidenced by the need for governments to enter the problem arena frequently and use their powers to mandate collaborative actions through, for example, emissions regulation or prohibitions on overharvesting various natural resources (e.g., fish, forests, etc.). Although the tendency to focus on firm-level problems and solutions is understandable, it highlights the urgent need for business scholars to study what would motivate firms to act with a system-level focus voluntarily and effectively. Furthermore, we need business models that examine cooperative solutions to system-level problems as opposed to competitive models (Christ, Burritt & Varsei, 2017; Nielsen, 1988). How can companies compete for customers and cooperate for the natural environment? As mentioned earlier, even the most common mechanisms developed to date (e.g., certifications and voluntary environmental programs) work best when there is governmental involvement to provide rewards for compliance, such as a temporary inspection moratorium (Henriques et al., 2013). More research is needed on how firms can broaden their thinking and embed themselves in social-ecological systems to co-create collaborative solutions to wicked problems. Why do firms choose to address wicked problems individually and eschew collaborative approaches with government and competitors? A myriad of micro-, macro-, and mezzo-level factors are likely at play and interacting in complex ways that have yet to be uncovered.

A common thread running through each of the quadrants is the role of institutions. In advanced and industrialized democracies, institutions are strong and generally effective. Hence, the solutions are somewhat clearer than in countries with weak institutional contexts. Governments can align the profit-motive of firms with the public good through command-and-control regulation, taxation, and market-based energy markets like the carbon market. Government purchasing can motivate private firms to include sustainability components in their products and services. One can understand the reluctance for heavy-handed regulation, but problems like climate change are clearly getting worse and need more drastic solutions. Given the urgency of the problems, the question for corporate sustainability experts is why these solutions have not worked and produced the results we have hoped for. Why have companies lobbied for less onerous solutions and opposed governments taking more drastic measures? Why have, for example, take-back laws, which require companies to take back their products at the end of their lifecycle, not been supported by industry?

Yet many of the examples raised in this book come from countries where institutions are weak, either because they are incomplete (i.e., institutional voids) or have been captured by elites (Dorobantu, Kaul & Zelner, 2017). The additional challenge for researchers is to understand how corporate sustainability can be effective under conditions of institutional weakness. The key is to ensure that corporate sustainability aligns with the interests of elites. So, the solution to wicked, systemic sustainability problems must ensure that, say, the business case for degrowth also generates benefits for elites. Successful business models will need to reconcile elite interests with sustainability in a four-way bottom line comprised of people, the planet, profits, and power. Such a pragmatic approach may be distasteful for many researchers but may ultimately be the only path to long-term sustainability. Hopefully, researchers will help in envisioning and developing such business models, because doing so may be more feasible than gaining control over the powerful.

Defining the equilibrium where government solutions are enough is a key issue for sustainability scholars. The issue of leveraging Leviathan should be central to corporate sustainability scholars. There appears to be a curvilinear relationship between the level of government participation in the solution and its effectiveness in harnessing all sectors of society—including business—to act sustainably. As Porter and Van der Linde (1995) explain, the right kind and amount of regulation can stimulate innovation for sustainability. However, management scholars need to analyze the interaction between different dosages of regulation and environmental impact as they are mediated by organizational innovation. This will help to find the sweet spot where companies innovate and respond sufficiently to deal with the climate crisis.

The key ideas behind Figure 9.1 are cooperation and collaboration. Clearly, government has the role of convenor, but that role is too often overshadowed by the voices of the private sector and civil societies calling for action. Yet no voice is louder than that of government, should it choose to speak up. Who needs to be invited to the table? What does each person bring to the table? How does one foster a space for co-creation? What can companies, government, and civil society achieve by working together?

A nagging question raised by the typology is where does science fit into sustainability strategies. Traditionally, firms' chief science officers have focused on the science relevant to the industrial processes that a firm may be innovating. However, science officers need to include within their routine duties the role of monitoring emerging issues and assessing how they might affect the ability of the firm to conduct business over time. Many sustainability problems were recognized by scientists much earlier than by private industry (Kowalok, 1993), yet issues such as biodiversity management were more driven by social legitimacy than by a keen scientific awareness. If there were deeper scientific involvement in sustainability strategy, it could help identify sustainability issues before they become sustainability crises (Boiral, Guillaumie, Heras-Saizarbitoria & Brotherton, 2018). We would all be better off if firms saw the smoke and acted to extinguish fires while they are still smoldering rather than facing a fire that has already engulfed an environmental structure. Hence, there is a need to go beyond the specific chemistry or efficacy of firms' products if we are to embrace a wider scope of scientific knowledge in looking at a firm's involvement in and positive influence on social-ecological systems.

3 CONCLUSION

Firms have a variety of incentives to create sustainability programs. But they lack the inclination and means to collaborate in the ways necessary to develop substantive solutions to our existential sustainability problems. A continued reliance on the firm to provide solutions will not be effective in addressing the greatest threat of our day. We need government. Our hope is that this book will open the eyes of strategy researchers, practitioners, government, and NGOs to the problems of the current sustainability approaches and encourage them to work together to address these critical issues. Greta Thunberg at the World Economic Forum in Davos on January 24, 2019 stated: "*I want you to act as if the house is on fire, because it is*." Let's do that. Let's act as if our house is on fire, because it is and has long been, and it may not stand for much longer if the fire is not soon brought under control. And let's work with, not against, Leviathan, to extinguish it.

BIBLIOGRAPHY

Alberini, A., & Segerson, K. 2002. Assessing voluntary programs to improve environmental quality. Environmental and Resource Economics, 22(1–2): 157–184.

Arimura, T. H., Darnall, N., & Katayama, H. 2011. Is ISO 14001 a gateway to more advanced voluntary action? The case of green supply chain management. Journal of Environmental Economics and Management, 61(2): 170–182.

Arora, S., & Cason, T. N. 1999. Do community characteristics influence environmental outcomes? Evidence from the toxic release inventory. Southern Economic Journal, 65(4): 691– 716.

Barnett, M. L. 2014. Why stakeholders ignore firm misconduct: A cognitive view. Journal of Management, 40(3): 676–702.

Barnett, M. L., Henriques, I., & Husted, B. W. 2018. Governing the void between stakeholder management and sustainability. In S. Dorobantu, R. V. Aguilera, J. Luo, & F. J. Milliken (Eds) *Sustainability, stakeholder governance, and corporate social responsibility*. Emerald Group Publishing Ltd: Bingley: 121–143.

Barnett, M. L., Henriques, I., & Husted, B. W. 2020. Beyond good intentions: Designing CSR initiatives for greater social impact. Journal of Management, 46(6): 937–964.

Barnett, M., Henriques, I., & Husted, B. W. 2021. Sustainability strategies. In I. M. Duhaime, M. A. Hitt, & M. A Lyles (Eds) *Strategic management: State of the field and its future.* Oxford University Press: New York: 647–662.

Batie, S. S. 2008. Wicked problems and applied economics. American Journal of Agricultural Economics, 90(5): 1176–1191.

Boiral, O., Guillaumie, L., Heras-Saizarbitoria, I., & Tene, C. V. T. 2018. Adoption and outcomes of ISO 14001: A systematic review. International Journal of Management Reviews, 20(2): 411–432.

Bourguignon, F. 2000, December. Crime, violence and inequitable development. In *Annual World Bank Conference on development economics 1999* (pp. 199–220). World Bank: Washington, D.C.

Christ, K. L., Burritt, R. L., & Varsei, M. 2017. Coopetition as a potential strategy for corporate sustainability. Business Strategy and the Environment, 26(7): 1029–1040.

Conroy, M. E. 2007. *Branded! How the "certification revolution" is transforming global corporations.* New Society Publishers: Gabriola Island, Canada.

Cuadrado-Ballesteros, B., Martínez-Ferrero, J., & García-Sánchez, I. M. 2017. Mitigating information asymmetry through sustainability assurance: The role of accountants and levels of assurance. International Business Review, 26(6): 1141–1156.

Cyert, R. M., & March, J. G. 1963. *A behavioral theory of the firm.* Prentice-Hall: Englewood Cliffs, NJ.

Dahlmann, F., & Bullock, G. 2020. Nexus thinking in business: Analysing corporate responses to interconnected global sustainability challenges. Environmental Science & Policy, 107: 90–98.

Dawkins, J., & Lewis, S. 2003. CSR in stakeholder expectations: and their implication for company strategy. Journal of Business Ethics, 44(2): 185–193.

Delmas, M., & Montes-Sancho, M. 2010. Voluntary agreements to improve environmental quality: Symbolic versus substantive cooperation. Strategic Management Journal, 31: 575–601.

Delmas, M. A., & Pekovic, S. 2015. Resource efficiency strategies and market conditions. Long Range Planning, 48(2): 80–94.

Devinney, T. M., Auger, P., & Eckhardt, G. M. 2010. *The myth of the ethical consumer hardback with DVD*. Cambridge University Press: Cambridge, U.K.

Dhara, C., & Singh, V. 2021, June 20. The delusion of infinite economic growth. Scientific American. Available at: www.scientificamerican.com/article/the-delusion-of-infinite-economic-growth1/#. Accessed June 25, 2021.

DiPrete, T. A., & McManus, P. A. 2000. Family change, employment transitions, and the welfare state: Household income dynamics in the United States and Germany. American Sociological Review, 65(3): 343–370.

Doonan, J., Lanoie, P., & Laplante, B. 2005. Determinants of environmental performance in the Canadian pulp and paper industry: An assessment from inside the industry. Ecological Economics, 55(1): 73–84.

Dorobantu, S., Kaul, A., & Zelner, B. 2017. Nonmarket strategy research through the lens of new institutional economics: An integrative review and future directions. Strategic Management Journal, 38(1): 114–140.

Duchon, D., & Drake, B. 2009. Organizational narcissism and virtuous behavior. Journal of Business Ethics, 85(3): 301–308.

Fajnzylber, P., Lederman, D., & Loayza, N. 2002. Inequality and violent crime. The Journal of Law and Economics, 45(1): 1–39.

Fancy, T. 2021, March, 25. BlackRock hired me to make sustainable investing mainstream. Now I realize it's a deadly distraction from the climate-change threat. *The Globe and Mail*. Available at: www.theglobeandmail.com/business/commentary/article-sustainable-investing-is-a-deadly-distraction-from-actually-averting/. Accessed January 27, 2022.

Fong, E. A., Misangyi, V. F., & Tosi, H. L. 2010. The effect of CEO pay deviations on CEO withdrawal, firm size, and firm profits. Strategic Management Journal, 31(6): 629–651.

Gao, J., & Bansal, P. 2013. Instrumental and integrative logics in business sustainability. Journal of Business Ethics, 112(2): 241–255.

Grant, T. 2013, November 16. How one company levels the pay slopes of executives and co-workers. *Globe and Mail*. Available at: www.theglobeandmail.com/news/national/time-to-lead/how-one-company-levels-the-pay-slope-of-executives-and-workers/article15472738/. Accessed January 27, 2022.

Gupta, S., Davoodi, H., & Alonso-Terme, R. 2002. Does corruption affect income inequality and poverty? Economics of Governance, 3(1): 23–45.

Haque, U. 2008. How to be a 21st century capitalist. Available at: http://discussionleader.hbsp.com/haque/2008/12/ how_to_be_a_21st_century_ capit.html. Accessed June 2, 2009.

Harrison, J. S., & Wicks, A. C. 2013. Stakeholder theory, value, and firm performance. Business Ethics Quarterly, 23(1): 97–124.

Hart, S. L. 1995. A natural resource-based view of the firm. Academy of Management Review, 20(4): 986–1014.

Hart, S. L. 1997. Beyond greening: Strategies for a sustainable world. Harvard Business Review, 75(1): 66–77.

Hart, S. L., & Ahuja, G. 1996. Does it pay to be green? An empirical examination of the relationship between emission reduction and firm performance. Business Strategy and the Environment, 5: 30–37.

Hart, S. L., & Milstein, M. B. 2003. Creating sustainable value. Academy of Management Executive, 17(2): 56–69.

Henriques I., Husted B. W., & Montiel, I. 2013. Spillover effects of voluntary environmental programs on greenhouse gas emissions: Lessons from Mexico. Journal of Policy Analysis and Management, 32(2): 296–322.

Henriques, I. & Sadorsky, P. 1996. The determinants of an environmentally responsive firm: An empirical approach. Journal of Environmental Economics and Management, 30(3): 381–395.

Henriques, I. & Sadorsky, P. 1999. The relationship between environmental commitment and managerial perceptions of stakeholder importance. Academy of Management Journal, 42(1): 87–99.

Hoffman, A. J. 2015. Laudato Si and the role of religion in shaping humanity's response to climate change. Solutions, 6(5): 40–47.

Islam, S. N. 2015. Inequality and environmental sustainability. Available at: www.un.org/sites/un2.un.org/files/1597341726.2653.pdf. Accessed May 25, 2021.

Kasuga, H., & Takaya, M., 2017. Does inequality affect environmental quality? Evidence from major Japanese cities. Journal of Cleaner Production, 142: 3689–3701.

Kelly, M. 2000. Inequality and crime. Review of Economics and Statistics, 82(4): 530–539.

Kenworthy, L. 1999. Do social-welfare policies reduce poverty? A cross-national assessment. Social Forces, 77(3): 1119–1139.

Kern, K., & Alber, G. 2009. Governing climate change in cities: Modes of urban climate governance in multi-level systems. In *The international conference on competitive cities and climate change, Milan, Italy, October 9–10, 2009* (pp. 171–196).

Khanna, M. & Anton, W. R. Q. 2002. Corporate environmental management: Regulatory and market-based incentives. Land Economics, 78: 539–558.

Klein, B., & Leffler, K. B. 1981. The role of market forces in assuring contractual performance. Journal of Political Economics, 89: 615–641.

Kourula, A., Moon, J., Salles-Djelic, M.-L., & Wickert, C. 2019. New roles of government in the governance of business conduct: Implications for management and organizational research. *Organization Studies*, 40(8): 1101–1123.

Kowalok, M. E. 1993. Common threads: Research lessons from acid rain, ozone depletion, and global warming. Environment: Science and Policy for Sustainable Development, 35(6): 12–38.

Laverty, K. J. 1996. Economic "short-termism": The debate, the unresolved issues, and the implications for management practice and research. Academy of Management Review, 21(3): 825–860.

Lazarus, D. 2020, April 28. Reagan was wrong. Government isn't the problem, as the pandemic makes clear. *Los Angeles Times*. Available at: www.latimes.com/business/story/2020-04-28/coronavirus-role-of-government. Accessed January 27, 2022.

Leal, A. R., Perez-Castillo, D., Amorós, J. E. & Husted, B. W. 2020. Municipal green purchasing in Mexico: Policy adoption and implementation success. Sustainability, 12: 8339.

Lenton, T. M., Rockström, J., Gaffney, O., Rahmstorf, S., Richardson, K., Steffen, W., & Schellnhuber, H. J. 2019. Climate tipping points—too risky to bet against. Nature, 575 (7784): 592–595.

Lepak, D. P., Smith, K. G., & Taylor, M. S. 2007. Value creation and value capture: A multilevel perspective. Academy of Management Review, 32(1): 180–194.
Li, H., Khanna, N., & Vidovic, M. 2018. The effects of third-party certification on voluntary self-regulation of accidents in the US chemical industry. Journal of Regulatory Economics, 53(3): 327–356.
Liu, J., Hull, V., Godfray, H. C. J., Tilman, D., Gleick, P., Hoff, H., ... & Li, S. 2018. Nexus approaches to global sustainable development. Nature Sustainability, 1(9): 466–476.
Lynch, J., Smith, G. D., Hillemeier, M., Shaw, M., Raghunathan, T., & Kaplan, G. 2001. Income inequality, the psychosocial environment, and health: Comparisons of wealthy nations. The Lancet, 358(9277): 194–200.
Lyon, T. P., & Maxwell, J. W. 2002. Voluntary approaches to environmental regulation: An overview. In M. Frazini and A. Nicita (Eds) Ashgate Publishing *Economic institutions and environmental policy*: Aldershot, U.K.: 75–120.
Mahedi, M., Binti, F., Banna, H., & Saifullah, K., 2018. Does income inequality affect environmental sustainability? Evidence from the ASEAN-5. Journal of the Asia Pacific Economy, 23(2): 213–228.
March, J. G. 1991. Exploration and exploitation in organizational learning. Organization Science, 2(1): 71–87.
Mazzucato, M. 2015. *The entrepreneurial state: Debunking public vs private sector myths*. Public Affairs: New York.
McNutt, P. 2002. *The economics of public choice II*. Edward Elgar Publishing: Cheltenham, U.K. and Northampton, MA, U.S.A.
Montiel, I., Husted, B. W., & Christmann, P. 2012. Using private management standard certification to reduce information asymmetries in corrupt environments. Strategic Management Journal, 33(9): 1103–1113.
Nielsen, R. P. 1988. Cooperative strategy. Strategic Management Journal, 9(5): 475–492.
North, D. C. 1990. *Institutions, institutional change and economic performance*. Cambridge University Press: Cambridge, U.K.
North, D. C., Wallis, J. J., & Weingast, B. R. 2009. *Violence and social orders: A conceptual framework for interpreting recorded human history*. Cambridge University Press: Cambridge, U.K.
Ostrom, E. 2009. A general framework for analyzing sustainability of social-ecological systems. Science, 325(5939): 419–422.
Pham-Kanter, G. 2009. Social comparisons and health: Can having richer friends and neighbors make you sick? Social Science & Medicine, 69(3): 335–344.
Piketty, T. 2014. *Capital in the twenty-first century*. Harvard University Press: Cambridge, MA.
Pogutz, S., Micale, V., & Winn, M. 2011. Corporate environmental sustainability beyond organizational boundaries: Market growth, ecosystems complexity and supply chain structure as co-determinants of environmental impact. Journal of Environmental Sustainability, 1(1): 4.
Porter, M. E., & Van der Linde, C. 1995. Toward a new conception of the environment–competitiveness relationship. Journal of Economic Perspectives, 9(4): 97–118.
Prakash, A., & Potoski, M. 2012. Voluntary environmental programs: A comparative perspective. Journal of Policy Analysis and Management, 31(1): 123–138.
Räthzel, N., & Uzzell, D. 2011. Trade unions and climate change: The jobs versus environment dilemma. Global Environmental Change, 21(4): 1215–1223.

Raval, A., & Hook, L. 2020, December 8. Shell executives quit amid discord over green push. *Financial Times.* Available at: www.ft.com/content/053663f1-0320-4b83-be31-fefbc49b0efc. Accessed July 12, 2021.

Reich, R. B. 1998. The new meaning of corporate social responsibility. California Management Review, 40(2): 8–17.

Richter, B. K., Samphantharak, K., & Timmons, J. F. 2009. Lobbying and taxes. American Journal of Political Science, 53(4): 893–909.

Ridzuan, S. 2019. Inequality and the environmental Kuznets curve. Journal of Cleaner Production, 228: 1472–1481.

Rittel, H. W. J., & Webber, M. M. 1973. Dilemmas in a general theory of planning. Policy Sciences, 4(2): 155–169.

Rodriguez, P., Uhlenbruck, K., & Eden, L. 2005. Government corruption and the entry strategies of multinationals. Academy of Management Review, 30(2): 383–386.

Sen, A. 1995. *Inequality reexamined.* Harvard University Press: Cambridge, MA.

Shiller, R. J. 2003. *The new financial order: Risk in the 21st century.* Princeton University Press: Princeton, NJ.

Sigman, H. 2005. Transboundary spillovers and decentralization of environmental policies. Journal of Environmental Economics and Management, 50(1): 82–101.

Stymne, S., & Jackson, T. 2000. Intra-generational equity and sustainable welfare: A time series analysis for the UK and Sweden. Ecological Economics, 33: 219–236.

Torras, M., & Boyce, J. K. 1998. Income, inequality, and pollution: A reassessment of the environmental Kuznets curve. Ecological Economics, 25: 147–160.

Turban, D. B., & Greening, D. W. 1997. Corporate social performance and organizational attractiveness to prospective employees. Academy of Management Journal, 40(3): 658–672.

Uzar, U., & Eyuboglu, K., 2019. The nexus between income inequality and CO_2 emissions in Turkey. Journal of Cleaner Production, 227: 149–157.

Vogel, D. 2007. *The market for virtue: The potential and limits of corporate social responsibility.* Brookings Institution Press: Washington, D.C.

Wade-Benzoni, K. A. 1999. Thinking about the future: An intergenerational perspective on the conflict and compatibility between economic and environmental interests. American Behavioral Scientist, 42(8): 1393–1405.

Wade-Benzoni, K. A., Sondak, H., & Galinsky, A. D. 2010. Leaving a legacy: Intergenerational allocations of benefits and burdens. Business Ethics Quarterly, 20(1): 7–34.

Wade-Benzoni, K. A., & Tost, L. P. 2009. The egoism and altruism of intergenerational behavior. Personality and Social Psychology Review, 13(3): 165–193.

Whelan, T., & Fink, C. 2016. The comprehensive business case for sustainability. Harvard Business Review, 21: 2012.

Wilkinson, R. G. 2006. The impact of inequality. Social Research: An International Quarterly, 73(2): 711–732.

Wilkinson, R. G., & Pickett, K. E. 2008. Income inequality and socioeconomic gradients in mortality. American Journal of Public Health, 98(4): 699–704.

Williams, A., Kennedy, S., Philipp, F., & Whiteman, G. 2017. Systems thinking: A review of sustainability management research. Journal of Cleaner Production, 148: 866–881.

Young, O. R., Berkhout, F., Gallopin, C. C., Janssen, M. A., Ostrom, E., & Van der Leeuw, S. 2006. The globalization of socio-ecological systems: An agenda for scientific research. Global Environmental Change, 16(3): 304–316.

Index

absorptive capacity 15
construct 14
Acott, T. G. 67
Adamic, L. A. 89
Agle, B. R. 13, 82
Aguilera, R. V. 59
Aguinis, H. 59
Amazon 43
Anderson, R. 18, 19
Argandoña, A. 45
astroturfing 85, 86

Bakshy, E. 89
Bansal, P. 151
Barnard, C. I. 78
Barnett, M. L. 15, 48, 52, 55, 110, 114–15, 151, 154
Baron, D. P. 83
Beasley, J. W. 85
Benediktsson, M. 113
Berman, S. L. 45, 47
Bettis, R. A. 23
Bhattacharya, C. B. 51, 53
Bismarck, Otto von 37, 38
Black, F. 17
Blowfield, M. 55
boundaries 96–8
Bridgeman, J. 58
business case 2, 6, 9, 13–15, 24, 32, 38, 43, 47–50, 53–4, 64, 68–72, 108, 109
biases of 64–72
consumption and 71–2
long-standing assumption 14–15
mapping 49
for sustainability 15, 68
technological solutions 70–71
thinking 69
"win–win" promise of 108
business conduct 132
business interrelating with government and stakeholders (BiGS) 122
business models 36
business risk 23, 24

calculative strategy 154
call option value 17
Carroll, David 86
Chaudhari, T. 58
"chemophobia" 114
Chong, A. C. Y. 86
Cisco 53
climate change 9
club theory 33
co-creative strategy 156
Coff, R. W. 83
cognition 67, 116
cognitive biases 90
cognitive mechanisms 92
Cohen, W. 14
Concerned strategy 155
consumption 12, 33, 64, 68, 70–72, 131, 149, 154, 157
control of corruption 147–8
Coombs, T. W. 80
cooperative strategy 155
Cornwell, T. 65
corporate citizenship 51
corporate financial performance (CFP) 14, 15
corporate misconduct 108–11, 114, 120
corporate ownership 113
corporate philanthropy 58
corporate policing 111
acting 116–20
assessing 115–16
noticing 111–14
corporate self-governance 6
corporate social initiatives 55
corporate social performance (CSP) 55, 56

corporate social responsibility (CSR)
 14–15, 18, 18, 45, 45, 48, 48, 51,
 53, 53, 55, 55, 56, 57, 57, 58, 58,
 59, 59, 98, 115
corporate sustainability 2–6, 18–24, 30,
 32, 35, 38, 71, 72, 79, 145, 158
 assets 22
 certifiable contributions 32–4
 initiatives 12, 24, 30, 32
 investments 19, 22, 23
 mapping out societal wins 30–32
 opening options 16–19
 option 19–22, 24
 programs 2, 3, 6, 30, 36, 38, 71, 72,
 109, 145, 156
 real option 18, 20, 24
 research framework for 154
 securing safety 19–24
 societal benefits of 31
corruption 114, 122, 131, 133–6, 145,
 147–8, 155
cost–benefit analysis 21
cost–reward analysis 117
"credence goods" 83
CSR logic model 56
Cuellar, M.-F. 136
culpability score 110

deforestation 5
Delmas, M. 12, 32, 33, 57, 70, 134, 150,
 155
Devika, K. 58
Dhara, C. 157
digital activism 94
digital age 78–81, 84, 85, 88, 91–4,
 96–9, 139
 stakeholder influence 86–92
digital detours 78–99
digitization 84
direct influence tactics 48
distant firms 97
Doonan, J. 151
Dowell, G. W. S. 11
Du, S. 51, 53
DuPont 64

Ebrahim, A. 58
The Ecology of Commerce, Paul Hawken
 18
Eden, L. 148
Edmunds, A. 85
Eesley, C. 82
Eisensee, T. 114
electronic vehicles (EVs) 70
Emerson, R. 88
energy management training 11
energy-saving opportunities, firms 11
entrepreneurs 84
environmental attitudes 65–6
environmental issues 23
environmental management models 65
environmental problems 5, 66, 70
 voluntary efforts by companies
 136–8
environmental protection 33
ethical concerns 117
externalizing machines 9
Exxon Valdez incident (1989) 20

Fancy, T. 156
Feddersen, T. J. 83
Figueres, C. 122
"filter bubble" 90
financial gains 4, 14
financial returns 50, 54
Fink, C. 150
firm misconduct 114
firm profitability 47
firms' approaches, conceptual
 classification 10
firm–stakeholder relations 78, 79, 88
Fombrun, C. 115
Freeman, R. E. 44–6, 108, 130, 132
free market 3, 6, 72, 122, 133, 137
free riding 34
Friedman, M. 44
Friedman–Freeman debate 44
Frooman, J. 95, 138, 148

Gao, J. 151
Garcés-Ayerbe, C. 82
general corruption 133–5
geographic proximity 96
Gifford, R. 67
Gilligan, T. W. 83
Glavas, A. 59
globalization 5
Godfrey, P. 110, 115

governance 3, 4, 6, 107, 109, 118–19, 139, 148
    systems 4
government
    agencies 130, 132, 133
    corruption 133–6, 147–8
    gripes against 129–40
    intervention 121
    regulation 6, 9, 129, 131, 145, 146
        costly and inefficient 131–3
        efficient and effective 145–7
    research agenda, solution 152–9
    sustainability and 129, 145–52
    voluntary corporate initiatives and 149–50
Graves, S. B. 45
green businesses 121
green consumerism 71
green consumption 12
Greenpeace 138
greenwashing efforts 120
Greyston Bakery 36
Griffin, J. 13

Hansen, J. 115
Haque, U. 147
Harrison, J. S. 150
Hart, S. L. 11
Hassan, N. B. B. A. 86
Hawken, P. 18
Hayibor, S. 13
health insurance plan 37
Henriques, I. 9–10, 83, 138, 149, 154
Hillman, A. J. 47
Hoover Dam 129
Husted, B. W. 66, 67, 135, 149, 154

indirect path 50–53, 55–9
industrial capitalism 37
information chaos 85
information disclosures 87–8, 92
information overload 79, 84–6, 89–90, 92
innovation 3, 14, 18, 19, 37, 129, 132, 159
    research 14
institutional theory 5
intangible benefits 24

Jafarian, A. 58
Jamali, D. 57
Jermier, J. M. 115
Jevons's paradox 70
Johnson & Johnson 19, 20
Jones, T. M. 47, 108

Kassinis, G. 81
Kaul, A. 58
Keim, G. D. 47
Khara, N. 57
King, A. 114, 138
King, G. 92
Kitzmueller, M. 57
Kogut, B. 17
Kotha, S. 47
Kourula, A. 139
Krupp, Friedrich Alfred (Fritz) 37, 38

Lafferty, B. 115
Lanoie, P. 151
Laplante, B. 151
Laplume, A. O. 45
La Trobe, H. L. 67
law 38, 130, 136
Lazarus, D. 145
leadership laboratory 36
lease agreement 16
Lenox, M. 82, 114
Leviathan
    learning to lean 145–60
    learning to loathe 130–39
Levinthal, D. 14
Litz, R. A. 45
Loosemore, M. 58
Lowrey, T. M. 65
Lund-Thomsen, P. 57
Luo, J. 58

Mahon, J. 13
Margolis, J. 13, 55
market governance 148
Mazzucato, M. 139
McCarty, J. A. 65
McCreary, E. C. 37
McGrath, R. G. 19, 22
McWilliams, A. 13, 58
media firestorm 86
Merrill, C. 115

Merton, R. C. 17
Messing, S. 89
Milstein, M. B. 11
misconduct 108–18, 120, 121
Mitchell, R. K. 82
"mom & pop" firms 96
Montiel, I. 135, 149
moral motivation 116
Morgan's portfolio 35
Morris, A. 85
Murillo-Luna, J. L. 82
Muthulingam, S. 11
myriad laws 108–9

net present value (NPV) 16
New Environmental Paradigm (NEP) 66, 67
"night watchman" state 131
non-primary stakeholders 48
nonstakeholders 47
Nourbakhsh, V. 58

operating assets 17
option pricing theory 17
Orlitzky, M. 13
Orts, E. W. 130
Ostrom, Elinor 122

Pan, J. 92
Pang, A. 86
Pariser, E. 90
Peloza, J. 59
Phillips, R. A. 46, 130, 132
photocopier 84
Pitt, L. F. 80
platforms, profiting 16
  opening options 16–19
Pogutz, S. 5
Polanyi, K. 129
policy-specific corruption 133
political leanings 113
Pope Francis 51
Porter, M. E. 132, 158
power 54, 88, 95, 107, 122
powerful stakeholders 46, 48, 50, 54
pricing power 12
primary stakeholders 47–9, 51–5, 81, 94
private corruption 134
private politics 81
private regulation 133, 134
process of punishment 109–11
profitability 4
proximity 96–8
Pucker, K. P. 138

Rands, G. P. 5
Rangan, K. 58
rational stakeholders 79
real corporate sustainability options 18, 19, 21, 23
  direct benefits 18
  exercise price of 21, 22
  indirect benefits 18
real options 18, 20, 24
  ups and downs, reputation 34–6
regulation 131–3, 136, 137, 145–7, 149, 154–9
resource systems 4
resource units 4
Rio Earth Summit 71
risk-free interest rate 22, 23
risk management 23
Rittel, H. W. J. 153
Rivera-Torres, P. 82
Roberts, M. E. 92
Rodriguez, P. 148
Roman, R. 13
Rowley, T. 45
Ruhr industrial elite 37

Sadorsky, P. 9, 10
safety-net benefits 23
Salomon, R. 15, 52, 55, 115
Scholes, M. 17
Schultz, Howard 53
Schwepker, C. 65
secondary stakeholders 47, 78, 81–3, 93–4, 139
Sen, S. 51, 53
Seo, H. 58
Shang, J. 59
shareholder management 130
Sharma, S. 83, 138
Shiller, R. J. 146
Shimshack, J. 57
short-term local benefits 30, 31
Shrivastava, P. 5
Shrum, L. J. 65

Siegel, D. 13, 58
Singh, V. 157
Sinha, S. N. 58
"slacktivism" 88
"slacktivists" 91
social bads 146, 147
social control 107–23, 135
business case 110
stakeholders as agents 108–9
social-ecological systems 6, 158, 159
social innovation 3, 37
socially responsible activities 13
social media 79, 84, 86, 90–93, 95–8
platforms 84, 86
social movements 83
political process model of 83
theory 84
social responsibility 52
social welfare 14, 37, 38, 48
plan 38
programs 37
societal benefits 30–32, 133
Sonpar, K. 45
Sparrow, B. H. 89
stakeholder influence 15, 79–84, 86, 92–5, 97–9
aggregate change 97
assumptions 80–81
digital age, reassessing 86–92
cognitive constraints 88–92
framing processes 83
implications of stalled 92–6
mechanisms 93
sources of 81–2
strategies and tactics 82–3
underlying assumptions 83–4
stakeholder influence capacity (SIC) 13–16, 24
stakeholders 9, 11, 15, 16, 33, 45, 46, 52, 54, 79, 82, 88, 90, 107, 109–13, 115, 117, 121, 138, 151
agents of social control 108–9
demands 46, 59, 80, 82, 95, 99, 151
government and 122
limits 112–14, 118
management 45, 121–2, 129, 130, 151
power 82, 95, 138
pressures, affect change 138–9
pressures, insufficient to change firm behavior 150–52
satisfying 43–59
as slipshod sheriff 109–11
and society 44–6
and sustaining society 120–21
theory 5, 44–6, 49, 80, 129–31
theory, primary concern 45
Starik, M. 5
Stead, J. G. 5
Stead, W. E. 5
Stephenson, M. C. 136
stress 31
strike/exercise price 17
Stromberg, D. 114
Strudler, A. 130
Sunstein, C. 90
supply and demand model 13
supply chain network design 58
sustainability 4, 9, 11, 13, 15, 16, 30, 44–7, 50, 52–5, 68, 122, 145, 153
business case 9–12
business case for 68
corporate benefits of 12
government and 145–52
impact 35
indirect path, charting 46–50
initiatives 12, 24, 30, 31, 34, 35, 50, 51, 53–5, 59, 64–5, 72
investment 11, 13
profiting 9–24, 53–5
programs 35, 36
stakeholders demand 68–72
strategy 4
surveying 2–6
sustainability goals 140, 156
process change 140
Sustainability Progress Report, 2019 43
sustainable competitive advantage 4
sustainable development 4
sustainable development goals (SDGs) 146
sustaining society 2–4, 9, 30–38, 43–5
and stakeholders 120–21
synchronicity 91
systematic risk 23

tangible benefits 11, 24
taxation 148
tax incentives 11

technological innovations 70, 71
Thunberg, Greta 159
Tost, L. P. 152
trade associations 119, 120
tragic consequences 4
trust 54
two-way communication 93
Tylenol poisoning crisis (1982) 19

Uhlenbruck, K. 148
Ullmann, A. 13
uncertainty 22
users 4

Vafeas, N. 81
Van der Laan, G. 47
Van der Linde, C. 158
Van Ees, H. 47
Van Witteloostuijn, A. 47
Vogel, D. 117, 120
voluntarism 130
voluntary environmental programs (VEPs) 32–4, 136, 137, 149–50, 155

Waddock, S. A. 45
Wade-Benzoni, K. A. 152
Wallace, C. 107
Wal-Mart 35, 51, 108
Walsh, J. P. 13, 45, 55
Webber, M. M. 153
welfare economics 131
welfare programs 38
Whelan, T. 150
wicked problems 121, 122, 145, 151, 152, 155, 156, 158
Wicks, A. C. 47, 150
Williams, A. 121
willingness to pay (WTP) 11, 64–8
Winn, M. I. 5, 83, 139
"win–win" outcomes 30
"win–win" paradigm 68
Wood, D. J. 45, 55, 82, 110
World Commission on Economic Development (WCED) 4

Zietsma, C. 83, 139